D1287173

WITHDRAWN

WITHDRAWN

The Arno Press Cinema Program

THE EARLY DEVELOPMENT
OF THE MOTION PICTURE
(1887-1909)

By

Joseph H. North

791. 43
N 865e

ARNO PRESS

A NEW YORK TIMES COMPANY

New York • 1973

26,367

This volume was selected for the
Dissertations on Film Series
of the ARNO PRESS CINEMA PROGRAM
by Garth S. Jowett, Carleton University

First publication in book form, Arno Press, 1973

Copyright © 1973 by Joseph H. North

THE ARNO PRESS CINEMA PROGRAM
For complete listing of cinema titles see last pages

Manufactured in the United States of America

- -

Library of Congress Cataloging in Publication Data

North, Joseph H
    The early development of the motion picture
(1887-1909)

    (The Arno Press cinema program. Dissertations on
film series)
    Reprint of the 1949 ed.
    Thesis--Cornell University.
    1. Moving-pictures--History. I. Title.
II. Series: The Arno Press cinema program.
III. Series: Dissertations on film series.
PN1993.5.A1N65   791.43'09   72-558
ISBN 0-405-04101-2

THE EARLY DEVELOPMENT OF THE

MOTION PICTURE

1887 - 1909

A Thesis

Presented to the Faculty of the Graduate School

of Cornell University for the Degree of

Doctor of Philosophy

by

Joseph H. North

September 1949

ACKNOWLEDGEMENTS

I wish to thank Professor A. M. Drummond for his guidance and continued interest in the preparation of this thesis.

I also wish to thank Professor W. H. Stainton for the many helpful conversations we have had relating to the development of the motion picture.

THE THESIS

Most writers covering the early history of the motion
picture pass over the first years of the medium's development
in a perfunctory fashion; and, in some cases, except for a brief
nod in the direction of Georges Melies and his magical films,
and Edwin S. Porter and his story films, they go so far as to
say that "before [David Wark] Griffith there was nothing." [1]

To be sure, nothing as mature as "The Birth of a Nation",
produced in 1914 and 1915, nor even anything as mature as "After
Many Years", produced by Griffith in 1908, the first year he
began directing motion pictures, was turned out by the pioneers;
but these men whose "very names have been all but forgotten",
performed, prior to 1908, jobs of inestimable value in preparing
the way for Griffith and the directors and producers who followed
him.

It will be the purpose of this thesis to outline the accomplishments of the pioneers, and to show the relationship and importance of their work to the work performed by Griffith, and
those who came later.

----

1. Seymour Stern, "D. W. Griffith: An Appreciation," The New
    York Times, August 1, 1948. Section 2, p. x3A.

TABLE OF CONTENTS

Producers of motion pictures are quick to
imitate Porter's technique
Production of one-reel story films on a
large scale delayed until nickelodeon
theatres become established in large
enough numbers to create a demand
The demand for motion pictures inspires
producers to expand studio facilities
Producers move to the west
Producers hire special writers to prepare
scripts
      Kalem brought into court for using
      "Ben Hur" without the consent of the
      publishers (1908)
Producers hire professional actors
Parallel lines of development traced by
Americans and Europeans during the first
decade
In 1908 American and European film
producers go off on different tangents
      In this year, at their congress of film
      producers which met on February 2, the
      French producers, in an effort to "raise
      the prestige of the cinema and erase the
      memory of its lowly past," decided to
      cast their lot with the theatre. They
      would photograph stage plays
          Film D'Art's "Assassination of the
          Duc de Guise." (1908)

During his first year as a director, Griffith
discovers the basic precepts of motion
picture production (as practiced by the
Americans, and later by the Europeans)
      In "For Love of Gold" Griffith moves his
      camera in close for a large full-length
      view of the actors (1908)
      In "After Many Years" Griffith moves his
      camera in for a large close-up of an
      actor's face (1908)
      In "After Many Years" Griffith employs a
      flashback
          By using a flashback Griffith places
          in juxtaposition shots which are dis-
          associated in time and space

In "The Drunkard's Reformation" Griffith
uses light with dramatic and pictorial
effectiveness (March, 1909)
Griffith goes to literature for his subjects
    Unlike the French, however, he
    never forgets the importance of
    movement and of the visual image
Griffith selects his casts with care
    He seeks actors who can adjust
    themselves to a realistic style
Griffith rehearses scenes before shooting
Griffith retakes shots which do not
satisfy him
Griffith's close shots make emphatic
gestures unnecessary
In "The Lonely Villa" Griffith experiments
with the last-minute-rescue (May, 1909)
    Griffith finds the disjunctive method
    of narration effective in creating
    tension

In his free use of the camera, and in his
editing, Griffith stands apart from the
Europeans
    The basic precepts he discovered during
    his first year as a director, underwent
    continual refinement as he turned out
    hundreds of motion pictures for Biograph
    during the following five years, and
    achieved their greatest maturity
    during 1914-1916 with his productions
    of "The Birth of a Nation," and
    "Intolerance."

Griffith's predecessors set the stage for
his appearance
Griffith consolidated the tools, materials,
and personnel in the creation of better
motion pictures

THE INTRODUCTION

This study covers the development of the motion picture during the period, 1887 to 1909.

In 1887, Thomas A. Edison and his assistant, William Kennedy Laurie Dickson, began work on a combination machine for seeing and hearing. In 1908, and during the early months of 1909, David Wark Griffith evolved the basic precepts of motion picture production as practiced by the Americans; and at the same time, in Europe, French motion picture producers, in an effort to "raise the prestige of the cinema," began photographing stage plays.

Many men, prior to Edison and Dickson, worked with the problem of motion record pictures. And claimants to the distinction of being the inventor of the motion picture are so numerous, it is doubtful if any one of the contestants will ever be identified for the honor to the satisfaction of the adherents of the other inventors for whom it is claimed.

The situation being such, and because the matter of priority has little to do with this thesis, we refrain from embroiling ourselves, and choose instead to start the study with the work of Edison and Dickson, who evolved the kinetograph camera. This practical machine may, without too much fear of contradiction, be said to have inspired the construction of the Lumiere, Paul, Armat, and K.M.C.D. motion picture machines, which in turn may be identified as the key machines used in helping lay the foundations of the vast motion picture enterprises we know today.

Below we have outlined very briefly the motion picture's development during the years 1887 to 1908. The outline has been included in the introduction with the thought that it may be helpful in holding together the details of the medium's development set forth in the thesis.

On inspection, the years 1887 to 1909 do not appear as empty and disorganized as some writers on the early history of the motion picture would have us believe. Rather, they seem to reveal a definite pattern of progress.

From 1887 to 1894, Edison and Dickson evolved the kinetograph camera; and the kinetoscope, a peep show machine, used to view the motion record pictures taken by the kinetograph. The years 1894-1896 saw work on, and development of, a series of machines, both American and European, which would project the motion record pictures on a screen for many people to see at one time. And the years 1896-1898 saw the motion pictures achieve a considerable popularity both in the houses where they were projected on a screen, and in the parlors where they were viewed in peep show machines. This latter period, though the producers concentrated almost

exclusively on the brief films of fifty feet, which could be shown
in both the projector and the restrictive peep show, also saw considerable experiment with longer and more elaborate motion pictures.

During 1898, however, motion pictures began to lose their hold
on the public's fancy. Audiences became impatient with the imper-
fections of projection; and they also began to tire of the episodic
films of fifty feet. The public's lack of interest in the motion
picture lasted until 1900.

In December, 1897, Edison started a series of court actions
against American producers for patent infringements. The legal
battles which followed involved the American producers to such an
extent that they were spending more time on lawsuits than they were
on motion picture production. The effects of such a situation are
obvious; and the lawsuits against the American producers must be
regarded as a factor in bringing on the depression.

Though the years 1898-1900 appear particularly unprofitable
in the development of the motion picture, a number of events took
place during the period which appear to have contributed considerably to the revitalization of the medium at the turn of the century.

Among other things "a new class of amusement buyers", who were
to become the real devotees of the motion picture, was being culti-
vated in the peep show parlors; mechanical flaws in the equipment,
which had constantly militated against the spectator's enjoyment
of the exhibition, were slowly being ironed out; scientists, like

Messter and Doyen, were discovering that the motion picture camera
was useful for something other than a mere recording instrument;
and European producers, free from the lawsuits which were vexing
American producers, found that the camera could be made to dis-
tort reality. Thus, by 1900, the motion pictures were once again
ready to start the drive towards the goal of public acceptance.

The transition from short subjects of fifty feet to story
motion pictures, one-reel long, was accomplished during the period
1900-1903.

Beginning in 1900, motion picture audiences seem to have begun
expressing a very marked preference for projected motion pictures.
Consequently, the producers, no longer constrained by the economic
necessity of producing short subjects for the peep show, began
turning out with considerable regularity, between 1900 and 1902,
subjects two hundred and fifty to four hundred feet in length.
These motion pictures "embodied very slight themes." Then between
1902 and 1903, as the public's taste for longer subjects developed,
motion pictures three hundred to six hundred feet in length began
to appear. These contained the framework of stories.

Though the first one-reel story motion pictures were produced
during 1902 and 1903, it was not until around 1906 that longer
films became a regular thing. Exhibition and distribution had
not advanced to the same relatively high level which had been
achieved by production, and until all three factors were on a
similar plane of development, production had to hold back.

The idea for an economical and expeditious method of distributing motion pictures was evolved in 1902-1903, with the establishment of the first exchange; and the idea for an economical and popular method of exhibiting motion pictures was evolved in 1905-1906, with the establishment of the screen theatre.

The solution of the distribution and exhibition problems resulted in the creation of well-defined channels through which motion pictures could reach the public. And now that there was an assured market, and an assured method of releasing the product to the market, the mass production of motion pictures began.

Thus, in 1908, when Griffith began directing at Biograph, the motion picture had already developed: one, an efficient business structure; two, a mass audience; and three, a large group of experienced technicians who were simply waiting to be shown how to make better motion pictures. A man with Griffith's imagination could hardly have wished for a more opportune moment to make an appearance.

Griffith's appearance was well-timed in another way, too. Almost on the very day he assumed his directorial duties, the European producers, in an effort to "raise the prestige of the cinema," began photographing stage plays. His conception and their conception of correct procedure in the production of motion pictures was worlds apart. Later, their successes were instrumental in spurring him on to gigantic and fruitful efforts.

The bibliography lists the books, newspapers, periodicals, and special data used in the preparation of the thesis. However, for those who wish to study the early development of the motion picture further, attention should probably be drawn to some of the sources which have been especially valuable.

Among the standard works Bardeche and Brasillach, Barry, Grau, Mrs. Griffith, Hampton, Hulfish, Jacobs, Lindsay, Low and Manvell, Munsterberg, Quigley, Ramsaye, Rotha, Seldes, and Talbot appear to contain the best information on the early history of the motion picture. Ramsaye's book, of course, is outstanding, and should probably be read first to obtain the most complete and most authentic picture of the medium's pioneer days.

Among the periodicals, the Optical Magic Lantern Journal and Photographic Enlarger, the Scientific American, and the British Journal of Photography are gold mines of information. The issues of these magazines contain contemporary, monthly, and bi-monthly reports which are important in checking the reliability of observations made by later writers.

For additional contemporary reports on the motion picture exhibitions in the metropolitan cities, the New York Times and the London Times are indispensable. Calling attention to these newspapers may seem obvious, but so many important "stories," like "New Things in the Movies" (the New York Times, June 29, 1902, p. 25 c,d,e.), appear to have been overlooked, it seems profitable to call attention to these sources once again.

The usefulness of several stories on the motion picture appearing in 1897 issues of the Ithaca (New York) Journal suggests that an investigation of the older issues of newspapers in other smaller communities might be worth while.

Books by Donaldson (published, 1912), Hepworth (1900--there is still an earlier edition of this book), Hopwood (1899), Jenkins and Depue (1908), Richardson (c.1911), Sargent (1913), and Trutat (1899) are valuable because these men were in the motion picture business, or very close to it; and because they did not wait until years later to record their observations.

For the best understanding of the motion picture's possibilities as an art medium, Bakshy and Spottiswoode, in the estimation of the writer, seem to say more that is orderly and intelligent than any other individuals who have reached print with their observations.

CHAPTER I

THE INVENTORS OF THE MOTION PICTURE

In 1887, Thomas A. Edison, assisted by William Kennedy
Laurie Dickson, began work on a combination machine for hearing
and seeing. Edison had already invented a hearing machine; now
he wished to complete the phonograph and give it a new significance by evolving a machine which would record and transmit things
seen, as well as things heard. [1]

Conditioned by his work with the phonograph, Edison first
experimented with the idea of recording motion record photographs
on cylinders. It was his notion that pictures could be recorded
spirally on a cylinder, just as sound waves were recorded spirally
in grooves on the cylinder of a phonograph. But there was a difference in the recording processes, as the inventor and Dickson
soon discovered. In recording sound for the phonograph, the sound
recording machine operated continuously, whereas in recording motion
pictures, the photograph recording machine had to be stopped at
regular intervals.

The need to stop the camera at periodic intervals to permit
the light to make an unblurred impression on the photographic emulsion had been established by other inventors prior to Edison, but

---

1. Terry Ramsaye, A Million and One Nights, pp. 54-55.

he was apparently unaware of the work others had done on the motion
picture before he had taken up the problem. Having discovered the
need for an intermittent movement, Edison concluded that it would
be necessary to devise a camera which would record photographs at
the rate of at least forty a second, if a correct motion record
was to be secured. With this idea in mind, he contrived a
cylinder picture recording camera which stopped and started forty-
eight times a second. The recorded pictures, hardly larger than
"the end of a dance program lead pencil," were capable of creating
the illusion of motion when viewed through a microscope in a transmitting machine, but they were apparently poor motion pictures
because they were so small. [1]

Edison now concluded that the cylinder had its limitations,
and that he must find a more likely contrivance on which he could
record his photographs. Celluloid, which was being used occasionally
as a substitute for breakable glass plates in snapshot cameras, was
tried. Strips of this material were covered with photographic
emulsion, and the camera was modified so that it would accommodate
the new material. As the celluloid moved past the lens and shutter
in the new camera, its progress was interrupted intermittently by
notches cut on the edge of the strip, and during this period of
interruption, or rest, the shutter in front of the lens opened and
exposed the film.

---

1. Ramsaye, pp. 56-57.

As Edison and Dickson worked on the camera, they introduced refinements. Sprocket wheels were employed to convey the strips of celluloid through the camera, and "a Geneva cross and spur wheel which engaged the film by jerks"[1] replaced the crude intermittent movement created by the notches cut on the edge of the film strip. And in order to give the film a very steady movement as it progressed through the camera, sprocket holes were cut into both sides of the strip of film.

Improvements were being made in the camera mechanism, but the celluloid strips were unsatisfactory -- they were heavy, and they were in exasperatingly short lengths. Strips of film with a collodion base were tried -- they were rough in texture, and fragile. Now the development of the motion picture waited upon the discovery of a satisfactory base for the photographic emulsion. The solution of this problem had to wait upon the experiments of George Eastman, in Rochester, New York.

At the same time Edison was working on the motion picture camera, Eastman was trying to produce a simple snapshot camera for the amateur photographer. He felt that by producing a small box camera, which was easy to operate and employed rollfilms rather than the cumbersome, fragile plates used in the cameras of that day, that he could make photography popular. He had demonstrated the practicability of rollfilms in 1884, when he introduced "the paper rollfilm

1. Ramsaye, p. 60.

as negative material, for use in a roll holder." [1] Now, like
Edison, he was trying to find a more suitable base for the photographic emulsion. In 1888-89, [2] when he hit upon a thin, flexible
base, not only his problems but also Edison's were about to be
solved.

It is not hard to believe that George Eastman could have been
the inventor of the motion picture if he had been interested in the
idea of making photographic motion records. By 1884, he had evolved
rollfilms, and by 1888-89, he had produced a thin, flexible base
suitable for motion picture use. Like all the experimenters who
worked on the idea of motion pictures, he certainly would have
immediately seen the necessity for an intermittent movement in the
camera, if he had been faced with the problem. But Eastman was
interested in still photography.

Edison, hearing about Eastman's new film base, instructed
Dickson to secure samples. As soon as he had a chance to inspect
the samples, he knew that the problem of motion picture photography
had been solved. Edison's preoccupation with the problem had been
intense as long as it had remained unsolved; now, in the year 1889,
having proved himself master of the situation, he was, as we shall
see, ready to forget all about motion pictures.

Edison called his motion picture camera the kinetograph, and
the transmitting machine for showing the motion record pictures made
by the camera, the kinetoscope.

---

1. Erich Stenger, The History of Photography, Trans. Epstean, p. 18.
2. Stenger, p. 18.

As the unexposed film passed through the kinetograph, it was stopped intermittently to permit the recording of photographic images at the rate of forty-eight pictures a second. In the kineto-scope, however, the film was run without interruption between an electric light and a shutter which exposed the picture by flashes. The kinetoscope was a peep show machine.

Concurrently, Edison and Dickson built a projector which threw motion pictures on a screen, but this particular aspect of the prob-lem was not given serious consideration at the time. The inventor felt that it would be impossible to sustain the public's interest in the motion picture, if pictures were projected on a screen so that many people could see them at one time.

Once the problem of the kinetoscope and the kinetograph had been solved, Edison immediately turned to other matters. He seemed no longer interested in the motion picture. This indifference cannot positively be explained, but certain of his attitudes may help us understand why he made no effort to exploit the kinetoscope for more than three years after perfecting it. For one thing, Edison considered the dynamo, the incandescent lamp, the telephone trans-mitter, and other of his projects of far more importance. This was certainly an understandable attitude, for it is impossible to deny the epochal nature of these works. From their inception, they were obviously important. On the other hand, the kinetoscope and the kinetograph had as antecedents the zoetrope and the magic lantern, which could hardly be classified as better than toys. It was a case of comparative values, and the inventor obviously had little respect for "a silly little device for making pictures that would dance." [1] Furthermore, the commercial exploitation of a toy would hardly appeal to a man who manufactured lamps and dynamos. It would be laughable.

But other people did not reflect Edison's indifference. They talked about his motion picture machine with interest. And Edison, being human, very likely, at moments when he desired relaxation, encouraged the talk by showing the kinetoscope to business associates and friends who visited the plant. This is how Thomas Lombard, who was responsible for getting the machine out of the factory and into the hands of the public, first became acquainted with the peep show machine.

Edison was certainly not reluctant to talk about motion pictures and the work he had done with them. In an article published in Harper's Weekly, June 13, 1891, with Edison's very certain knowledge, for he provided the author, George Parsons Lathrop, with side and planned views of the kinetoscope, and specific information relating to the mechanical operation of the kinetograph and kinetoscope is given. All of this information became public property before Edison

---

1. Ramsaye, p. 56.

had even applied for a patent. Certainly the man thought little,
and worried less, about the future of his invention.

On August 24, 1891, Edison made application for a United States
patent covering the kinetoscope and kinetograph. Because application for foreign patents would have cost him an additional $150.00,
Edison, according to Ramsaye, decided that they were not worth the
money.

This decision lost Edison millions, for later when foreign
inventors began producing motion picture projectors, they could
proceed with their work without paying the American royalties. But,
in fairness to his judgment, it must be said that "it had been
Edison's experience that the more patents he took out abroad, the
more he lost." [1] In many cases, patents seem to have advertised
possibilities to infringers and pirates.

It is interesting to note that in his patent application of
August 24, 1891, Edison disregarded the screen possibilities of the
motion picture; he only mentioned the camera and the peep show
machines.

Thomas Lombard, of the North American Phonograph Company, which
was organized to exploit Edison's phonograph as a dictating machine,
was the first to see the commercial possibilities of the kinetoscope.
In 1893, he and two associates, Frank R. Gammon and Norman C. Raff,
acquired from Edison the rights of sale for the machine. Lombard,
Raff, and Gammon, who organized under the name, the Kinetoscope

---

1. Ramsaye, p. 76.

Company, were interested in selling territorial rights on the
business of the machine, and in establishing exhibition halls in
the choicer locations like New York, Chicago, and San Francisco.

With the formation of the Kinetoscope Company, Edison was
forced to manufacture kinetoscopes, and produce motion pictures
for the machine.

As a first step in the solution of the motion picture production problem, Edison and Dickson built a studio mounted on a
revolvable platform. It was an unpretentious, somber, tarpaulin-
covered affair, which cost $637.67 to construct. But, even though
it was not much more than a shack in the eyes of the general popu-
lace, William Kennedy Laurie Dickson found every square foot of it
to his liking, and he called it "The Kinetographic Theatre." The
name did not hold, however, for the men around the Edison plant,
finding that it reminded them of a certain black closed wagon
operated by the police, ended up by calling it the "Black Maria."

The turntable arrangement on which the studio was constructed
permitted the producers to swing the building around so that they
could obtain the fullest possible benefit of the sunlight, and at
the same time obviated the constant shifting of the heavy kinetograph camera with its battery-driven motors.

With the completion of the studio in February, 1893, Dickson,
who was director, cameraman, and laboratory staff, began preparing

films for the kinetoscope. He chose subjects from the variety
stage, which were full of movement; dancers, contortionists, ani-
mal acts, slapstick comedy scenes. These subjects were recorded
on short strips of film, fifty feet in length, which took considerably less than a minute to photograph.

The camera was regarded as a recording instrument; it was
placed in the same category with the phonograph machine. Its creative possibilities were unknown. Dickson would set the camera in
position and delimit its field with strings. Any subject moving
outside the area created by the two strings which ran out from the
camera in spoke-like fashion was simply not photographed; and even
if the idea of panning [1] the camera had occurred to Dickson, he
would have been unable to accomplish this simple movement, because
the first kinetographs were inflexibly fixed to photograph straight
ahead at eye-level.

Because film in 1893 was not sensitive enough to record subtle
shadows, all kinetograph subjects were filmed in the brilliant sunshine, against a black background. Maximum contrast was the desideratum.

It is interesting to note that the limitation of fifty feet
per motion picture was imposed by another mechanical shortcoming.

The reel of motion pictures of to-day is approximately
one thousand feet in length, and many pictures have been

---

1. "Panning. The Camera Pivots Round on a Vertical Axis, Taking
A Panoramic View of the Subject." Raymond Spottiswoode, A
Grammar of the Film, p 47.

presented in twelve such reels, or two and a quarter miles
of film. This limitation to fifty feet existed because the
camera operated with jerky, intermittent motion as it stepped
the film past the lens. These jerks against the weight of
the film had to overcome the inertia of the roll at each
jerk. If the film was much longer than fifty feet, the jerk
would break it. [1]

Raff, Gammon, and Lombard had wanted to exhibit the kinetoscope at the Columbian Exposition in Chicago in 1893, but Edison
was tardy with his delivery of the machines, and it was not until
the spring of 1894, after the exposition had closed, that Edison
was ready with his first shipment of kinetoscopes. These were
delivered to the Holland Brothers, eastern agents of the Kinetoscope Company, who gave them their first public display on April
14, 1894, at 1155 Broadway, New York City.

The Kinetoscope exhibitions on Broadway were attended by two
young men, Otway and Grey Latham. They were enthusiastic about
the commercial possibilities of the new wonder. With two friends,
Samuel J. Tilden and Enoch Rector, they made application to Edison
and received his permission to organize the Kinetoscope Exhibition
Company, which had as its purpose the exploitation of peep show
machines with prize fight pictures. "It seems that it was on this
restricted and special basis that the deal escaped the strictures
of the prior contract with Norman C. Raff" [2] and his colleagues.

The Lathams wished to take a battery of kinetoscopes and

---

1. Ramsaye, p. 72.

2. Ramsaye, p. 107.

exhibit one round of a prize fight in each one of these machines
at a time. Since the kinetoscope designed by Edison was limited
to fifty feet, Enoch Rector, a Latham partner, tripled the capacity
of the machine so that it could show abbreviated rounds.

By July, 1894, having overcome the limitations of the older
kinetoscopes, Rector arranged a prize fight between Michael
Leonard and Jack Cushing, to be staged in the Edison studio.
Nearly a thousand feet of film was exposed. The fight picture
was by far the longest motion picture attempted up to this time.

The fight pictures were exhibited at 83 Nassau Street, New
York City, during August, 1894. They were well received.

It soon became evident that a change of program was in order,
so James Corbett and Pete Courtenay were signed for a motion
picture fight. New success inspired the Lathams to wish that they
could project these pictures on a screen, so that many people
would be able to see the films at one time. In line with these
thoughts, the Lathams began experimenting with motion picture projection.

The Lathams were not alone in their desire to project motion
pictures. At the very time that they were experimenting with their
ideas, Raff, of the Kinetoscope Company, was urging Edison to take
up the idea. The inventor had little confidence in projected pictures. Ramsaye reports the following remarks made by Edison to
Raff:

"No," replied the Wizard, "if we make this screen machine that you are asking for, it will spoil everything. We are making these peep show machines and selling a lot of them at a good profit. If we put out a screen machine, there will be use for maybe about ten of them in the whole United States. With that many screen machines, you could show the pictures to everybody in the country -- and then it would be done. Let's not kill the goose that lays the golden egg." 1

But Raff persisted in his argument, and Edison finally obliged him by assigning one of his mechanics, Charles H. Kayser, to work on the project. This was apparently the best way to get rid of Raff -- for a while, at least.

In the meantime, the Lathams, less inspired but more determined than Edison, evolved a motion picture projector. Though their projector, the pantoptikon, threw pictures on a screen, it was not an altogether satisfactory machine, for it adhered to the continuous movement of the kinetoscope. The Lathams had discovered the need for an intermittent movement in the camera, but they failed to comprehend the need for an intermittent, or step by step, presentation in the projector.

Because of this imperfection, the pantoptikon had a short and unsuccessful history. But the camera which was used to photograph subjects for the projector did incorporate an important new feature which later machines employed. This new device, "the Latham loop," served to release the camera from its restrictive limitation of film strips fifty feet long.

The loop had been created when Enoch Rector, who had extended

1. Ramsaye, p. 119.

the capacity of the kinetoscope for the Leonard-Cushing prize fight pictures, decided to construct the Latham camera so that it would accommodate longer strips of film. He accomplished this objective by introducing into the camera an additional feed sprocket which formed a loop in the film just before it reached the intermittent. Thus when the intermittent jerked the film down into position in front of the lens, it drew down slack film, rather than taut film directly from the feed reel.

The Latham projector was exhibited to the press on April 21, 1895. This showing was designed to publicize the first public exhibition of the pantoptikon, which was given on May 20, 1895.

Like the Lathams, other men were inspired to undertake the solution of motion picture projection. And, in every case, as with the Lathams, their desire was stimulated by witnessing an exhibition of Edison's kinetoscope.

In England, the business of motion pictures began when two Greeks, George Georgiades and George Trajedis, set up a kinetoscope parlor in London with Edison machines imported from New York. The showing was successful, and the two exhibitors decided it would be profitable to operate additional machines. At this juncture, they evolved an interesting line of action. Instead of importing comparatively expensive machines from the United States, they decided to have duplicates made in England, and with this idea in mind, they appealed to a maker of precision instruments, Robert W. Paul. Paul questioned the legality of their contemplated action, but they persisted, and the instrument maker was prompted to investigate the British patents records. As we know, he found that Edison had not applied for foreign patents.

The Edison decision not to make application for patents in Europe cost the inventor a large personal monetary loss, but on the other hand, his indifference accelerated the development of the motion picture, for it gave Paul and other European inventors a free hand.

Finding that he was not restrained by patents, Paul filled the order of Georgiades and Trajedes and made other machines on his own account. These machines he sold to an eager market.

Meanwhile, back in Orange, William E. Gilmore, Edison's manager, was fuming because of the sudden demand for motion pictures from the owners of machines made by Paul. He was annoyed on two counts: first, that he had lost a lot of sales to Paul; and secondly, that the owners of the English-made machines had the temerity to come to him for films. Obviously he could not prosecute them, but he could cut off their source of film supply since the Edison studio produced the only motion pictures made in the world at that time. This would teach them not to buy "illegal" machines in the future. And in order to better oversee the market

in Englad, Gilmore dispatched Frank Z. Maguire and Joseph D.
Baucus to London as Edison agents for the kinetoscope. They were
instructed to sell films only to those exhibitors who owned kinetoscopes made by Edison.

The following advertisement, apparently originating in the
London office of Maguire and Baucus, appeared in the Personal &
c. column of the London Times of October 30, 1894:

THOS. A. EDISON'S
LATEST and MOST MARVELLOUS INVENTION
THE KINETOSCOPE
Sole Agents for Mr. Edison in Europe, & c.,
Continental Commerce Company
70, Oxford-street, London, W.
Machines earning 1,000 per cent. on investment [1]

Wishing to exhibit as well as sell kinetoscopes, Maguire
and Baucus apparently also operated a parlor in connection with
their sales room, for the following advertisement appeared in the
Entertainments & c. column of the London Times on October 19, 1894:

EDISON'S MARVELLOUS KINETOSCOPE
Day and evening on EXHIBITION, 70, Oxford-street [2]

This advertisement, or a variation of it, appeared in the
Times, daily, from October 19, 1894, through November 21, 1894.
An advertisement in the November 15, 1894, issue indicates that
business was good enough to justify the opening of a second parlor.

––––––––––

1. "Personal & c.", The London Times, October 30, 1894, p. 1c.
2. "Entertainments & c.", The London Times, October 19, 1894, p. 1c.

EDISON'S MARVELLOUS KINETOSCOPE
Day and Evening on EXHIBITION
70, OXFORD STREET, and 432, STRAND
Buffalo Bill's Wild West Show scenes, Sandow
Carmencita, Bertoldi, dancers, and comic scenes. [1]

When the motion picture program was listed in the advertisements appearing in the London Times it did not vary at any time
from the one appearing in the November 15th issue of the paper.
This seems to indicate that new films were scarce, and also that
Gilmore and Edison were more interested in selling kinetoscopes
than they were in producing motion pictures.

Paul was in a difficult position. Realizing that the market
for his machines would be lost if he failed to provide his customers
with films, he set about making a camera so that he could produce
motion pictures. Immediately understanding the need for an intermittent in the camera, he set to work and progressed so rapidly
that by March 29, 1895, [2] he had devised a camera and was prepared
to make motion pictures for his kinetoscope customers.

Paul's camera was an improvement over the Edison kinetograph
in that it was comparatively small and portable, and in that it
recorded photographs at the rate of approximately twenty pictures
a second.

The portability of his camera enabled Paul to move around
freely in search of new subjects. This camera quality constituted
progress, for the great size and weight of the Edison kinetograph

---

1. "Entertainments & c.", The London Times, November 15, 1894, p. 1E.
2. Ramsaye, p. 149.

with its battery driven motor made excursions outside the studio exceedingly difficult. Now it was possible for Paul with his hand-operated camera to move into the street and country without being compelled, like Edison, to hire a wagon and horse to transport his machine. During this early period when the creative capacities of the camera were unknown, and the novelty of the motion picture subjects was of tremendous importance in sustaining interest in the medium this mobile quality in the camera was an important asset.

When Paul discovered that he could make satisfactory motion records at the rate of approximately twenty frames [1] a second he of course extended the temporal length of the film, for it took more than twice as long for a film strip of fifty feet to run through his camera at the rate of twenty frames a second as it took a strip of the same length to run through the kinetograph at the rate of forty-eight frames a second.

It was not long after Paul had evolved the camera that he saw the desirability of projected motion pictures. Like the Lathams he first attempted projection with the continuously running movement of the kinetoscope, but he soon saw the need for an intermittent in the projector, as well as in the camera, and by October, 1895, [2] at the latest, Paul had solved the projection problem.

---

1. Each picture on the strip of film is known as a frame.
2. Ramsaye, p. 161.

The first demonstration of his projector was given before an audience at the Finsbury Technical College on February 20, 1896, and the second before another group in the library of the Royal Institution on February 28, 1896. As a result of the second demonstration on February 28, his projector, the animatograph found its way into the professional entertainment world.

The kinetoscope found its way into France in the early fall of 1894 when Lionel Werner established a parlor at 20 Boulevard Poissoniere in Paris with Edison kinetoscopes imported from the United States. The showings met with enthusiasm, and, as was to be expected, they excited in the minds of some of the spectators the idea of projected motion pictures. In this case Louis Lumiere, a maker of photographic materials, was the man destined to solve the problem.

With his brother August as a collaborator, Louis began work with his idea. The two brothers fell into a familiar pattern of action. First they started working with the continuous movement of the kinetoscope as a basis for motion picture projection, then they saw the inadequacies of the method, and finally they comprehended the need for a step by step presentation of the pictures.

The understanding of the Lumieres had interesting results. Seeing the need for an intermittent in both the camera and projector they devised a machine which could accomplish both operations.

As a camera, the shutter on their machine operated speedily in order to allow the recording of the pictures, and as a projector the shutter operated slowly in order to allow the light to soak through the film and project the pictures on a screen. Later the Lumieres outdid themselves by making the machine available for the third operation in motion picture photography—developing.

In addition to being a combination camera-projector-developer, the machine, which they named the cinematograph, had the additional advantage of being even more mobile than the Paul machine. Louis Lumiere when he went away from the studio carried his camera in one hand.

The mobility and flexibility of the cinematograph made it possible for Lumiere cameramen to travel all over the world in search of subjects, and actually pay their way enroute by giving local exhibitions. Motion pictures of the crowds wandering around the Prater in Vienna were interesting to the people in Paris, London, and New York, but they were no less interesting to the Viennese, who gladly paid to see the films before they were sent to Paris for world distribution.

While building the cinematograph, the Lumieres experimented with the number of pictures they needed to record a second in order to secure a satisfactory motion record for projection purposes. They established sixteen frames a second as the desideratum, and the hand crank in the cinematograph was regulated to expose eight

NORTHEAST NEBRASKA TECHNICAL
COMMUNITY COLLEGE · LIBRARY

frames with each turn. The Lumiere standard of sixteen frames
a second was later accepted by the motion picture world.

The Lumieres exhibited their motion picture projector for
the first time March 22, 1895, at their plant in Lyon before
several members of the Society for the Encouragement of National
Industry. This was followed by other showings on the 10th and 11th
of July in the salons of the General Review of Science, and on the
16th of November in the auditorium of the Sorbonne at the meeting
of the Science Faculty. [1] Regarding the motion picture as a
scientific wonder, and having little faith in its commercial possibilities, the Lumieres were in no rush to exhibit the machine
publicly. [2]

In the United States Thomas Armat of Washington, D. C.,
duplicated the work of Paul and the Lumieres. But his machine
incorporated features which made it a better projector than either
the cinematograph or the animatograph, and established it as the
basic machine on which modern projectors are modelled.

Armat had discovered that satisfactory projection was dependent on not only long periods of rest as the film passed through
the machine, but also on long periods of illumination as the picture
on the film was projected on the screen. To secure this long
period of illumination Armat simply used a shutter cut away so that

1. Rene Jeanne, "L'Evolution Artistique Du Cinematographe," Le
   Cinema, p. 169.

2. Maurice Bardeche and Robert Brasillach, The History of Motion
   Pictures, Trans. Iris Barry, p. 10.

it gave to the screen long periods of illumination and relatively
short periods of darkness. The cinematograph was like the Armat
projector in that it employed the intermittent which gave the
film the desired long periods of rest, but it was unlike the
Armat machine in that it employed a shutter which gave the screen
equal periods of light and darkness. The shutter on the cinematograph "did not permit the machine to operate at its full efficiency." [1]

The Armat projector, which was created in collaboration with
C. Francis Jenkins, was exhibited publicly September, 1895, at
the Cotton States Exposition in Atlanta, Georgia. This showing
did not result in immediate public acceptance of the projector,
but it did give Armat, perhaps as compensation for the money he
lost in the venture, an opportunity to study the machine under
actual operational conditions. This study revealed deficiencies,
the most obvious of which was the terrific strain imposed on the
taut film by the intermittent as it jerked the film into position
in front of the lens. The continual jerks frequently damaged
the film, tended to make the projected picture unsteady, and
limited the length of film which could be projected. Armat now
accomplished for the projector what Rector had accomplished for
the camera. He introduced a sprocket which fed slack film into the
beater movement. This little device, because it reduced the tension

---

1. Ramsaye, p. 165.

on the film, rectified all of the deficiencies mentioned above.

Armat's feed sprocket was so obviously similar to "the Latham loop," that it is perhaps a matter of wonder that Rector and the Lathams did not manage to anticipate Armat.

There are a couple of explanations why the Lathams never introduced the feed sprocket into their projector.

Because the pantoptikon adhered to the continuous movement of the kinetoscope, it did not employ an intermittent movement; thus Rector and the Lathams were not faced with the problem of having to eliminate the strain imposed on the taut film by the intermittent as it jerked the film into position in front of the lens. If, eventually, an intermittent had been introduced into the pantopti-kon, it seems very probable that Rector would have immediately seen the desirability of introducing an extra feed sprocket into the machine in order to eliminate the continual jerks which played havoc with the film.

The failure of Rector and the Lathams to introduce an inter-mittent movement into the camera is another matter which probably needs explanation. Perhaps they were too much influenced by what Edison had done: his kinetograph employed an intermittent movement, so did their camera; his kinetoscope operated continuously, so did their pantoptikon. Or perhaps the hard feeling, which led to a break between the Lathams and Rector during the summer of 1895, prevented the partners from sitting down and calmly analyzing the pantoptikon's deficiencies.

The exhibition at the Cotton States Exposition had served Armat as a test demonstration, just as the Lumiere exhibitions before the scientific and industrial groups had served them as test demonstrations. The Armat machine was now ready for its first real public demonstration. This matter simply had to wait upon a deal that Raff and Gammon of the Kinetoscope Company were arranging.

Somewhat later than the Lathams, Paul, the Lumieres, and Armat in their search for screen projection came the K.M.C.D. Syndicate, made up of E. B. Koopman, H. N. Marvin, Herman Casler, and William Kennedy Laurie Dickson.

The history of the Syndicate began with an argument between William E. Gilmore, Edison's manager, and W. K. L. Dickson, who had assisted Edison in his work on the kinetoscope. As a consequence of the argument Dickson had resigned from the Edison Company. For a short while he had a half-hearted interest in the Latham's enterprises, but this association also failed to last because of personal differences.

In spite of his unhappy experiences with Edison and the Lathams, Dickson continued to be interested in motion pictures, and when he thought of an idea for a new peep show machine which could be made simply and inexpensively, he communicated with H. N. Marvin, whom he had met in one of the Edison plants in New York.

Dickson's idea was to put pictures on a book of cards, and create the illusion of movement to the eye by flipping the pictures over one by one. Marvin saw merit in the idea and passed it on to his business associate, Herman Casler of Canastota, New York.

In his factory at Canastota, Casler developed a hand cranking machine which would exhibit a wheel of pictures. Like the Paul, Lumiere, and Armat machines, the peep show instrument devised by Casler had an intermittent which momentarily stopped each picture in front of the viewing lens.

Now Casler and his associates needed pictures for their new peep show machine, the mutoscope. In their experiments they had used the little pictures from a strip of kinetoscope film; these had worked rather well and Marvin, and E. B. Koopman, the financier of the group, thought possibly they could make an arrangement with Edison whereby kinetograph negatives could be used to make pictures for the mutoscope.

Edison rejected the proposition.

Now that they were in the same position that Paul had found himself when Edison had cut off the supply of films to owners of English-made kinetoscopes, Casler and Dickson decided to devise a camera so that they could produce their own motion pictures.

Because the mutoscope pictures were viewed by reflected light, like ordinary photographs, rather than by light cast through the film as in the kinetoscope, the K.M.C.D. camera was designed to take unusually large pictures. Frames nearly two and three quarters inches wide and two inches high were employed. Thus the area of the picture was almost eight times as great as the area of the pictures on the kinetoscope film strips.

Use of this very wide film strip distinguished the camera, but the primary difference between the Casler-Dickson camera and the Edison-Dickson camera lay in the method of conveying the film through the machines. In the kinetograph, sprocket wheels engaged the perforated film and carried it regularly through the machine. The motion record pictures on the film were equally spaced. In the K.M.C.D. camera, on the other hand, unperforated film was carried through the camera irregularly over rollers which permitted slippage. At the moment of exposure, however, two fingers which punched holes in the film held it steady so that a photographic record could be made. Because of the slippage the motion record pictures on the film were unevenly spaced.

Since the Casler-Dickson camera was designed to make picture cards for the mutoscope it was unnecessary to have equally spaced motion record pictures. The two holes punched in the film as the

pictures were made assured the correct placing of the negatives
on the positives during the printing process.

The K.M.C.D. camera was completed sometime during September,
1895. By this time motion picture projection was an accomplished
fact both in Europe and in this country. The Lumieres were giving
exhibitions of their cinematograph before scientific groups; Paul
was on the verge of making application for patents on his animatograph; Armat was exhibiting his machine at the Cotton States
Exposition; and the Lathams were giving commercial exhibitions
of their pantoptikon.

In view of what was happening elsewhere in the world, it
seems natural enough, once the mutoscope had been set on its commercial way, to find the K.M.C.D. Syndicate solving the motion
picture projection problem. Their projector, which was named the
"American Biograph," was devised sometime between September, 1895,
and October, 1896, when it was given its first public exhibition.

The kinetoscope was exhibited publicly for the first time on
April 14, 1894. Many men as soon as they saw the Edison invention
were attracted by the idea of projected motion pictures. They
wanted to combine the magic lantern and the peep show machine.
These men worked independently, but the realization of projected
pictures was so inevitable that within two years after the kinetoscope had been released all of them had evolved projection machines.

From what has been related thus far it is evident that the field of motion pictures from 1887 to 1896 belonged exclusively to the men who knew machines. And these men because of the mechanical nature of the medium were to continue to dominate the field for many years to come.

Men of artistic culture, on the other hand, because they associated the motion picture with the zoetrope and the magic lantern, and because they failed to find artistic merit in the feeble production efforts of the mechanics, ignored the medium.

The prevailing attitudes during the first years are summed up by Alexander Bakshy:

> Its very singularity among all other emanations of the mechanical genius explains a great deal of the history of the motion picture as a branch of purely commercial activity and a vehicle of art. It was natural that it should have been fastened upon by men to whom the mechanical nature of the medium was its strongest appeal; these men knew the commercial value of mechanical processes, and they could appreciate the particular market value of this novelty. It was equally natural that people of artistic culture should have failed to see the essential difference between the motion picture and other mechanical devices. Whatever creative powers this new medium possessed, they were certainly not very conspicuous in the manufactured productions of its early sponsors. To believe in their existence required more than an effort of imagination; one had to forget the sorry results of the innumerable other attempts at producing works of art by mechanical means. Hence, the prejudice against the motion picture was natural, the contempt for its puerile efforts in art inevitable. [1]

---

1. Alexander Bakshy, "The New Art of the Moving Picture," Theatre Arts Monthly, XI, (April, 1927). 277-282.

CHAPTER II

FIRST PUBLIC EXHIBITIONS OF THE
MOTION PICTURE IN THE METROPOLITAN CITIES

As soon as the motion record pictures were released from
the confines of the peep show, and were boldly projected on a
screen for all the world to admire, the men who participated in
the delivery began considering how the new projected pictures
should be dealt with.

Some, like the Lathams, because they were driven by the need
for money, insisted on immediate exploitation, even though their
new brain child was really not yet ready to leave the laboratory;
while others, like the Lumieres, who were not financially pressed,
and who regarded the motion picture more as a scientific wonder
than a device to be exploited commercially, limited their new
machine to private showings for almost a year.

Though some of the inventors may have hesitated at first,
wondering what to do with their projected pictures, they soon
enough began to see the little marvel's commercial possibilities.
And beginning just a year and a few days after the Holland Brothers
first publicly exhibited the Edison peep show kinetoscope on
Broadway, the inventors started exploiting projected motion pictures.
The first exhibition, which took place in New York, was followed
by other exhibitions in the United States and Europe, so that by
the spring of 1896 projected motion pictures were being presented

publicly in New York, Paris, and London.

The speed with which the transition from peep show exhibitions to projected motion picture exhibitions took place was indicative of the tremendously rapid development which the motion picture was to experience during the ensuing years.

The first public exhibition of a motion picture projector was given by the Lathams on May 20, 1895, at 153 Broadway, New York City. [1] Because it had the advantage of novelty, the Latham pantoptikon was received with some acclaim. But actually the projector was inferior because it operated on the continuous movement principal of the peep show kinetoscope.

The machine was given a number of exhibitions in this country and abroad, but the showings were never altogether satisfactory. Rich G. Holloman, manager of the Eden Musee in New York City, like many others who saw the machine, appreciated the pantoptikon's possibilities, but he was dissatisfied with its operation. However, he did tell the Lathams that the Musee was ready to install the first perfected motion picture projector available.

These commercial exhibitions had little importance because of the projector's shortcomings. It remained for the machines devised by other inventors to create a significant impression on the public.

The Latham exhibitions did help accomplish several positive

---

1. Martin Quigley, Jr., _Magic Shadows_, p. 157.

bits of good however. They annoyed Edison, and as a consequence made him more amenable to the idea of projected motion pictures. And later they probably emboldened Raff and Gammon to the point where they dared suggest to Edison that he make a deal with Armat. Competition was speeding up the development of the motion picture.

The various inventors may have labored in ignorance as to who specifically was trying to develop motion picture projectors during 1894 and 1895, but it was very unlikely that any of them, here or abroad, were living such detached lives that they were unaware of the fact that a "race", as the Optical Magic Lantern Journal and Photographic Enlarger calls it, was on. [1]

Some seven months after the first Latham exhibition, the Lumieres introduced their projector to the public. The cinematograph had been in fair operational order by March, 1895, but the Lumieres because they had no great confidence in the motion picture withheld their machine from public exhibition and simply demonstrated it on occasion to scientific groups. This delay was beneficial in that the brothers, during this period, were able to make adjustments in the machine.

The cinematograph was exhibited publicly for the first time on December 28, 1895, at the Grand Cafe, Boulevard des Capucines, Paris. [2] Because the Lumiere brothers considered the commercial

1. The Dreamer, "Topical Notes," The Optical Magic Lantern Journal and Photographic Enlarger, VII, (April, 1896). 71.
2. Bardeche and Brasillach, p. 4.

exploitation of motion pictures a "rather delicate enterprise"
for which they were not entirely qualified, they thought it
prudent to call upon the photographer, Clement Maurice, for help. [1]
He responded by arranging the first Lumiere exhibition, and the
others that followed.

The December program was made up of ten films, each sixteen
meters long:

1. Leaving the Lumiere Factory at Lyon
2. Tuileries Fountain
3. The Train
4. The Regiment
5. Cavalry Sergeant
6. A Game of Cards
7. Weeds
8. The Wall
9. The Sea
10. Quarrel of the Babies [2]

Each film was nothing more than the recording of a brief
moment of action. Considering the fact that one of the newspaper
men covering the Latham preview on April 21, 1895, found satisfaction in seeing the motion picture of a man smoking a pipe, [3]
it is very evident that the recording of an action in these early
films did not always have to be something as obvious as a train
coming into a station. A motion picture recording something as
simple as Professor Trewey and Antoine Lumiere, father of Auguste
and Louis, playing cards was enough to elicit "une merveille

---

1. Jeanne, p. 169.

2. Jeanne, p. 170.

3. The New York Sun, April 22, 1895, Article Reproduced by
Ramsaye, opposite p. 143.

photographique" from one of the Parisian newspapers. [1]

The Lumiere motion picture exhibition was the first of many exhibitions in which the cinematograph was featured. This good projector was destined not only to stimulate the development of the motion picture in France, but in England, the United States and other countries as well.

In England the first public exhibition of motion pictures was given at a polytechnic institution, the Marlborough Hall. It was not unnatural that the motion picture should find immediate endorsement at an institution which was interested in the many practical branches of art and science. The exhibition at Marlborough Hall Polytechnic, which was begun during February, 1896, was announced on page one of the London Times of Monday, February 24, 1896, in the column, "Entertainments".

> The Cinematographe.
> Living Photographs Reproduced life size by means of the Cinematographe, of Messrs. A. and L. Lumiere, Marlborough-hall, the Polytechnic, Regent-street, W. Daily, at 2, 3, 4, 5, 6, 7, 8, 9, and 10 o'clock. Every hour from 2 till 10. One shilling. [2]

A note in the April issue of the Optical Magic Lantern Journal and Photographic Enlarger establishes the exhibition priority of the Lumiere cinematograph at Marlborough-Hall:

----

1. Le Radical, December 30, 1895, quoted by Jeanne, p. 170.

2. "Entertainments & c.", The London Times, February 24, 1896, p. 1E. Rachael Low and Roger Manvell (The History of the British Film, p. 113) say that the first exhibition of motion pictures at the Polytechnic took place on February 20, 1896.

In the race for first place as regards public exhibition priority, the foreigner wins, Messrs. Lumieres's projection kinetoscope being on view in Marlborough Hall, Regent Street. [1]

In quick succession during the month of March, 1896, London showmen "raced" to exhibit the new motion pictures. Here was a seven-day wonder which needed to be exploited quickly before the novelty wore off. [2]

A preview showing of the Lumiere cinematograph had been given for the press at the Empire Theatre in London on February 7, 1896, [3] but public exhibitions at the Empire seem to have been delayed until the following month. An advertisement in the London Times of Saturday, March 7, 1896, announced the showing. This apparently was the first exhibition of motion pictures in a London variety house.

Empire. - The Cinematograph. - Under the management of Trewey. - Animated Pictures, Monday, March 9th, at 10 o'clock. These pictures accomplish everything but speech. Seats may be booked at the box-office. [4]

At the Polytechnic where motion pictures were given their first public exhibition in England, films were projected continuously throughout the afternoon and evening with brief intermissions between each showing, whereas at the Empire the cinema-

---

1. The Dreamer, "Topical Notes," The Optical Magic Lantern Journal and Photographic Enlarger, VII, (April, 1896). 71.

2. Frederick A. Talbot, Moving Pictures, pp. 40-41.

3. Ramsaye, p. 238.

4. Advertisement, The London Times, March 7, 1896, p. 10 D.

tograph was exhibited once or twice a day, as one number, in
an evening of variety turns. An advertisement on page eight
of the London Times of April 16, 1896, reveals the motion
picture's position in the variety house program:

Empire - Grand Varieties

Egger-Reiser. Tyrolean Singers and Dancers	7:45
'La Danse,' New Ballet	7:55
Schwarz Bros.	8:55
The Lusinskis, Russian Dancers	9:10
(First appearance in England)	
The Schaffers, Acrobats	9:20
Fred Mills, Ventriloquist	9:35
Lumiere Cinematographe, under the sole	
management of Monsieur Trewey	9:45
Paul Cinquevalli (Juggler)	10:10
'Faust Ballet' (Second Edition)	10:30
Griffin and Dubois, Eccentrics	11:35

[1]

Shortly after the Empire included motion pictures in its
program, Egyptian-Hall, "England's House of Mystery"; and the
Alhambra, a variety house; and Olympia, an amusement park,
followed suit.

An advertisement in the London Times of March 19, 1896,
indicates that the Egyptian-Hall engagement began less than two
weeks after the first Empire exhibition. [2] And both the Olympia
and Alhambra engagements seem to have followed the "House of
Mystery's" showings within a few days.

_____

1. Advertisement, The London Times, April 16, 1896, p. 8 E.

2. "Entertainment & C.", The London Times, March 19, 1896, p. 1 E.

The film exhibitions at Olympia were announced in the
London Times of March 24, 1896, [1] while the first exhibition
of films at the Alhambra was announced in the Times of the
following day, March 25, 1896. The Alhambra announcement follows:

> Alhambra. - The Animatographe.
>   Animated Pictures
> For the first Time, To-night, at 10 o'clock
>
> _____
>
> Alhambra. - The Animatographe.
>   To-night, at 10 o'clock
> Exhibited under the personal superintendence of
> the inventor, Mr. R. W. Paul. [2]

Both Olympia, which was managed by Sir Augustus Harris,
and the Alhambra, which was managed by Mr. Moul, employed the
animatograph, the projector constructed by Paul.

The Alhambra, like the Empire, presented the motion picture
as one number in a series of acts. But at Olympia, which was
an amusement park, the motion picture was probably presented
continuously, from noon to closing, as a side-show attraction.
The following advertisement taken from the London Times of June
27, 1896, reveals the character of Sir Augustus Harris' Olympia:

> Olympia. - Open from 12 to 11 p.m. Continuous amuse-
> ment. Wet or fine. International Cycle Races. Splendid
> Company of Variety Artistes. Charming Illuminated Pleasure
> Gardens. Open-air Cafe Chantant. Popular Concerts. Every
> Evening by Riviere's Grand Orchestra and Band of H. M. Scots

_____

1. "Entertainments & C.", The London Times, March 24, 1896, p. 1 E.

2. Advertisement, The London Times, March 25, 1896, p. 8 E.

Guards. The Rontgen 'X' Rays. Merry Macbeth by Whimsical
Walker. Animated Pictures. Crystal Gardens, &c. Admissions, One Shilling. Thousand of free seats. Refresh-
ments at Popular Prices. Book to Addison-road (Kensington)
Station. [1]

It is easy to understand why the motion picture immediately

found an outlet in the variety houses, and in the recreation

centers of a similar character. The very method of presenting

ten or twelve acts, as an evening's entertainment, permitted a

variety theatre manager to gamble frequently with new acts which

he thought might strike the public's fancy. While taking a

chance with a new number, he could easily maintain the reputation

of his house with eight or nine favorite acts. The same situation,

of course, existed in an amusement park like Olympia.

F. A. Talbot asserts that Robert Paul's animatograph was

the first motion picture projector to be given a public demon-

stration in Great Britain. [2] But on the authority of the London

Times, and the Optical Magic Lantern Journal and Photographic

Enlarger, Talbot is in error; the Lumiere cinematograph was the

first projector to be given a public demonstration in Great

Britain.

Talbot also relates that when Paul's machine was demonstrated

at the library of the Royal Institution on February 28, 1896,

Lady Augustus Harris was present. Unlike the members of the Royal

----

1. "Entertainments & C", The London Times, June 27, 1896, p. 1 E.

2. Talbot, p. 39.

Institution, who were interested in the projector as a scientific instrument, Lady Harris, according to Talbot, regarded the motion picture from a theatrical point-of-view, and was much impressed with its possibilities as an entertainment medium. Her impressions, which were related to her husband that same night, excited him to such a degree that he communicated with Paul and made a breakfast engagement with him for the next morning. [1] Harris was eager to book the projector for an exhibition at Olympia.

After concluding a deal with the inventor on the following day, Harris, again according to Talbot, surprised Paul by telling him that he had heard of a French invention being used in Paris similar to Paul's animatograph. This information "took the experimenter by surprise, for he had been labouring in absolute ignorance that other men were at work in the same field." [2]

Now it is possible that Paul, while constructing his machine, did work in absolute ignorance that other experimenters were working toward the same goal. But it seems very unlikely that neither Paul nor Harris had heard of the motion picture exhibitions which were taking place at the Marlborough-Hall Polytechnic on the very day the above remarks were supposed to have been made. As a matter of fact, if Sir Augustus, while having breakfast with Paul on February 29th, had turned to the first page of

----

1. Talbot, p. 39.
2. Talbot, p. 40.

the London Times he would have found:

> MARLBOROUGH-HALL   the Polytechnic
> Regent-street, W.
> Living Photographs, Life Size,
> by LUMIERE'S CINEMATOGRAPH
> The most perfect illusion of living actuality,
> already the talk of London. Punctually at
> every hour, from 2 to 10. One shilling. [1]

Ramsaye also indicates that neither Harris nor Paul,
during their conversation of the 29th, were aware of the
Marlborough-Hall exhibitions, or of any previous exhibitions
of the Lumiere projector in London. But Ramsaye's report of
the press showing of the cinematograph at the Empire Theatre
on February 7, 1896, [2] make the unawareness of both Paul and
Harris *seem* still more unlikely.

The truth of the matter is probably this. Harris was impressed with the cinematograph exhibitions at the Marlborough-
Hall Polytechnic and wanted very much to find another machine
to install at Olympia so that he could compete for the trade.
The Lumiere machine was already engaged, so he was temporarily
prevented from realizing his wish. But as soon as he heard his
wife's report he considered it a windfall, and depending on her
judgment, immediately engaged the animatograph.

Talbot complicates matters further by declaring that the
Lumiere machine failed to create a sensation in England because

---

1. "Entertainments & C", The London Times, February 29, 1896. p. 1 D.
2. Ramsaye, p. 238.

Paul's animatograph had already been seen at Olympia and held
first place in public esteem. [1] We know, of course, that the
exhibition of the French projector antedated the exhibition of
Paul's machine at both Olympia and the Alhambra. But this
point aside, we wonder if the Lumiere machine did not prove more
of a sensation than Talbot would have us believe when we consider Sir Augustus Harris' advertisement in the London Times
of Thursday March 26, 1896:

> Olympia
>   'The Theatrograph' (Paul's)
>   Animated Pictures
> The most startling scientific marvel of the age [2]
> Similar to the Cinematographe at the Empire

If Harris felt that the theatrograph, or animatograph,
was better or even as good as the cinematograph, it seems
unlikely that he would have acknowledged that Paul's projector
was "Similar to the Cinematographe at the Empire."

Grau repeats the mistake of Talbot and Ramsaye by placing
the Alhambra and Olympia exhibitions of the Paul machine before
the Marlborough-Hall Polytechnic, and the Empire showings, but
he declares that the cinematograph "was simpler, more accurate,
and immeasurably more scientific than Paul's Animatographe." [3]

---

1. Talbot, pp. 46-47.

2. "Entertainments & C", The London Times, March 26, 1896, p. 1 E.

3. Robert Grau, The Theatre of Science, p. 6.

Before discussing the first commercially successful exhibition of the Armat projector it is necessary to consider
briefly a business arrangement that made the exhibition possible.
The events leading up to the arrangement can be traced to the
indifference of Edison, with his lack of faith in projected
motion pictures.

During the period, 1894-1895, when other inventors in
France, England, and the United States worked to achieve projection, Edison had, as we have noted, assigned this problem
to an assistant, Charles H. Kayser, and devoted his own efforts
to the job of manufacturing the kinetophone, a combination
phonograph and peep show machine. In the inventor's mind there
was no question as to which was the more important undertaking;
to Edison, motion pictures were simply a supplement to the phonograph. He had felt that way in 1887, and by 1895 he had not
changed his mind.

With the kinetophone a patron was able to put tubes to his
ears, look through the viewing lens, and hear as well as see
subjects which had been recorded both on the phonograph and
kinetograph. Sound was synchronized with film movements by
mechanical means.

While Edison was bringing the kinetophone around to a
marketable condition, Kayser was not having a happy time with
the problem of motion picture projection, and Raff and Gammon,

at whose instance Kayser had been set to work, were becoming
very annoyed and worried.

This uneasiness on the part of the Kinetoscope Company
managers can probably be traced to the pantoptikon exhibitions
during the spring of 1895, and to the commercial release of
the mutoscope during the fall of the same year: the first event
suggested great profits if Edison would develop a satisfactory
projector; and the second event introduced competition which
depressed the company's income. Desperation letters sent to
Edison were ignored, and Raff and Gammon, though they were
reluctant to break with the inventor, were ready for extreme
measures in the face of this treatment.

Stories of the unrest existing in the Kinetoscope Company
spread, and Armat, having succeeded in bringing his projector
into good working order, decided that he might take advantage
of the situation. He wired Raff and Gammon information about
his projector. The telegram was viewed with scepticism, but
during December, 1895, Frank Gammon visited Armat in Washington,
and was given a demonstration. Gammon was impressed, and he
and his partner, Raff, decided, even though it meant a break
with the inventor, to finance Armat's projector. But knowing
the commercial value of Edison's name they determined first to
feel him out, and see what he thought about the idea of manu-

facturing Armat's projector. Obviously Edison was not pleased,
but in the end Raff and Gammon prevailed and arrangements were
made to manufacture the projector at the Edison plant in Orange.

Because the magic name of Edison would be helpful in
selling the projector, it was agreed among Armat, Edison, Raff
and Gammon that the machine, which was named the vitascope,
should be released as an Edison product.

The vitascope was exhibited to the press on April 3, 1896,
and exhibited publicly on April 23, at Koster and Bials' Music
Hall, Herald Square, New York City. The music hall showing was
advertised in the New York Daily Tribune of April 23, 1896:

> KOSTER & BIAL'S MUSIC HALL   34th-st.
> Tonight, first time   VITASCOPE
> Edison's Marvel, The   VITASCOPE
> CHEVALIER   and all the   1
> CHEVALIER   Foreign Stars.

Following the introduction of the vitascope at Koster and
Bial's, J. Austin Fynes, manager of Keith's Union Square Theatre,
decided that he too would like to exploit the new motion pictures.
Being unable to secure the vitascope, because his Herald Square
competitors had secured exclusive rights to the Edison-Armat
machine for showings in New York City, Fynes began looking for
other machines. Of course his field was limited, but he did
have the pantoptikon, the cinematograph, and the animatograph to
choose from. After considering and rejecting the Latham's pro-

---

1. Advertisement, New York Daily Tribune, April 23, 1896, p. 9 F.

jector, he decided to investigate the Lumiere and Paul machines.

At the same time Fynes was trying to secure a projector,
B. F. Keith was preparing to sail for Europe on a business-
pleasure trip, so Fynes took advantage of the opportunity and
advised his employer to investigate both machines when he arrived
abroad. Keith after inspecting both the cinematograph and the
animatograph decided to negotiate for the cinematograph, but
when he prepared to buy the French machine he discovered that
the American rights had been sold to W. B. Hurd, who had just
sailed for New York. Keith cabled this information to Fynes,
who made it a point to meet Hurd at the pier when he arrived.

After being given a demonstration of the cinematograph,
Fynes agreed to pay Hurd $350 a week for each Keith theatre in
which the machine was employed. Robert Grau observes that "This
was, in fact, the inauguration of the moving pictures as a theatrical attraction of importance." [1]

There is no question that the exhibition of the cinematograph at the Keith theatres was an event of tremendous importance
in the development of the motion pictures in the United States.
Fynes was regarded highly by vaudeville managers throughout the
country, and his acceptance of the new machine was a signal for
other theatre managers to include motion pictures in their programs.

---

1. Grau, p. 8.

The first exhibition of the cinematograph at Keith's Union
Square Theatre was given on June 29, 1896. The showing was
announced in the New York Times of June 28, 1896:

> KEITH'S   New Union Square Theatre
>   Continuous Performance
> First Exhibition in America
> of the Celebrated
> "LUMIERE'S CINEMATOGRAPHE"
> The Sensation of Europe
> Exhibited before all the crowned heads and
> hailed universally as the
> GREATEST MARVEL OF THE 19TH CENTURY
> Also big vaudeville show, headed by
> Bus Williams, Chas. Dickson and 40 others
> Noon to 11 p.m. - No Stop
> Orch., 50 c.; Balcs., 25 c.   1

And the same issue of the Times carried a story by a
reporter who had attended a private showing of the machine on
June 27. The story follows:

> One of the several English equivalents of the
> vitascope, called the Lumiere Cinematographe, will be
> placed on exhibition at Keith's Union Square Theatre
> to-morrow night. It is much better than its name, as was
> proved at a private view yesterday morning. It is said
> to be the first stereopticon kinetoscope exhibited. Its
> pictures are clear and interesting. One represents the
> arrival and departure of mail trains in a railroad station,
> another the bathing pier at Nice at the height of the
> season. 2

Fynes' competitive move bore fruit quickly, for in September,
1896, two of the Proctor vaudeville houses installed vitascopes.
The Proctor engagements were announced in the New York Times of

---

1. Advertisement, The New York Times, June 28, 1896, p. 11 G.

2. "Shows of the Summer," The New York Times, June 28, 1896,
   p. 10 A.

September 13, 1896:

  Edison's Vitascope will be the main attraction at
Proctor's Pleasure Palace this week. A number of new
views have been arranged, including the arrival of Li
Hung Chang, the firing of cannon at the Peekskill en-
campment, the sinking of the Rosedale, and the arrival
of an elevated train at the Twenty-third Street Station; [1]

and

  Edison's Vitascope will be on exhibition this week
at Proctor's Theatre in West Twenty-third Street at
1:04, 3:50, and 10 P.M. [2]

On October 12, 1896, the biograph made its first appearance

in a theatre in New York City, the Olympia Music Hall. [3] The

New York Times of October 18, 1896, reported the exhibition a

"big hit". [4]

  It is interesting to note that the vitascope which had

opened at Koster and Bial's in April had moved on to the Proctor

theatres by September. And the biograph which had opened at

the Music Hall in October had moved on to Koster and Bial's by

November. [5] The motion picture was beginning to spread its

wings.

  Ramsaye writes that Rich G. Hollaman introduced the cinemato-

---

1. "Notes of the Week," The New York Times, Sept. 13, 1896, p. 18 B.

2. "Notes of the Week."

3. "A Moving Picture of McKinley," New York Daily Tribune, Oct.
13, 1896, p. 7 B.

4. "Notes of the Week," The New York Times, Oct. 18, 1896, p. 11 B.

5. "Notes of the Week," The New York Times, Nov. 8, 1896, p. 11 B.

graph to the Eden Musee patrons on the very same night that Fynes introduced the machine to the Union Square audiences. Hollaman, it seems, argued Fynes into allowing the Musee to engage the cinematograph right along with the Keith theatres on the grounds that "the unique institution of thrills in wax work was a museum not a theatre." [1]

However, the New York Times article of June 28th which gave an advance notice of the film exhibitions to be given at the Union Square Theatre, and which Ramsaye quotes in part, [2] gives no indication that the Eden Musee presented films at the same time, though it did cover the museum's program for the week.

Ramsaye no doubt has evidence to support his statement that Fynes and Hollaman introduced the cinematograph in New York at the same time, but as yet I have not discovered the source of his information. Grau says that Hollaman established motion pictures at the Eden Musee shortly after the Union Square Theatre success. [3]

Talbot recognizes the importance of Rich G. Hollaman and the Musee engagements in the development of the motion picture in the United States, but again some of his facts are confused.

---

1. Ramsaye, p. 263.
2. Ramsaye, p. 264.
3. Grau, p. 10.

Talbot ignores Fynes' enterprise, and credits Hollaman with
having introduced the cinematograph to America. [1] This
mistake is perhaps of little consequence, but the further
assertion that screen projection in the United States was
unknown prior to the introduction of the Lumiere projector [2]
makes unreliable his final assertion that the French machine
laid the foundation of the motion picture industry in America. [3]
This remark is as much subject to doubt as his statement that
the Lumiere machine failed to create a sensation in England
because Paul's machine had already been seen in England and consequently held first place in public esteem.

Toward December, 1896, "the Edison Projecting Kinetoscope
was coming on the open market as a mere piece of machinery,
available to any purchaser, regardless of territory or intended
use." [4] This was a new method of distributing projecting equipment, which was bound to have a stimulating effect on the development of the motion picture in the United States. Hitherto, in
New York City, at any rate, the booking of a biograph, a cinematograph, or a vitascope, by a theatre, or by a chain of theatres,
seems to have included exclusive exhibition rights for the projector engaged. The different makes of projection machines up

---

1. Talbot, p. 47.
2. Talbot, p. 47.
3. Talbot, p. 47.
4. Ramsaye, p. 323.

to this time seem to have been as limited in their capacity
to be in more than one place at one time as the vaudeville
actors performing in the theatres where the motion pictures
were being shown.

CHAPTER III

FIRST PUBLIC EXHIBITIONS
OF THE MOTION PICTURE ON THE ROAD

While the films were finding a place in the vaudeville
and variety theatres of London and New York, the motion picture
showmen had taken to the road. With their brief one-night
stands, and sometimes more extended engagements in the smaller
towns and cities, the road showmen did as much to introduce the
motion picture to new audiences, and keep the film alive during
these early precarious years, as did the vaudeville managers in
the larger cities.

The Lumiere camera-showmen, who started their long tours
in the summer of 1895, [1] were the first in the field. But they
did not go without competition for long. In England the magic
lantern lecturers accepted the motion picture with such prompt-
ness that the Optical Magic Lantern Journal commented in the
issue of April, 1896:

> The present boom, as regards the lantern, appears
> to be in the direction of 'animated projection.' [2]

It was natural for the lanternists to accept the motion

---

1. Ramsaye, p. 314. There seems to be no question about the
precedence of the Lumiere showmen, but the summer of 1895
seems a bit beforehand. Ramsaye himself gives December 28,
1895, as the date for the first commercial showing of the
cinematograph.

2. The Dreamer, "Topical Notes," The Optical Magic Lantern
Journal and Photographic Enlarger, vii (April, 1896). 71.

picture so readily. They knew where lecturers were welcome,
and furthermore many of them had a certain amount of technical
knowledge which would enable them to adjust to the requirements
of the new machine. But even if the lecturers were not handy
with machines they knew where they could find experienced lantern
operators, who would have no trouble learning how to operate a
motion picture projector.

The extent of some of the tours which the lanternists
undertook is illustrated by an article in the Optical Magic
Lantern Journal of November, 1896, which reports the activities
of Mr. C. W. Locke. The article, headlined "Animated Photographs
at Brechlin," reports that Mr. Locke, who manipulated the
cinematoscope, as well as the slide lantern, at Trechin, was
also booked to operate animated photographs at Aberdeen, Peter-
head, Montrose, Inverness, Macduff, Elgin, and "other places." [1]

But the lanternists frequently went very far afield. In
1899 and 1900, E. H. Stevenson, a reverend gentleman as well as
a motion picture operator, undertook a series of lantern lecture
engagements in out-of-the-way settlements maintained by the church
in Australia. [2]

While enroute to the continent down under, Mr. Stevenson

1. "Notes," The Optical Magic Lantern Journal and Photographic
Enlarger, vii (November, 1896). 173-174.

2. E. H. Stevenson, "Cinematographic Entertainments at Sea,"
The Optical Magic Lantern Journal and Photographic Enlarger,
xi (February, 1900). 15.

contributed to the entertainment of the passengers and crew
aboard the ship R. M. S. "Omrah" by presenting motion picture
entertainments on four different occasions. The following bill
was prepared for the first showing:

R. M. S. "Omrah," Mediterranean Sea.

———————————————————————————————————

A CINEMATOGRAPH ENTERTAINMENT

will be held

THE SALOON

on Wednesday, October 25th, 1899, at 8 o'clock

by Mr. E. H. Stevenson

———————————————————————————————————

REALISTIC MAJESTIC ARTISTIC COMIC [1]

The exhibitions were well received; indeed, Mr. E. H.
Stevenson received a compliment from the carpenter's mate,
Mr. R. H. Long, which unquestionably stirred up envy in the
breasts of fellow exhibitors in the year of 1900. Mr. Long
wrote:

The Two Stevensons -- R. L. and E. H.

The one with fluent pen can keenly throw
Pictures of life upon his book, and lo!
We look thereon and see men come and go,
          As on this earth;
And love and pain and passion flow
          In tears and mirth.

———————————

1. E. H. Stevenson.

The other with a film before a light,
The whole world marshals to our startled sight;
And flings broadcast in dancing black and white
           Upon a screen,
Till scarce we dare to think we see aright,
           But in a dream. [1]

The foremost English showman of these early years seems to have been T. J. West. According to Talbot he organized traveling motion picture shows that not only toured England, but the colonies as well. [2]

In America, as in England and France, the motion picture was finding an outlet to the public through the traveling film shows, as well as through the vaudeville theatres in the larger cities.

Le Roy Latham, nephew of Woodville Latham, was the first American motion picture showman. In the summer of 1895 he bought the territorial rights to the Latham machine for Virginia. His enterprise was not successful, however, for after exhibiting his program of five films in Norfolk, Newport News, and Richmond he gave up the motion picture business altogether. An inferior projector and a scarcity of films contributed to his failure.

But other showmen soon took Latham's place, especially after Raff and Gammon began selling territorial rights to the Armat-Edison machine.

---

1. E. H. Stevenson.

2. Talbot, p. 130.

Among the first to acquire a projector from Raff and Gammon was William T. Rock, who purchased the vitascope rights to Louisiana for $1,500. Rock opened a motion picture "store" theatre in New Orleans on June 28, 1896, and continued to operate in this one location for three months.

The length of this engagement -- unusual for 1896 -- can probably be attributed to the fact that Rock was among the very first of the showmen in the field and consequently had the advantage of novelty in his favor. He was certainly not assisted in his enterprise by being able to secure an unlimited supply of new subjects since he was dependent on one motion picture producer for all of his films, Edison.

After exhausting the market in New Orleans, Rock moved out into the smaller cities of the state showing the same films he had exhibited in New Orleans.

The exhibitors very real problem of securing subjects during the first ten years of the motion picture's existence precluded the possibility of a motion picture theatre as we know it today. But this condition did not prevent some showmen from attempting to establish permanent quarters for the new medium. During the summer of 1897, Alexander F. Victor, finding a vacant store room in Newark, New Jersey, fitted it up with two hundred chairs and proceeded to give motion picture exhibitions. Endeavoring to strengthen his weak film programs, very much as his fellow exhibitors do today with their bingo games, beauty contests, and symphony orchestra programs, Victor added Bowman's Military Band to the program. But films of sufficient interest were difficult to be had, and Victor's customers, who paid twenty-five cents admission, soon found his programs uninteresting, and not worth the money, so Victor was forced to close.

T. L. Tally, who opened a "Phonograph and Vitascope Parlor" in Los Angeles in August, 1896, did a better job of hedging than Victor. Not only did Tally exploit the vitascope and the phonograph, he also exploited the peep-show machines, the kinetoscope and the mutoscope. In this way he survived. His amusements were cheap, and furthermore he offered his customers variety.

In New England, between 1896 and 1900, the traveling show-men made money by playing to capacity houses on Sundays when the legitimate theatres were closed. [1] Illustrated song slides on the screen added to the pleasure of the customers.

Grau declares that the tremendous popularity of the Sunday film programs first revealed to the theatre managers of New England the new theatre public created by the motion picture:

---

1. Grau, p. 27.

In a city like New Britain, Conn., where moving
pictures created little or no interest during the week,
as a number in the vaudeville house, all of the three
playhouses, and every available hall was utilized on
Sundays, and though admission prices were higher than
now, the attendance was overwhelming for all. [1]

Harry and Herbert Miles, of whom we shall hear more

later, were American showmen who exhibited films far from home

during the early years. In 1901 the brothers presented motion

pictures in Juneau, Alaska, and in the gold camps in the vicinity.

The program for their first exhibition in Juneau on July 26,

read:

THE GREAT AMERICAN BIOGRAPH

Showing life Motion Pictures of the Scenes and
Incidents that have engaged the attention of the entire
World, selected from 10,000 feet of film, which includes:
President McKinley's Triumphal Western Tour; The Galves-
ton Disaster; Beaumont, Texas, Oil Fields; Paris and Pan
American Exposition; Chinese, Philippine and Boer Wars;
Carrie Nation, the Kansas Saloon Smasher. [2]

A brief review of the motion picture programs presented

by the traveling showmen in Ithaca, New York, during the year,

1897, is helpful in revealing how widespread motion picture

exhibitions were in the smaller cities during the second year

of projected motion pictures. It must be remembered, however,

that Ithaca is a university town, and was extremely theatre

conscious, and therefore is not altogether a typical small city.

---

1. Grau, p. 27.

2. Ramsaye, p. 403.

Lyman H. Howe, employing a special machine called the animotiscope, [1] gave a motion picture exhibition in Ithaca on May 8, 1897, at Library Hall. [2] This showing was so popular that the Ladies' Alliance of the Unitarian Church, which had sponsored the exhibition, engaged Howe for a second exhibition on June 3. This time 850 people, paying 25 cents apiece, filled Library Hall to capacity. [3]

Mr. Howe's program consisted of "songs, conversations, etc., well given by the phonograph, after which pictures of moving objects were thrown on the screen." [4]

During August a motion picture of the Corbett and Fitzsimmons prizefight, "by counterpart", was shown at Renwick Beach, an amusement park. This exhibition was not successful for the engagement was cancelled after only one showing, and the management expressed its apologies for a bad performance in the following day's paper:

> The management of the Beach feel that an apology is due the people who attended there last evening, for the very bad vitascope pictures given them. [5]

---

1. Ramsaye, p. 313, and Advertisement, The Ithaca Daily Journal, June 3, 1897, p. 2 A.Ramsaye's spelling-Animatoscope. The Journal's spelling-Animotiscope.
2. Advertisement, The Ithaca Daily Journal, May 8, 1897, p.2 A.
3. "The Animotiscope a Great Hit", The Ithaca Daily Journal, June 4, 1897, p. 6 D.
4. "A Remarkable Exhibition," The Ithaca Daily Journal, May 10, 1897, p. 6C.
5. "Renwick Beach," The Ithaca Daily Journal, August 10, 1897, p. 6C.

The newspaper does not explain what the trouble was, nor does it mention who operated the projector, though it does identify the machine as a vitascope. This motion picture of the prizefight may have been the motion picture produced by Sigmund Lubin, who hired two freight handlers from the Pennsylvania terminal in Philadelphia to re-enact the fight.

On October 4 and 5 the veriscope motion pictures of the real Corbett-Fitzsimmons fight were shown at Ithaca's leading theatre, the Lyceum. The newspaper advertisement declared that "the entire 14 rounds, and the scene 10 minutes before and 5 minutes after the knockout"[1] would be shown. Orchestra seats sold for 75 cents, balcony seats for 50 cents, and gallery seats for 25 cents.

Two days after the veriscope left town the biograph was engaged by Mr. Dixie, who had had the bad luck with the vitascope at Renwick Beach, for a showing at Library Hall. The biograph exhibitions, described as a "great success," were given on October 7, 8, and 9 with a matinee on October 9.[2] Only about 200 people attended the first showing, and Mr. Dixie allowed that the 50 cents admission price may have been responsible for the poor attendance. At any rate, he reduced the admission to 25 cents for the last three exhibitions.

---

1. Advertisement, The Ithaca Daily Journal, October 4, 1897, p. 2 A.

2. "Biograph A Success," The Ithaca Daily Journal, October 8, 1897, p. 6 E.

The last motion picture exhibition of the year was given
on December 10 at the Lyceum. The Alonzo Hatch Company presented
the animatoscope as one number in a series of acts. [1]

The travelling showmen while providing an outlet for the
motion picture during the period 1896-1900 were also laying the
foundation for the permanent establishments which would house
motion picture exhibitions in later years.

But the realization of motion picture theatres as we know
them today had to wait upon the establishment of large, efficient
producing and distributing companies to provide the theatres
with films regularly, and at low prices.

The speed with which projected motion pictures found their
way out into the country should be noted.

In both England, and in the United States, metropolitan
exhibitions antedated provincial exhibitions by only a matter of
months, and in some cases weeks. For example, Mr. Locke, by
November, 1896, slightly more than nine months after the London
premier, was booked to exhibit motion pictures in Scotland; and
Mr. Rock, by June 28, 1896, slightly more than nine weeks after
the New York premier, was exhibiting motion pictures in New Orleans.
And, even though he failed because of an inferior projector, we
must not forget LeRoy Latham's exhibitions in Virginia during the

----

1. Advertisement, The Ithaca Daily Journal, December 10, 1897, p 2 A.

summer of 1895.

Today the impact of the motion picture is felt throughout
the world. In 1895 and 1896, the motion picture's outposts in
the hinterlands were already being established.

CHAPTER IV

THE EXHIBITOR AND HIS PROBLEMS

When motion pictures were first presented in the vaudeville houses, and on the road, the showmen had to determine the most effective ways of presenting films to the public. Perhaps the method of presentation, apart from the mere business of threading and operating a projector, does not appear too important during this early period when subjects fifty feet in length were the rule, but frequently the selection and arrangement of film programs did influence audience receptivity and comfort, and this in turn had a bearing on the motion picture showmen's success or failure.

When vaudeville managers determined to introduce motion pictures into their programs it was natural to include them as one turn in a number of acts. And since a vaudeville turn lasts approximately fifteen or twenty minutes it was necessary to arrange a schedule of approximately ten of the standard one-and-two minute films to fill the time allotted an act. There were some variations, but this method of presenting films in the vaudeville houses seems to have persisted for the first ten years of the motion picture's existence.

The film program shown at Koster and Bial's in New York, and that shown at the Empire in London, seem to remain typical of the period. The Empire film program, which ran 25 minutes, [1] and was one vaudeville number in a program of ten, [2] consisted of eleven subjects:

> Landing passengers from a steamer,
> Two babies pulling each other's hair,
> Boys bathing at the seashore,
> Boys sailing boats on a pond,
> Scene in Trafalgar Square at noon,
> Arrival and departure of a train,
> Laborers tipping a brick wall over,
> Man watering a garden,
> Boatman rowing a boat,
> Two acrobats,
> Scene in a public park. [3]

The Koster and Bial's film program, which was one vaudeville act in a series of eight given before the first intermission, [4] consisted of twelve subjects:

> Sea Waves,
> Umbrella Dance,
> The Barber Shop,
> Burlesque Boxing,
> Monroe Doctrine,
> A Boxing Bout,
> Venice, showing Gondolas,
> Kaiser Wilhelm, reviewing his troops,
> Skirt Dance,
> The Bar Room, [5]
> Cuba Libre.

---

1. Advertisement, The London Times, April 16, 1896, p. 8.
2. Advertisement, The London Times, April 16, 1896, p. 8.
3. Ramsaye, p. 241. From a Letter by Charles H. Webster, Raff, and Gammon's agent in London, who saw the program.
4. Ramsaye, opposite p. 249. From a reproduction of the Koster and Bial program.
5. Ramsaye, opposite p. 249. From a reproduction of the Koster and Bial program.

According to Charles H. Webster, Raff and Gammon's vitascope
agent in London, the wait between films at the Empire was between
fifteen and twenty seconds. [1]

There was probably a corresponding wait between pictures at
Koster and Bial's, for film in the vitascope, at first, was
threaded on a spool-bank, as in a kinetoscope peep-show machine. [2]
This arrangement permitted continuous projection of a single film,
but it most certainly delayed the threading of the projector because
of the numerous sprocket wheels over which the film had to be
threaded.

And even though two projectors were used at Koster and Bial's, [3]
it is likely that the shortness of the films would have prevented
an exhibitor from having all twelve subjects projected continuously
without a break even if he had thought it desirable.

Actually the exhibitor probably desired a very brief intermission between subjects to allow the audience to accommodate itself
to the change in film subjects. Talbot advises this policy as
late as 1912. [4] And furthermore, the second machine may have been
installed for the sake of having a reserve apparatus handy in case

---

1. Ramsaye, p. 240.

2. Illustration, New York Herald, May 5, 1896.

3. Illustration, New York Herald, May 5, 1896.

4. Talbot, p. 135.

the first machine broke down. Talbot, again in 1912, suggests
this as a reason for installing two projectors in a motion
picture theatre. [1] He does not suggest that the exhibitor project
films continuously, one after the other, as we do in our motion
picture theatres today.

In the "shop" theatres, and out on the road the exhibitors
faced a problem unlike that faced by the vaudeville motion picture
exhibitor. Whereas the latter could depend on his vaudeville
performers to carry the program, and give the audience its money's
worth, the travelling showman depended almost entirely on films
to carry off the honors of the evening, as well as provide the
time bulk in respect to the evening's entertainment. As a consequence, the travelling showman was forced to employ a method
of presentation unlike that used in the vaudeville theatres, where
ten or twelve heterogeneous film subjects could be shown in the
allotted time of fifteen or twenty minutes without causing weariness.

Faced with the responsibility of organizing a film program
lasting an hour or more the travelling showman, at first, exhibited
very little ingenuity or imagination. He merely threaded and projected one by one a miscellaneous assortment of one-minute subjects

---

1. Talbot, p. 135.

for the required length of time. That the exhibitor managed to
prosper despite such indifferent showmanship can only be explained
by the public's tremendous initial interest in a machine which
could create the illusion of movement.

But once the novelty of films wore off, some of the exhibitors realized that they would have to revise this method of
exhibiting films if they were to retain the interest of their
audiences.

Of course, to begin with, they would have to show greater
care in the selection of subjects, and then too they would have
to equip themselves with better projectors.

But it was the method of presentation that needed a great
deal of attention.

One of the foremost schemes advanced suggested the inter-
mingling of films and slides. This method of showing slides
between each film was scored by the Showman on the grounds that
an audience when it came to see animated photographs, did not
want to have the "time taken up with ordinary lantern views." [1]
Hopwood, however, recommended this method because he thought that
the effect of the dynamic motion pictures was heightened when
contrasted with the static slides. [2]

---

1. The Showman, "Animated Photographs and Projecting Machines,"
   The Optical Magic Lantern Journal and Photographic Enlarger,
   viii (June, 1897). 103-105.

2. Hopwood, p. 212.

Cecil Hepworth, who was the foremost exponent of the alter-
nating slide and film method, thought that the introduction of
slides, because "of these there is always a greater variety to
choose from," gave the exhibitor a better chance to string his
motion pictures and slides together into episodes or sets. [1]
And if the entertainers were ingenious enough and careful enough,
Hepworth comments, they could actually construct a "plot" on
which to hang their animated pictures and slides. This latter
Method would, of course, facilitate transition from motion picture to slide to motion picture, etc. Secondly, Hepworth thought
that the slides provided a thorough rest for the eyes after the
more or less tiring motion pictures. There was probably considerable point to this argument, for M. Gaumont, annoyed by
the flickering of the projected picture, had devised a black hand
fan, pierced with many holes, called "La Grille," which a spectator might hold with a waving movement between his eyes and the
screen in order to eliminate the flickering. [2] Hopwood, noting
that fingers are far anterior in point of time to the Grille, suggests that a vibrating black-gloved hand with fingers slightly
spread provides almost as much relief as the Frenchman's device.

In practically no time at all the more enterprising exhibitors

---

1. Hepworth, pp. 83-34.

2. "Notes," The Optical Magic Lantern Journal and Photographic
   Enlarger, viii (June, 1897). 101-102.

began assembling their short films into sets, so that they told
a little story, or had more meaning. When Lyman Howe gave his
showing in Ithaca on May 10, 1897, he attempted this very thing
with four fire department scenes, and the Ithaca Daily Journal
reviewing the motion pictures he exhibited, observed:

> Perhaps the most effective were a series of four,
> representing a fire alarm in New York City. [1]

Howe and his fellow exhibitors found precedent for this
practice in the lantern lectures. A study of the Advertisements
in the Optical Magic Lantern Journal and Photographic Enlarger
reveals the type of program presented by the lanternists:

> SLIDES, set 25, Temperance, 'Which side wins,' life models
> (sale or exchange). P.E.W., 52 Fairfield Road, Bow. [2]

> Lantern Slides. - The Tower of London, twenty-four slides,
> 12s.; 'A Day at the Zoo,' thirty slides, 15s.; and fifty
> London slides, 25s. - John Stabb, 154, Queen's-road,
> Bayswater. [3]

Appropriate music and sound effects seem to have been arranged
for film exhibitions in the vaudeville and variety houses from
the very beginning.

---

1. "A Remarkable Exhibition," The Ithaca Daily Journal, May 10,
   1897. p. 6 C.

2. "General Wants & c.," The Optical Magic Lantern Journal and
   Photographic Enlarger, vi (February, 1895).

3. "General Wants & c.," The Optical Magic Lantern Journal and
   Photographic Enlarger, v (November, 1894).

The New York Times in speaking of the cinematograph exhibition at Keith's Union Square Theatre during the summer of 1896, says:

> This week new military views are to be added, one scene representing an actual battle between two troops of cavalry. There will be the flashes of sabres, noise of the guns, and all the other realistic theatrical effects. [1]

And Henry V. Hopwood in his book, "Living Pictures," which was published in 1899, says that a motion picture of the "Albion" launch disaster, exhibited only thirty hours after the tragedy, was accompanied by an orchestra playing "Rocked in the Cradle of the Deep." [2]

These were interesting early uses of music and sound effects employed in connection with motion picture exhibitions; but Messrs. West and Son, who presented a program entitled, "Our Navy", at the Regent Street Polytechnic in London, during the fall of 1899, seem to have achieved the ultimate in sound accompaniment for motion pictures during the years before 1900.

The Optical Magic Lantern Journal, which enthusiastically endorsed the program, indicates that the sound effects contributed appreciably to the success of the program:

> The pictures, which include about 40 sets of 'animated,' are perhaps the finest collection ever given at any one entertainment. Some of the best subjects are physical exercises (with band accompaniment), cutlass exercise (with

---

1. "The Summer Shows," The New York Times, July 5, 1896, p. 10 B.

2. Henry V. Hopwood, Living Pictures, p. 231.

audible hits), gun firing, yacht races, etc. All the fakes possible, such as the boom of the guns, the swish of the water, and so on, are realistically manoeuvered behind the scenes, and the two hours of entertainment goes along without a hitch; yet the time seems short, and one wishes there had been more. [1]

It seems reasonable to assume that large, versatile orchestras accompanied all of the film shows presented in the vaudeville and variety theatres. The orchestras were already there to accompany the vaudeville performers, and certainly the idea of sound accompaniment for films was not new. Edison, as we have seen, thought of the motion picture as a complement to his phonograph, and he persisted in associating the two instruments, even though he failed to realize a completely satisfactory combination of the machines. An expression of his opinion is found in the June 16, 1894, issue of the Electrical World:

> I believe that in coming years, by my own work and that of Dickson, Muybridge, Marie and others who will doubtless enter the field, that grand opera can be given at the Metropolitan Opera House at New York without any material change from the original, and with artists and musicians long since dead. [2]

But even without this Edison tradition to influence them, the theatre orchestras of the day having been reared in the tradition of melodrama appreciated fully the value of descriptive

---

1. "A Lantern Entertainment Well Worth a Visit," The Optical Magic Lantern Journal and Photographic Enlarger, x (November, 1899). 143.

2. "The Kineto-Phonograph", The Electrical World, xxiii (June 16, 1894). 799-801.

music. [1] And to add to the loveliness of the heroine, and to
the sinisterness of the villain, and to the urgency of a fight,
and to the innumerable passions and moods of stage characters
in a play was their stock and trade. So it seems likely that
even if the theatre managers had not instructed them to accompany
with music and sound effects the motion picture of "a battle
between two troops of cavalry," they probably would have
instinctively fallen into playing a von Suppe overture, or some
other appropriate piece of music, upon witnessing such an
exhibition.

Music served still another purpose during the early film
exhibitions. Frequently, motion picture showmen were forced to
set up their projectors in an auditorium along with the spectators,
rather than in sound-proof booths. This arrangement caused the
audience discomfort, for the noisy machines "disturbed visual
enjoyment to no small extent." [2] As a result of this situation
the exhibitors resorted to mechanical instruments like the barrel-
organ, the orchestrion, the music box and the phonograph to
minimize the unpleasant noise with one more agreeable. [3]

The mechanical instruments served to drown out the unpleasant

---

1. Frank S. Ferguson, English Melodrama in the Early Nineteenth
   Century, p. 4.
2. Kurt London, Film Music, Trans. Bensinger, p. 27.
3. Kurt London.

NORTHEAST NEBRASKA TECHNICAL
COMMUNITY COLLEGE · LIBRARY

noise of the projectors. But that was probably the limit of
their servicability, since it is unlikely that the exhibitors
undertook the difficult task of synchronizing the "canned"
music pouring out of these machines with the action being portrayed on the screen.

Later, in the small houses which could not afford orchestras,
a piano was employed. This was a step forward, for the piano
player, while providing a pleasant sound which neutralized the
unpleasant sound of the projectors could also by following the
action on the screen provide descriptive music to suit the
action.

As a still later development, pipe organs replaced pianos.
The public endorsed the change with enthusiasm because the organ
was more flexible and more dynamic than the piano. And the
managers were pleased with the change because the organ cost
much less than the orchestra, and proved as satisfying. [1]

Sometimes a musical accompaniment at a film exhibition was
ignored altogether. Jenkins and Depue indicate that this was
occasionally the case even as late as 1908, for in commenting on
the management of a motion picture theatre in their book, "Handbook for Motion Picture and Stereopticon Operators," they remark
that "appropriate music is usually rendered during the exhibition

_____

1. Benjamin B. Hampton, A History of the Movies, pp. 99-100.

of a picture." [1]

Apart from the selection and arrangement of subjects, and
the preparation of music and sound effects to accompany the
exhibitions, there were other problems besetting the motion
picture exhibitor.

The hazard of fire attendant upon the exhibition of motion
pictures, encouraged no doubt by the inflammable nature of
motion picture film, and by the frequent use of exhibition halls
which were veritable fire traps, seems to have made "going to
the movies" during the early years a precarious business.

Though the movement for fire prevention in the legitimate
theatres had been "steadily growing since the early eighties or
before," [2] motion picture exhibitions during the first year or
two escaped official regulation. This free condition probably
existed at first because machines were scarce, expensive, and
fairly difficult to operate; and because the early machines were
operated by men who had been trained by the manufacturers to
appreciate the dangers connected with such work. These were
probable factors which acted as a break on the widespread use of
the motion picture projector, and as a consequence eliminated the
need for fire regulations.

———————

1. C. Francis Jenkins, and Oscar B. Depue, Handbook for Motion
   Picture and Stereopticon Operators, p. 13.

2. Arthur Edwin Krows, Play Production in America, p. 80.

But as soon as the manufacturers released machines on the open market, and as soon as prices were reduced, the projectors fell into the hands of men who were not always aware of the dangers involved in motion picture exhibition. As a consequence a series of fires occurred which created a great deal of public apprehension.

The most serious and sensational of these catastrophes was the Charity Bazaar Fire which took place in Paris on May 4, 1897. Nearly one hundred and fifty persons, mostly women, lost their lives in the disaster. [1] It seems that one of the operators of the motion picture machine used at the bazaar refilled the tank in the light house with fuel while a second operator foolishly struck a match for him to see by. [2] The fuel vapors ignited and spread to inflammable materials near the machine, and the fire was under way. The Paris police, under orders of the Minister of the Interior, responded to the calamity by listing all of the motion picture machines and shows in the city. This was one of the first steps toward regulation of motion picture exhibitions.

Ramsaye remarks:

> If we are to credit the statements given out, it is obvious that it was not at all a film fire, but a result of careless handling of the lamp fuel, which might as well have happened with a stereopticon show or any other use of

---

1. "The Tragedy of the Charity Bazar Fire," Scientific American, lxxvi, (May 15, 1897). 307.

2. Hepworth, p. 79.

similar illumination. But the films got the blame and they have it yet. [1]

And Ramsaye might have gone on to say that the exhibition hall in which the films were shown at the bazaar had only one exit "at all familiar to the ill-fated crowd of 1,500 souls within;" [2] and that the building itself was nothing more than a match box structure which could not have been erected in a city like New York "as long as the building laws were literally interpreted and rigidly enforced." [3]

But Ramsaye's effort to relieve the films of responsibility for fires seems futile. Consider the panic and fire which occurred at a motion picture show held in a tent in Market Place, Bilston, Stafford, on July 4, 1898:

> It appears that one of the gas tubes at the limelight jet became detached, and a slight blaze occurred. This in itself was a small matter and was at once rectified, but someone gave the cry of 'fire,' when a stampede immediately took place, and the 200 people who were present made a mad rush for the exits, where many were knocked down and trampled upon. In the hurry to get out the crowd knocked over the lantern apparatus and a film took fire, which in turn caused the canvas roof of the tent to take fire, necessitating the calling out of the fire brigade, who speedily extinguished the flames. Fortunately none of the audience were seriously injured. [4]

---

1. Ramsaye, p. 354.

2. "The Tragedy at the Charity Bazar, Paris," Scientific American, lxxvi, (May 20, 1897). 307.

3. "The Tragedy at the Charity Bazar, Paris."

4. "Notes," The Optical Magic Lantern Journal and Photographic Enlarger, ix, (December, 1898). 174.

Though a hysterical member of the audience started the panic which led to the fire, it is difficult not to call it a film fire. Clearly, if the projector had been placed in a fire-proof booth, there would have been no trouble.

Such occurrences as the Charity Bazaar, and the Market Place fires were not uncommon during the first years; and considering the lackadaisical practices of some of the men who ran the motion picture machines it is not surprising that fires at motion picture shows happened as often as they did. For example, some of the operators, because they had only one machine and needed to make a number of changes during a program, generally allowed the film to run into a basket, rather than attach it to the take-up reel. [1] The procedure reduced the length of the intermission, but it also, because celluloid is highly inflammable, increased the fire hazards a hundred fold. If a spark were to fall into the basket of loosely packed film the resultant conflagration would be "so sudden and so energetic as to almost equal an explosion." [2]

And other operators, when electricity was not available, frequently employed an ether-oxygen light rather than a mixed-jet limelight. The latter, though safer, was not popular because it required a second cylinder containing hydrogen, which meant ad-

_____

1. Hopwood, p. 215.
2. Hopwood, p. 216.

ditional work for the operator. While the ether-oxygen light
is not dangerous if properly handled, a slight error in its
handling might lead to unfortunate results. "It is undeniable
that the more serious accidents at Living Picture entertainments
have resulted from the employment of this light." [1]

In connection with the Charity Bazaar fire, Hopwood says
that while it is admitted that the projectionist was either
ignorant or forgetful in his attempts to fill his ether reservoir
in the neighborhood of a naked light, "it must not be forgotten
that a similar amount of carelessness in the use of oxy-hydrogen
limelight could not, with gas in cylinders, have led to similar
fatal results." [2]

Ramsaye feels that the bazaar fire seriously "impaired the
status of the screen in the minds of the upper classes and their
followers." [3] He is certainly right; and other film fires unquestionably stirred up similar feelings among all classes of
people. After all, calamaties of this kind were not new, for the
public had seen the great theatres of London and Paris burn down
with regularity during the nineteenth century [4] and they knew that
"once the fire begins, all is over." [5] While this apprehension

1. Hopwood, p. 218.
2. Hopwood, p. 219.
3. Ramsaye, p. 356.
4. Percy Fitzgerald, The World Behind the Scenes, p. 249.
5. Fitzgerald, p. 249.

may have been calmed somewhat by the enactment of regulations which helped reduce the menace in the legitimate houses, the public's fears were probably revived by this new outburst of destruction in the theatres housing motion pictures. Speculation would say that some people stayed away from motion picture exhibitions out of fear.

Large cities saw the need for regulation sooner than cities less densely populated. On November 8, 1898, the London County Council moving to protect the citizenry approved a code aimed to regulate the exhibition of motion pictures. Some of the stipulations are listed below:

1. The Council must be notified of all motion picture showings six days in advance of the exhibition.
2. The motion picture projector shall stand in a suitable fire-proof room which shall be entirely enclosed. The floor of the room must also be fire-proof.
3. The location of the projector must not interfere with an exit.
4. A fireman must be in attendance near the projector with a wet blanket and two buckets of water.
5. The audience must be at least 8 feet away from the lantern.
6. Films must be enclosed in a metal case when not in use.
7. When the film emerges from the projector it must be rewound as fast as it emerges from the machine.
8. Not less than 2 nor more than 3 operators shall be engaged within the lantern space.
9. The entire duty of one of the operators shall consist in taking charge of the film after it has passed from the projector.
10. Smoking within the lantern space shall be forbidden at all times.

11. The exhibitor shall be held responsible for employing competent, experienced and trustworthy operators.
12. No naked gas or oil flames, or matches shall be allowed in the lantern space. [1]

The Optical Magic Lantern Journal and Photographic Enlarger regarded the regulations as "very stringent." [2] And, no doubt, the exhibitors too, after the free and easy methods of the early years, found the new rules irksome and difficult to comply with. But the regulations were sensible, and it was not long before they demonstrated their soundness:

> Cinematograph Fire. -- On the 4th ult. at a Hammersmith Theatre the film for the Cinematograph became ignited, but being enclosed in the fireproof room designed by the London County Council, even those in close proximity were unaware of any mishap. Unfortunately the operator was rather severely burned, and the show had to be postponed. [3]

Film exhibitors out of reach of the London County Council, and similar safety code committees, had the insurance companies to contend with. While not empowered to enforce laws, the companies, if they felt that proper precautions were not being taken, had the privilege of running up rates on premises insured by them. That they did not hesitate to take this line of action is evident:

> The committee controlling the Birmingham Town Hall has decided to allow no cinematographic exhibitions therein, as the insurance rates would be considerably increased if any form of cinematograph apparatus is used. [4]

---

1. "New Cinematographic Regulations," The Optical Magic Lantern and Photographic Enlarger, ix, (December, 1898). 175.

2. "New Cinematographic Regulations."

3. "Cinematograph Fire," The Optical Magic Lantern Journal and Photographic Enlarger, x, (April, 1899). 45.

4. "The Cinematograph and Birmingham Town Hall," The Optical Magic Lantern Journal and Photographic Enlarger, x, (April, 1899). 45.

So the insurance companies as well as organizations like
the London County Council enforced rules which acted as a brake
on indiscriminate film exhibitions; and by the early months of
1899 showing motion pictures in many places was no longer merely
a matter of threading a machine and projecting pictures on a
screen. The exhibitor had to comply with rules relating to
audience safety which made the business of exhibition more complicated and more expensive. These factors were probably influ-
ential in preventing some men and organizations from becoming
exhibitors. This was certainly true of some schools which "merely
because they did not possess a fire-proof chamber in which to
operate them," [1] gave up at least temporarily the idea of showing
motion pictures. Non-inflammable film, which is used in 16 mm.
projectors today, and which can be safely employed in a machine
set up in the midst of an audience, was unknown in the early years.

Ramsaye's effort to minimize the hazards in connection with
film exhibitions seems a trifle overdone. He says: "Motion picture film is in truth about as explosive and about as dangerous,
pound for pound, as yellow pine shavings from a carpenter's work
bench." [2] The dangers of yellow pine shavings aside, we prefer
to quote Hepworth who seems to have a greater appreciation of human

---

1. Talbot, pp. 54-55.

2. Ramsaye, p. 353.

frailty than Ramsaye does:

> It would be idle to deny the fact that there is a
> certain amount of danger connected with the cinematograph
> in careless or incompetent hands. Some there are, I know,
> who deny its existence altogether in this connection;
> but it will generally be found, upon inquiry, that these
> persons are interested in the sale of cinematographs or
> films or other accessories. It is a most short-sighted
> policy, and is sure to recoil on the heads of its
> originators sooner or later, apart from the moral aspect
> of the question. And when it is remembered that the
> inevitable relaxation of precautions, which follows upon
> the assurance from high places that there is no danger,
> jeopardises hundreds of human lives, the matter becomes
> something more than one of sharp business practice. [1]

Hepworth, of course, assumes maximum precautions. But
he apparently was a rare individual, for he made these observations in 1897, one year before the London County Council
enacted the laws governing the management of motion picture
exhibitions.

Another big problem besetting motion picture exhibitors
was the mechanical failure of motion picture equipment. Machine
vibrations, creeping film, inadequate illumination, imperfectly
perforated film, and flicker, all made trouble for the producers
and exhibitors. These problems were unquestionably very serious
for complaints about the motion picture's mechanical shortcomings were common throughout the early years.

---

1. Hepworth, pp. 79-80.

In the editorial, "The Veriscope," which appeared on May 26, 1897, in the New York Times, the writer observed that the veriscope, which was used to project the Corbett-Fitzsimmons fight pictures, left much to be desired; and that the chief trouble with the machine "is the constant quiver that destroys the illusion which might otherwise be created and at last comes to operate actively and unpleasantly on the nerves of the spectator." [1]

The writer goes on to say that to obviate this trouble should be, and no doubt is, the goal of persons operating this machine, but "toward this result they have not thus far made perceptible progress." [2]

Rich G. Hollaman strove continually to improve the quality of his projectors. The Joly machine which he installed at the Eden Musee in February, 1897, was advertised to operate without noise or flicker, and the machine he installed six months later, in August, 1897, was advertised to have stronger light, clearer pictures, and less vibration than other machines. Comparatively the Hollaman machines were probably better than most, but they evidently were not altogether satisfactory for Hollaman organized

---

1. "The Veriscope," The New York Times, May 26, 1897, p. 6 D.
2. "The Veriscope."

a machine project which continued to grapple with the problem of projection.

Cecil Hepworth's advice to prospective purchasers of motion picture equipment is further evidence that mechanical failure was a pressing matter:

> There is a wonderful array of instruments to choose from, and they vary through all degrees of efficiency from the most abominable of 'St. Vituscopes' - as it has been suggested that all cinematographs should be generally called - to the nearest approach to perfection that has at present been obtained. [1]

But perfection seems to have been just as remote two years later, for Hopwood wrote in 1899: "The shutter and its varied failings are, in fact, a weariness of the flesh." [2]

And in 1900 Maclean complained:

> In many instances the unsatisfactory action of projection machines has been due less to their own imperfections than to the perforations of the film not accurately registering with the feeding device. [3]

Mechanical failure of motion picture equipment made trouble enough; but the problem was further aggravated by inexperienced operators who "being neither mechanics nor lanternists, and possessing no knowledge of technicalities, were quite unable to

---

1. Hepworth, p. 12.

2. Hopwood, p.

3. Hector Maclean in Cecil Hepworth's _Animated Photography,_ p. 112.

tell a good machine from a bad one." [1] This situation, which
led to the manufacture and distribution of machines which under
ideal conditions would never have been foisted on the public,
moved the Showman to warn "cinematograph users" that the employment of inferior apparatus badly managed was in good part
responsible for the decline of lantern lectures, and that it
might very well lead to the decline of motion picture exhibitions. [2]

Though motion picture equipment continued to be imperfect,
refinements in the mechanism were frequently being introduced
and within a short period of time a number of the early aggravations were eliminated, or at least partially reduced.

For example, Albert E. Smith of Vitagraph, after having
experienced numerous interruptions during exhibitions because
the outline of the projected picture slipped out of alignment
with the outline of the projected beam of light, devised a movable
framing aperture which could be adjusted while the projector was
in operation. This device which enabled the projectionist to
align the picture and the beam of light, gave Smith's machine
such a tremendous advantage during the months it remained the
sole projector with a framer, that it might "without too much of

_____

1. The Showman, "Animated Photographs and Projecting Machines,"
   The Optical Magic Lantern Journal and Photographic Enlarger,
   viii, (June, 1897).

2. The Showman.

a stretch of fact, be credited as a deciding factor in the career of the famous Vitagraph [Company]." [1]

Smith also seems to have done much to eliminate screen flicker. By adding blades to the then single blade shutter he discovered that in effect he could eliminate the flicker by multiplying it. "The resultant betterment of projection was extraordinary." [2]

Clearly, before the motion picture could progress it would be necessary to eliminate mechanical flaws which "operated actively and unpleasantly on the nerves of the spectator," and which probably kept many people away from the motion picture exhibitions.

During the first years of the motion picture, films were sold outright to the exhibitors. [3]

This method of distribution appeared unfortunate in two respects. For one thing, it seemed wasteful because a single exhibitor could hardly expect to exhaust the usefulness of a motion picture print, which, if given ordinary care, could be

---

1. Ramsaye, p. 351.

2. Ramsaye, p. 352.

3. Bardeche and Brasillach, p. 7.

projected "about three hundred times." [1] And secondly, it
appeared to have the disadvantage of imposing a high percentage
of the production costs on the individual exhibitor, who was
forced to pay as much as 10 or 12 cents a foot for a black and
white subject, [2] and 24 to 30 cents a foot for hand-colored
subjects. [3] These prices mentioned above meant that black
and white motion pictures, 50 feet in length, cost between 5
and 6 dollars, and that hand-colored motion pictures, 50 feet
in length, cost between 12 and 15 dollars.

The durability of the prints, and the amount of money it
took to purchase enough films to organize a proper program,
probably explains, in part, why it was that motion pictures
found an outlet in the vaudeville houses, and in the theatres
on the road.

The vaudeville houses in the big cities were probably
attractive to the exhibitors because they offered the opportunity
of an extended run, and because they required fewer of the costly
films to make up a program. The theatres on the road were
probably attractive to the exhibitors because they permitted the
exhibitors to show the same film night after night to different

---

1. "Life of a Cinematograph Film," The Optical Magic Lantern
   Journal and Photographic Enlarger, viii (November, 1897). 177.

2. Bardeche and Brasillach, p. 7. Ramsaye, p. 427.

3. Bardeche and Brasillach, p. 7.

audiences.

Of course, the scarcity of good subjects, [1] let alone passable subjects, was also very instrumental in encouraging the exhibition of films in the vaudeville and road theatre. In these spots frequent changes of program were less necessary than elsewhere.

Though the outright sale of motion pictures seems to have had its drawbacks, no real effort was made to change the system. As early as 1895, Raff and Gammon, when they first began distributing kinetoscope subjects, evolved a plan whereby exhibitors paid ten dollars for the first subjects they purchased, and thereafter two dollars when they exchanged old for new subjects. [2] Thus, disregarding the initial expenditure, which might almost be regarded as a deposit guaranteeing return of the films, the kinetoscope exhibitor paid four cents a foot for his film compared to the ten or twelve cents paid by the later motion picture showman. This plan was developed slightly by Percy Waters and Edson Raff during 1897 and 1898, but thereafter it seems to have been discarded. [3] Showmen apparently found it more advantageous to own the films outright.

----

1. Grau, The Theatre of Science. p. 28.

2. Ramsaye, p. 252.

3. Ramsaye, p. 428.

Several explanations can be given for the exhibitors rejection of the film rental system. They probably did not want to be bound by the time limit which Raff and Gammon very likely imposed on their films; they probably did not wish to be constantly bothered with the business of shipping films back to New York; they probably found the initial fee of ten dollars exorbitant; they probably were not positive that they, or Raff and Gammon, would last long enough in the business so that the reduced rental on trade-in films could be enjoyed; and they probably discovered that Raff and Gammon were capable of sending them inferior films.

In regards to this last point, a letter written by William T. Rock reveals his dissatisfaction with the stock and the editorial content of films sent him by Raff and Gammon through the mail.

New Orleans, Nov. 25, 1896

Raff & Gammon
Gents:-
    Your letter of November 20th to hand and would say I will except some of your 2nd hand films of yours in exchange for the 6 I send you I do allow that 3 of them were bad, but only sent them for you to see how bad the stock was in them expecting you would make some allowance on them to us. I expressed you from New Iberia back a very poor film a new one you sent me of the Steamship St. Louis and asked you to send me Cissy Fitzgerald

not colored in place of it I have not received it yet will
you please send it if you have not done so already....
                & oblige
                 Yours truly
                    Wm. T. Rock [1]

The points enumerated above were probably instrumental in
bringing about the discontinuance of Raff and Gammon's system
of distribution.

While the exhibitors apparently found the trade-in system
unsatisfactory, they soon discovered that the outright purchase
of films did not eliminate all of their problems. Apparently,
because most exhibitors were located away from the big cities
where the dealers had their headquarters, most films were "purchased through the post without being seen." [2] This condition
seems to have led to the distribution of films which "under more
normal circumstances would be unsaleable." [3] That the producers
and dealers would take advantage of such a situation is excused
by the Showman who says that "with customers clamouring to be
attended to, and orders in hand far ahead of the output, to 'make
hay while the sun shines' is only natural." [4] Very likely the
situation was made even more unbearable because most films pur-

---

1. Ramsaye, pp. 271-272.

2. The Showman, "Animated Photographs and Projecting Machines,"
   The Optical Magic Lantern Journal and Photographic Enlarger,

3. The Showman.

4. The Showman.

chased through the mail were unreturnable. [1]

Several months prior to the period when the dealers were trying to "make hay while the sun shone," Messrs. Watson & Son of 313, High Holborn, set aside a room in their establishment where exhibitors might see films before purchasing them. [2] This arrangement, of course, was of no value to the showmen who could not come to the city; but it certainly was satisfactory for those nearby, and for those outside the city who cared enough to make the trip.

The note announcing the Watson's projection room also advertised the availability of "about one hundred different subjects." Since exhibitors were apparently having "great difficulty" obtaining films during the latter part of 1896, this note evidently pleased them. It is not known whether the Watsons bothered to maintain their projection room during 1897 when the demand for films reached a peak.

Owning films outright, especially good ones, probably gave some of the exhibitors a sense of well-being, for with twenty or thirty good subjects on hand, the exhibitor, if he were any kind of a bargainer at all, could probably exchange them with a fellow showman, [3] for other subjects equally as good. On the

---

1. The Showman.

2. "Films", The Optical Magic Lantern Journal and Photographic Enlarger, vii (October, 1896). 162.

3. Jacobs, p. 52.

other hand, if the exhibitor sent Raff and Gammon a dozen good subjects he no longer could use he might very well receive in return a dozen inferior subjects. At any rate the exhibitors seemed to prefer to exchange subjects among themselves. This way they knew what they were getting.

There is a suggestion that the salvation Army may have evolved a trading system which possibly worked very well. When the Army in West Australia determined to equip each of its colonies with a motion picture projector the promotors of the idea probably organized a clearing house of some kind so that each film could be shown in each colony. A note in the Optical Magic Lantern Journal and Photographic Enlarger suggests the possibility, by remarking: "This will be interesting, as their system will permit a great interchange of subjects." [1]

The film exchanges, as we know them today, "had to wait for the emergence of the screen theatre, a permanently located exhibition, with a demand for changes of program." [2] But until the motion picture subjects improved to a point where they could justify the establishment of a motion picture theatre, the outright sale of motion pictures, and trade system persisted.

---

1. P. Newland, "A Few Lantern Notes From West Australia," The Optical Magic Lantern Journal and Photographic Enlarger, x (February, 1899). 27-28.

3. Ramsaye, p. 428.

This chapter is designed to reveal, in a small way, a number of the many problems which confronted the exhibitor.

His problem was not as simple as it might seem, for it was his job to present to the public, in as attractive a manner as possible, the, on the whole, only mildly-interesting episodic films of fifty feet, characteristic of the period 1895-1900.

In the vaudeville houses where the film program occupied only a few minutes of the entire program, and where the motion picture was not the principal attraction, the problem of exhibition was not too complicated because the films were simply introduced into an already well-established routine; but on the road, where the exhibitor was compelled to rely on the motion pictures to carry off the honors of the evening, he frequently had to rely on slides, a good lecture, phonograph records, and a great deal of ingenuity in his efforts to assemble an attractive program.

Furthermore, the exhibitor both in the city and on the road was faced with the everlasting problem of finding the best motion picture equipment available; he was also oftentimes engaged with the authorities in settling matters pertaining to fire regulations and public safety; he was constantly struggling with the business of buying and trading motion pictures, discovering during the course of such transactions the most efficacious manner of distributing films; he was frequently engaged in experimenting with the best music and sound effects to be employed as an accompaniment to the motion picture programs; he was always learning what the public liked and disliked about the motion pictures he presented.

These were just a few of the problems which the exhibitor began settling during the first five years of projected motion pictures.

That the exhibitor learned his elementary lesson well is borne out by the manner in which he managed the nickelodeons during the great period of expansion which began in 1905.

If this period of motion picture development appears at all disorganized, it should be remembered that order of a high degree began to come out of the alleged chaos within the space of a few years, and that a good part of the later efficient organizational pattern was being determined during the first five years.

CHAPTER V

MOTION PICTURE PRODUCTIONS, (1895-1900)

The average length of a motion picture during the period, 1896-1900, seems to have been fifty feet, [1] but in spite of this limitation on length the producers managed to turn out films with considerable variety. Not only did they produce topical and scenic motion pictures, similar in an abbreviated form to those which can be seen in any Newsreel Theatre today, but they also from the very beginning, it seems, produced, on a limited scale, motion pictures of little dramatic incidents, comedies, trick films, and vaudeville turns. The topical and scenic films were photographed in all parts of the world, while the prearranged scenes, or scenes arranged explicitly to be photographed by the motion picture camera, were shot either on location, [2] or in a studio, which generally consisted of a stage in the open air.

The illusion of realistic movement created by the motion picture was the factor which thrilled the film audiences; and cameramen, at first, had to do nothing more than photograph subjects like trains, dancers, firetrucks, and crowds in order to

---

1. "A Cinematographic Feat," British Journal of Photography, xlvii (April 13, 1900). 230.

2. A place outside of a studio where a picture or part of it is filmed.

secure a satisfactory audience response. The effect stimulated

by these films is borne out by Benjamin Hampton, who believes

that nothing in the million-dollar spectacles of later years

ever excelled the "punch" delivered by the motion picture of

the onrushing train; [1] and by Edmund A. Robbins, who as a

member of the motion picture audience of fifty years ago, relates

some of the emotional reactions created by the early films:

> The marvellous accuracy of these pictures in depicting
> natural phenomena, etc., is often demonstrated in a curious
> manner by the audience, a sea-scene in which a large wave
> breaks through the mouth of a cave, the realism of which
> is so great that a shudder can hardly be suppressed, and
> the splash can be quite easily imagined. In another, when
> a turn out of a fire engine was being shown, the engine
> dashes down the street towards the audience and appears
> to come right upon them. On one occasion, an old lady
> in the audience, quite unable to suppress a scream, started
> up in her seat and tried to scramble out, and in doing so
> knocked over the person behind her in her endeavour to get
> away from the horses; many more cases of the same sort have
> been known. [2]

Shown right along with the "punch" films were the topical

and scenic films, which were the more staple numbers of the

motion picture programs for the first three or four years. Scenes

of the gondolas in Venice, the crowds in Trafalgar Square, a

parade in Herald Square, the fountain in the Tuileries, Kaiser

Wilhelm reviewing his troops, the British royal family participating

---

1. Hampton, p. 14.

2. Edmund A. Robins, "Animated Pictures," The Optical Magic Lantern
   and Photographic Enlarger, viii (June, 1897). 99-101.

in a public event, and Major McKinley receiving a delegation
of adherents, were perhaps common enough as postcard subjects,
or as illustrations in a book or magazine, but when presented
with the realistic movement of a motion picture they were regarded
with a new enthusiasm. Interestingly enough, not only the public accepted the topical and scenic films with delight, but
even the British Museum authorities, as early as 1897, consented
to accept "films of recent public ceremonies and events" for
their archives. [1]

In the field of the scenic and topical films, the Lumieres,
with their portable camera, were preeminent. The secret of the
camera's compactness was zealously guarded because the Lumieres
fully appreciated the advantage they had in this field. [2]

The Frenchmen's preoccupation with the scenic and topical
films, while it probably discouraged other producers from attempting to seriously compete with them, turned out to be their
undoing as motion picture producers, for later when public interest was directed more and more towards staged motion picture
productions, to the disadvantage of travel films, the Lumieres
were unable to adjust and had to retire from production. In
Bardeche and Brasillach, Louis Lumiere is quoted as saying:

---

1. Edmund A. Robins.

2. Hampton, p. 18.

After 1900,. . ., films turned more and more towards the theatre and towards the use of staged scenes, compelling us to abandon production since we were not equipped to do this kind of thing. [1]

Precedent for photographing prearranged scenes had been established by Edison and Dickson who had made motion pictures of small comedies and vaudeville turns for the kinetoscope in the studio at Orange. The inventor and his assistant, because the kinetograph camera was so heavy and awkward, found it easier to bring subjects to the kinetograph, rather than take the camera out to meet the subjects.

Though the disadvantages of heavy, awkward cameras had been overcome in part by the construction of more compact machines, and though the filming of topical and scenic films apparently required only the possession of a camera, the early producers in time turned to the seemingly more complex studio productions. A partial explanation for this phenomenon can probably be found in the aggravations experienced by the travelling cameramen, as well as by the producers unwillingness to seriously compete with the Lumieres in their chosen field.

The travelling cameramen's job, though it might appear simple enough at first glance, did not consist solely of setting up a camera at eye level and shooting an actual scene from a

---

1. Maurice Bardeche, and Robert Brasillach, pp. 8-9.

single point of view; it also involved a number of mundane problems which sometimes made the business vexatious.

In the first place a camera was still a camera, and it was a laborious job to move it from one place to another. [1] In the second place it was frequently very difficult to photograph a public event when surrounded by a crowd. People, in spite of exhortations, had a way of "passing just in front of the camera and blotting out the whole picture for a time with their huge and ill-defined forms." [2] In the third place, the early cameras often got out of order, [3] and it was difficult to make anything but minor repairs on the machine while on the road. And finally it was expensive and time-consuming to travel. The uncertainties of the weather added to complexities of this last point, for the public event in Dublin would go on even though cloudy skies meant inferior pictures.

The early studios were nothing more than open-air stages where a prearranged scene could be enacted before a bit of scenery in the bright sunlight. A rather elaborate example of this type was the stage constructed by the American Mutoscope and Biograph Company on the top of their building in New York,

---

1. Lewis Jacobs, The Rise of the American Film, p. 10.

2. Hepworth, p. 97.

3. Jacobs, p. 10.

no later than April, 1897. [1] In a picture of this open-air
studio it appears that the stage which was mounted on wheels,
could be revolved on a slightly less than semi-circular double
track, and that the mutograph camera, which was also mounted
on wheels in a squarish tin hut, could be tracked [2] from the
axis of the semi-circular double track right up to the stage
itself. The tracks over which the camera hut apparently could
run appear to be fixed permanently at right angles to the center
of the stage. Such an arrangement would of course eliminate the
possibility of any kind of shot [3] except a right angle shot.

The Frenchman, Georges Melies, constructed his studio in
1896, [4] or 1897. [5] While he was becoming acquainted with the
camera he had emulated Paul and the Lumieres by photographing
little scenic and topical films in and around Paris; but by the
end of 1896 he had given up this kind of work and devoted himself
to the making of motion pictures with prearranged scenes. His
first fictional films were photographed in his garden, but freakish
weather soon drove him indoors.

---

1. "The Art of Moving Photography," Scientific American, 76 (April
   17, 1897). 248-250.

2. Raymond Spottiswoode, A Grammar of the Film, p. 46. "Tracking.
   The camera is moved bodily up to its subject."

3. Spottiswoode, p. 44. "The Shot. A portion of film portraying
   physical objects without visible spatial or temporal discontinuity."

4. Iris Barry, "Georges Melies, Magician and Film Pioneer: 1861-
   1938." Film Notes.

5. Bardeche and Brasillach, pp. 11-12.

He designed a studio which looked like a conservatory but was in reality very like a theatre except that, instead of an audience, there was a camera to observe what took place on the stage. [1]

Paul's first comedy, "The Soldier's Courtship," was photographed on the roof of the Alhambra Theatre in London. Properties and scenery from the Alhambra were utilized in the staging of the production. [2]

Finding that the public liked "The Soldier's Courtship" Paul decided to construct a studio where he could produce other motion pictures similar to the little forty-foot comedy. [3] His studio which was built at New Southgate in North London was a small building, two floors high, with a sloping glass roof on the north side. The second floor was used as an acting area; and the second floor wall on the north side of the building could be parted to create a "proscenium" opening, "measuring 18 feet in width by 13 feet in height," [4] through which the cameraman photographed the scene from a platform which was on the same level as the stage, and outside of the building. The cameraman's platform was mounted on rollers, and on a track placed at right angles to

---

1. Barry, "Georges Melies."

2. Talbot, pp. 103-104.

3. Talbot, p. 104.

4. Talbot, p. 104.

the stage. The ground floor level was available for "working effects from below; such as bridges, stage traps, and other artifices of the playhouse." [1] The Paul studio according to Roger Manvell was constructed in 1902.

There are indications that Paul may have met a fate similar to the Lumieres. Like the Frenchmen he was a business man, an instrument maker. And again like the Frenchmen he had a compact hand-operated camera. Instrument makers with portable cameras may not object to photographic scenic and topical views, but photographing staged scenes was an altogether different matter -- it required a new technique. Paul apparently tried to adjust to the new trend in motion picture production by constructing a studio in 1902, but by 1908 he had retired from motion pictures. [2]

By constructing studios the producers could approach mechanical regularity in their work. And this factor was no less important to Melies, Paul, and the American Biograph than it is to Paramount and British Gaumont today. To be sure, the studio productions required scenery, properties, costumes, and actors, but when lighting conditions were right for shooting, there was no chance of missing fire because of some whimsey.

The studio eliminated many of the uncertainties of motion

---

1. Talbot, p. 104.

2. Talbot, p. 42.

picture production. But the matter of adequate lighting remained a problem, and it was necessary for cameramen both in the studio and on location to wait for clear, sunshiny days before shooting. This situation existed because both the lenses and film used in the camera were excessively slow. [1]

Working with artificial light was probably attempted, but with little success because arc lights were unsatisfactory. Successful indoor motion picture photography, not employing sun light for illumination, had to wait upon the introduction of the mercury vapor lamp in 1906.

Iris Barry says that Georges Melies "used a close-up as early as 1896 and made the first film by artificial light," [2] and Bardeche and Brasillach imply that Melies used artificial illumination when he photographed the singer Paulus in 1897. [3] If these writers are correct the reliable Ramsaye is wrong.

He says that artificial lights were employed for the first time during the filming of the Sharkey-Jeffries fight at the Coney Island Athletic Club on November 3, 1899, when approximately 400 arc lamps were suspended over the ring. [4] As a regular thing, productions like the Sharkey-Jeffries motion picture were simply

---

1. Jacobs, p. 10.

2. Iris Barry, Film Notes, Series I, Program 1.

3. Maurice Bardeche and Robert Brasillach, pp. 11-12.

4. Ramsaye, p. 408.

not feasible because of the lighting problem.

Early studio productions were simple affairs, but they did demonstrate that the motion picture needed no longer to depend on passing events for subject matter.

J. Stuart Blackton and Albert E. Smith of the Vitagraph Company following the declaration of war between Spain and the United States on April 21, 1897, rushed up to the roof of the Morse Building in New York City and photographed "Tearing Down the Spanish Flag." [1]

Blackton in a lecture at the University of California in 1929 told how it was made:

> It was taken in a 10-by-12 studio room, the background a building next door. We had a flag pole and two 18-inch flags. Smith operated the machine and I, with this very hand, grabbed the Spanish flag and tore it down from the pole and pulled the Stars and Stripes to the top of the flag pole. That was our very first dramatic picture and it is surprising how much dramatic effect it created.... The people went wild. [2]

Along with "Tearing Down the Spanish Flag" were shown comedies like "Sausages from Dogs and Cats." This little comedy is described in the Optical Magic Lantern Journal of May 1897:

> Sausages from Dogs and Cats. – A very humorous set of animated photographs has recently been made in New York. A man is seen turning the handle of a huge sausage machine,

---

1. Ramsaye, p. 389.

2. Jacobs, p. 11.

from the spout of which sausages are pouring out. During the operation, several men come on the scene, and drop small dogs and cats into the large hopper. These run through an opening behind and can be used over and over again. [1]

In 1897, Cecil Hepworth in discussing the business of taking animated photographs, says:

Little made-up comedies, carefully arranged and well acted (there's the rub) make perhaps the most pleasing of all subjects for the living photographs, just as, when indifferently performed or evilly conceived, they are ineffectual or repulsive. [2]

The remark seems to indicate that the staging, and particularly the acting, were the two most important factors in the production of "made-up" motion picture comedies.

While acting and staging may have been the most important factors in staged motion picture productions, there were cameramen-producers during these first five years, and especially Melies, who were evolving a technique which would give the camera a more conspicuous role in the production of comedies and other staged motion picture productions.

Though Jacobs says that Melies' "Cinderella," produced in 1900 was his first outstanding motion picture, [3] the Frenchman's films were already being described by the Warwick Trading Company

1. "Sausages from Dogs and Cats," The Optical Magic Lantern Journal and Photographic Enlarger, viii (May, 1897). 78.

2. Hepworth, p. 98.

3. Jacobs, p. 25.

advertisements, in 1899, as "The Celebrated 'Star' Films;" [1]
and their influence even then was probably being felt in Europe
among the producers of motion pictures.

In their issue of June, 1900, the Optical Magic Lantern
Journal describes a film produced by Robert Paul in a manner,
which suggests the Melies method:

> Trick Film Tableau. — Those who have had much experi-
> ence in connection with taking pictures on cinematographic
> film, know that it is by no means a difficult task to pro-
> duce the most absurd, yet realistic looking effects by means
> of judicious stops, rejoining and other devices. One of
> the latest 'fakes' has been produced by Mr. R. N. Paul,
> entitled 'Kruger's Dream of Empire.' When the scene opens
> the stage is occupied by a bust of Oom Paul and a large
> frame on which is boldly written 'on Majuba Day England
> was defeated.' Oom Paul enters and observes this with evi-
> dent delight. He sits down in an arm-chair and dozes. The
> legend in the frame changes to a striking cartoon entitled
> 'Kruger the Conqueror,' in which Kruger himself is seen
> with one foot on a recumbent figure of Lord Roberts, and a
> rifle in one hand and a Bible in the other. To the real
> Kruger in his chair enters Mr. Joseph Chamberlin with the
> British crown on a silken cushion. He kneels and presents
> this to Kruger, but, as Kruger stretches forth his hands
> to grasp it, it vanishes in a puff of smoke. Kruger is
> rudely awakened from his illusion, and while he gazes on
> the cartoon it suddenly changes to the words 'on Majuba
> Day Cronje Surrendered.' In his rage he rushes to seize
> Chamberlain, but the latter suddenly disappears, and at
> the same time the bust of Kruger changes to a bust of
> Queen Victoria, which Kruger endeavours to overthrow. While
> doing so four men in khaki enter and seize him, placing
> him on the pedestal. They drape him with the Union Jack.
> Two of the men step forward and fire on Kruger. As the shot
> is fired Kruger vanishes and his place is taken by a stately
> figure of Britannia. [2]

---

1. Hopwood, p. XIV.

2. "Trick Film Tableau," The Optical Magic Lantern Journal and
   Photographic Enlarger, xi (June, 1900).

The motion picture studio cameramen, who stayed home and
lived fairly normal lives, seldom regretted their positions,
except possibly when the travelling cameramen produced some excellent scenes of the Spanish-American War, or the Boer War.
These subjects, because they stirred up enthusiasm in the motion
picture audiences, created envy and consternation among the
studio workers.

Finding themselves in the unhappy position of being scooped,
the home operators countered with an enterprising line of action.
They faked the dramatic war incidents in the studio: Edward
Amet of Chicago refought the naval battle of Santiago in a tub
with miniature ships; [1] and Edison conducted the Boer War with
stovepipe cannons and two armies of Bowery drifters attired in
costumes rented from Eaves. [2]

Before the advent of the sham war films, and the magical
or trick films "seein' was believin'," but now the adage did not
hold. In some cases, common sense may have helped reveal faked
from real, but, considering their reply to a worried correspondent, it does not seem improbable that even the staff of the
Optical Magic Lantern Journal would have been "put to it" to
tell the difference.

-----

1. Ramsaye, p. 390.
2. Ramsaye, pp. 402-403.

Sham War Cinematograph Films. — A correspondent asks us how he is to know real from sham war films, seeing that several subjects are made up at home from life models? The subject lends itself so well to life model work that one has to a great extent to rely on common sense; for instance, in one film we have heard about, there is a hand-to-hand encounter between Boers and British, all realistic in its way, but the effect is somewhat spoilt by reason of the fringe of an audience appearing on the picture occasionally. Thus, when one sees gentlemen with tall hats, accompanied by ladies, apparently looking on, common sense would at once pronounce the film of the sham order. The same may be said of soldiers lying and firing from behind 'earthworks,' composed of nicely arranged straw. [1]

But common sense did not help the sailors at the United States Naval Training Station at Lake Bluff, Illinois. They were completely fooled when Amet showed them his faked motion pictures of the Battle of Santiago. [2]

Jacobs says that during these early years,

Pictures were made in the streets. There were no studios, and only crude laboratories behind the business offices. The making of pictures depended entirely upon the ingenuity and ability of the cameraman. He was director, photographer, laboratory expert, and sometimes even the leading actor. [3]

The picture he draws is not quite accurate. While most of the early motion pictures were produced as simply as he says, there were on the other hand a number of early productions requiring

---

1. "Sham War Cinematograph Films," The Optical Magic Lantern Journal and Photographic Enlarger, xi (March, 1900). 30.

2. Ramsaye, p. 391.

3. Jacobs, p. 9.

a considerable cooperative effort; and by the spring of 1897,
at the latest, the work being accomplished by the American
Mutoscope and Biograph Company, Melies "Star Films," and others
already suggested the complexities of present day production.

When Paul photographed "Kruger's Dream" in 1900, and Melies
produced "The Conjurer" in 1899, and Biograph the sausage factory
scene in 1897, all of these productions involved special problems of staging or costuming. And because they were staged
scenes they all required the employment of men and women performers who needed direction. The direction may have been simple;
but it was necessary, as Hector Maclean, in his discussion of
"rehearsed effects" affirms:

> With these, however, it is strongly advisable to have
> an assistant, a kind of combination of stage manager, drill
> sergeant, and timekeeper, who will keep the actors up to
> their parts and see that they finish before all the film
> is used up. 1

In connection with this remark it is interesting to note
that the picture of a scene being photographed on the Biograph
stage in the April 17, 1897, issue of the Scientific American
seems to include "a stage manager, drill sergeant, and time-
keeper" person. Looking at the stage from the camera point-of-
view, he sits down stage left, apparently looking at a watch.

----

1. Hector Maclean in Cecil Hepworth's Animated Photography, p. 128.

Furthermore, pictures of the Biograph laboratories appearing
in the above mentioned issue of the Scientific American indicate
that they were anything but "crude" laboratories. Numerous individuals appear to have worked in the drying and retouching room,
and in the dark room. Both rooms are large, and seemingly well
equipped.

Speaking elsewhere about the cameraman and his job Jacobs
has this additional remark to make:

> Once set up for shooting, the camera was seldom if
> ever changed for another viewpoint; the whole subject was
> photographed in one shot, without any shift in the camera's
> position. [1]

He goes on to say that this rigidity of technique was finally
overcome by the introduction of a flexible tripod head which
enabled the cameraman to pan his camera, and that one of the
earliest records of such a shot appears in the Edison catalogue
of 1901-1902. [2] However, there is evidence, admittedly not con-
clusive, which suggests that pan shots might have been undertaken
with the mutograph as early as 1897, or 1896. This camera was
supported by three adjustable legs mounted on a turntable. According to the Scientific American, "This combination of the
turntable with the vertical adjustment....enables the camera to

_____

1. Jacobs, p. 10.

2. Jacobs, p. 10.

be shifted so as to take in the required field." [1] Now it is
conceivable that the mutograph could have been panned as it
photographed the "Pennsylvania Limited" rushing by at sixty
miles an hour, and a picture of the camera shooting this scene
suggests it, but the possibility exists that the turntable was
only employed prior to shooting when the cameraman was establishing his field of vision.

Tracking the camera during a shot was probably not undertaken, but certainly the tracks, fixed at right angles to the
Biograph stage, over which the camera hut could move, indicates
that various length shots were tried. The Scientific American
suggests that this was true when they write that the stage was
erected "for taking photographs of celebrated scenes from plays
or of individual performances in which it is desired to reproduce
the motions as well as the features of the subject." [2] "Features"
suggests a rather close shot.

Several of the early producers of motion pictures had two
sets of customers whom they served. The American Mutoscope and
Biograph Company, for example, had the mutoscope as well as the

---

1. "The Art of Moving Photography," Scientific American, 76
   (April 17, 1897). 248-250.

2. "The Art of Moving Photography."

biograph; the Lumiere's had the kinora [1] as well as the cinematograph; and Edison had the kinetoscope as well as the projecting
kinetoscope.

This fact may have had considerable to do with the establishment of fifty feet as the average length of a motion picture
during the period 1896-1900, for the producers by holding down
the length of their motion picture productions could accommodate
the projection machines as well as the peep shows with their
limited capacities.

Edison's film could be used either in his peep-show machine
or his projecting machine. But the kinora and the mutoscope
employed cards mounted radially from a drum which necessitated
the printing of a second set of positives. This was a small matter, however, for the economy was insured by the possibility of
printing both the projection positives and the peep show positives
from the one negative.

The positives for the kinetoscope, though transparent, were
"somewhat dense so as to bring out the detail." [2] But, even
though it was found more desirable to use films of less density
for projection purposes in order to permit more light to pass

1. Henry Hopwood, Living Pictures, p. 39.
2. Talbot, p. 31.

through the film, kinetoscope prints were frequently used in projection machines. Later, of course, adjustments were made, but they were minor; the size of the picture and the perforation gauge were identical in both kinetoscope and projecting kinetoscope films. [1]

---

1. Talbot, opposite p. 33.

CHAPTER VI

"LONG" MOTION PICTURE PRODUCTIONS. (1895-1900)

Though the average length of a motion picture between 1895 and 1900 was fifty feet, longer films were produced. These films were important because they suggested something beyond the episodic motion pictures of fifty feet, and because they revealed that there were audiences and exhibitors who would accept the longer productions.

Apparently the first long film undertaken was Enoch Rector's production of the Corbett-Fitzsimmons championship prizefight which was staged on March 17, 1897. During the fight Rector exposed eleven thousand feet of film. [1]

Paul Rotha's remark,

> Gradually the fifty-feet length of film used in the kinetoscope lengthened until, in 1897, eleven thousand feet of film were shown by Enoch Rector in America, being a cinematic record of the Corbett-Fitzsimmons fight at Carson City, Nevada," [2]

is incorrect because it suggests that motion picture producers had gradually extended the length of their productions, during the period 1895-1897, and that the prizefight represented a new standard length. The long Corbett-Fitzsimmons motion picture

---

1. Ramsaye, p. 286.

2. Paul Rotha, The Film Till Now, p. 23.

was, however, a conspicuous exception to the standard production
of fifty feet.

Rector produced the motion picture independent of the
Lathams. Like Dickson, who had been his associate in the Latham
Company, Rector found the personal conduct of the Lathams unbearable,
and he left them in 1895. When he parted company with the brothers
he took with him, as his share of the concern's assets, the exclusive fight contract with Corbett.

With the contract in hand he made a deal with Edison whereby
the proposed fight between Corbett and Fitzsimmons would be
photographed with the kinetograph camera. This was the year 1896.

Though the fight did not materialize at this particular time,
because of legal complications which ended with Corbett turning
his championship belt over to Peter Maher, Rector made the best
of a bad situation by helping arrange, with the aid of a $10,000
guarantee, [1] a fight between Fitzsimmons and Maher, which eventually took place in Mexico, just over the Rio Grande from Langtry,
Texas, on February 21, 1896.

The project turned out to be a pictorial and financial
fiasco. Rector "failed to get any pictures, as the light was too
poor;" [2] and the paid admissions -- one hundred and eighty-two

---

1. "Fitzsimmons is Champion," The New York Times, Feb. 22, 1896,
   p. 5 D.

2. "Fitzsimmons is Champion."

men who paid $20 apiece to see the fight [1] -- did not even come close to equaling the guarantee. Almost needless to say, the business relationship of Rector and Edison terminated with this affair. Later, Rector may have found some consolation in the fact that Fitzsimmons disposed of Maher in exactly ninety-five seconds, hardly a suitable length for a prizefight motion picture even in that day. Rector, it will be remembered, had tripled the capacity of the kinetoscope to accommodate one hundred and fifty feet of film, and in July, 1894, had exhibited, round by round, a film of the Leonard-Cushing fight nearly one thousand feet long in a battery of six kinetoscopes.

The Fitzsimmons-Maher prizefight took place almost six weeks before the press showing of the Edison-Armat vitascope on April 3, 1896. If Rector had been successful in photographing the bout, the pictures would very likely have been projected in the vitascope, as well as transmitted in the kinetoscope.

Rector's experience with the huge electrically-driven kineto-graph had revealed to him many of the instrument's limitations, so the young engineer decided to build a more "facile instrument." [2] Though evidence is lacking to establish the fact, he may have been influenced in his decision by hearing of the work of Lumiere

1. "Fitzsimmons is Champion."

2. Ramsaye, p. 284.

and Paul, who, by this time, had produced less bulky, crank-operated machines. At any rate, he did construct such a camera, and, here again possibly influenced by the Lumiere sixteen-a-second cinematograph which was exhibited in this country for the first time in June, 1896, he did reduce the number of ex-posures in his camera from the Edison standard of forty-eight to his own standard of twenty-four. In this particular camera the Edison standard gauge film was employed.

Ramsaye also remarks that Rector "struggled for capacity against another possible rainy day" by trying to achieve "higher photographic speed." [1] Ramsaye does not indicate how this problem was solved, if at all. But he does say that Rector designed a special camera for the event. [2] Its capacities are not explained, but the machine did carry a special film two and three-sixteenths inches wide. This wide film enabled him to bring his camera closer to the ring and, at the same time, take in the entire field encompassed by the posts about the ring. Also the large size film enabled Rector to make larger photo-graphs, which would probably be of some advantage in bringing out the detail in the picture if the lighting was poor.

_____

1. Ramsaye, p. 285.

2. Ramsaye, opposite p. 296.

While Rector was working on his camera the public began to clamor for a fight between Fitzsimmons and Corbett. And finally when the arrangements for the fight were made, Rector was as ready, it seems, as he could possibly be.

Again the motion picture was compelled to finance the prize-fight. Before Fitzsimmons and Corbett would enter the ring Rector, and his associate, Samuel Tilden, and the promotor, Dan Stuart, had to agree to finance the fight, as well as share the motion picture profits: twenty-five per cent for Corbett; twenty-five per cent for Fitzsimmons; and fifty percent for Rector, Tilden, and Stuart. [1]

The prizefight was staged in Carson City, Nevada, on March 17, 1897. Fitzsimmons won in the fourteenth round. With three cameras and forty-eight thousand feet of film Rector stood by the ring and photographed the fight.

Ramsaye says:

> Rector and Tilden were not sure of an avenue to the market for their picture. There was considerable discussion with Raff and Gammon of the Vitascope Company; [2]

then,

> Under the new name of the Veriscope Company, Rector and Tilden determined to present the picture in New York and market it territorially themselves. [3]

---

1. Ramsaye, p. 286.

2. Ramsaye, p. 286.

3. Ramsaye, pp. 286-287.

With the help of Corbett and his manager, William A. Brady, publicity of the fight film was very well handled.

Immediately following the fight, Corbett returned to New York City and appeared on the stage at the Academy of Music in a play called "A Naval Cadet." His appearance was a "triumph." "The crowd was almost hysterically enthusiastic. 'Corbett' they wanted, first and last. The play was incidental." [1] And the play was "incidental" to Corbett and Brady too. Here was a fine opportunity to publicize the fight film, which was scheduled to be exhibited at the Academy a few weeks later.

Between the second and third acts Corbett made a curtain speech. He told the audience that on the basis of his showing he wanted another chance to win back the crown. And he did not forget to add: "The pictures taken of the fight are here, and you may judge for yourself, how I stood in the fight." [2]

Mr. Brady, who had just as keen an appreciation of the possibilities of twenty-five per cent, made an even better curtain speech:

> I think him entitled to the victory at Carson, and the pictures will bear me out. In the sixth round when Fitzsimmons was down, the fight should have been stopped. For the pictures show me and Corbett's timekeeper claiming the time limit had been overstepped. But Mr. Muldon thought differently. [3]

---

1. "Corbett at the Academy," The New York Times, April 20, 1897, p. 9 B.
2. "Corbett at the Academy."
3. "Corbett at the Academy."

The reporter went on to say that Brady also claimed that the
pictures would show Fitzsimmons striking a foul blow in the
fourteenth round.

With this send-off it is not surprising that the Corbett-
Fitzsimmons fight motion picture had a very nice run at the
Academy of Music during the months of May and June, 1897. The
top admission price was one dollar.

Following the New York exhibition, the film was distributed
throughout the country.

According to an advertisement in the Ithaca, New York, Daily
Journal of October 4, 1897, the film showed "the entire 14 rounds,
and the scene 10 minutes before and 5 minutes after the knockout." [1]
The advertisement suggests that the film ran approximately seventy
minutes -- three minutes for each round, one minute between each
round, and fifteen minutes of motion pictures taken before and
after the fight.

Sigmund Lubin, motion picture producer of Philadelphia,
employed two freight handlers to re-enact the fight for the
camera. When the finished picture was projected on the screen
a narrator read during the course of the struggle a round by
round account of the fight from the newspaper. [2] This was very

---

1. Advertisement, The Ithaca Daily Journal, October 4, 1897, p. 2 A.
2. Ramsaye, p. 288.

likely the motion picture which was given an unsuccessful exhibition at Renwick Beach in Ithaca, New York, during August,
1897. [1]

The Corbett-Fitzsimmons fight motion picture seems to have
terminated Enoch Rector's period of usefulness as far as motion
picture production is concerned. He apparently spent a good
deal of time talking about "dramatic pictures," [2] but his decor-
ous friends pooh-poohed his ideas, and Rector never got beyond
the fight film.

The motion picture's association with prizefighting was
not altogether good, for numerous individuals found the sport
incorrigible, and many states at the time forbade fighting
altogether.

As a consequence the fight motion pictures, and especially
the Corbett-Fitzsimmons production, served to "bring the odium
of pugilism upon the screen all across America." [3] This view,
which is held by Ramsaye, is verified by Westbrook Pegler who
reveals that:

---

1. See pp. 63-64.

2. Ramsaye, p. 288.

3. Ramsaye,

This fight had chivvied all over the wild and wooly
west of that day because the hardy frontiersmen regarded
it as an obscene proceeding, and a retreat toward the
twilight of the dawn of civilization. [1]

On the other hand the attention which the fight motion

picture provoked, prompted a great newspaper like The New York

Times to stop and take stock of the medium.

It is not very creditable to our civilization perhaps
that an achievement of what is now called the 'veriscope'
that has attracted and will attract the widest attention
should be the representation of a prizefight. Moralists
may deplore this fact, and the kindred fact that the
fight in question 'sold more extras' than would be sold
by a presidential election. But they will have to eradi-
cate a great deal of human nature before they can alter it. [2]

While the New York Times' statement that the great

commonalty interested in prizefighting included many of the

washed as well as the unwashed is interesting, it is the last

paragraph of the editorial which deserves attention.

Even in its present state the invention yields wonderful results. By means of it the fruits of travel are con-
veyed, more than by all other inventions, to those who stay
at home. Whoever has seen the reproduction of such pageants
as the coronation of the Czar or his reception in Paris has
little to envy those who witnessed the actual event. With
the improvement in its mechanism it will no doubt be applied
to more valuable purposes than those to which it has thus
far been confined; and we may foresee that it will serve
for the solution of many scientific problems for which the
unaided human eye is too slow to furnish the necessary data. [3]

---

1. Westbrook Pegler, "Prizefighting of Yore," The Syracuse Post
Standard, October 7, 1947. p. 8 A.

2. "The Veriscope," The New York Times, May 26, 1897. p. 6 D.

3. "The Veriscope."

The Times had admired the topical film of the Czar's reception in Paris, but had not felt compelled to comment on the motion picture's potentialities until the Corbett-Fitzsimmons motion picture was exhibited.

The K.M.C.D. Syndicate, which exploited the mutoscope and the biograph, seems to have conducted its business along slightly bolder lines than most of the commercial producers of the time. Some of their major efforts, compared to the obviously long fight film seem ridiculously short, but compared to the standard film of fifty feet they command attention.

W. K. L. Dickson's photographing of a life-saving crew at work is one example of their enterprise. This job was accomplished in Worthing, England, with the help of the Mutoscope and Biograph Syndicate, Ltd., of London, a subsidiary of the American company.

Dickson's first shot showed the life-saving crew quickly donning their cork coats, and hitching the horses to the boat in order to bring it to the water's edge; the second shot taken from the pier showed the launching and departure of the boat; while the third shot which concluded the film showed the landing of the crew. The article in the Optical Magic Lantern Journal and Photographic Enlarger is rather long, but so good in describing this staged motion picture production that it is quoted in its entirety:

On the 6th of April the inhabitants of Worthing were suddenly startled by the report of a cannon, which meant, to those 'not in the know,' a ship in distress. Consequently crowds gathered quickly on the sea front, hastening westwards along the Marine Parade as far as the flagstaff opposite the coastguard station, where the lifeboat was ominously emerging from its shelter. Great excitement prevailed; four horses were connected, the crew donning their coats of cork and mounting with all speed their pet life-saving apparatus — one of the many monuments of England's beneficience.

Soon the command was given, 'Let her go!' On this occasion, however, that command had a double meaning, and many in the crowd were greatly puzzled as to the meaning of all they saw. Close to the esplanade stood a horse with electric batteries, which sent their mysterious powers through a red double cord up to a huge camera mounted on a rigid iron tripod, and inside of this instrument there was a reel holding a sensitised film about 200 feet long. This, too, was 'let go,' to run its entire length down behind a lens, recording many impressions per second of the interesting procession rushing by towards the scene of the action.

'This big camera was the "Mutograph," of the Mutoscope and Biograph Syndicate, Ltd., of London. The instrument is the invention of Mr. Herman Casler, and was brought here and manipulated by Mr. Wm. K. Laurie Dickson, Elet. Eng. Technician to the American Mutoscope Co. (with Edison, 1881-1895). As soon as the first performance was completed, the whole machinery was erected on the pier to take the launching and departure of the lifeboat. When this had been accomplished the mutograph was loaded for the third time to photograph also the landing of the Worthing gallant corky crew. For this event the spectators had to wait nearly two hours, during which time many of them dispersed. As the boat was nearing the shore and surmounting the last few breakers, Mr. Dickson shouted once more, 'Let her go!' When the lifeboat struck the beach many rushed forward to assist in pulling her up, while some of the crew jumped hastily out of the boat into the foaming waves, and quick as lightning, yet most carefully, laid upon the sand the body of a man drowned (?) for the purpose of pleasing sightseers and in the interest of science. Medical aid was, however, at hand, and by means of proper restorative and a most scientific manipulation of the breathing apparatus, the drowned mariner was soon able to return to his home and friends. And thus ended the noble work of life-saving and animated photography.

The sun was shining all the time, there was a good breeze blowing and plenty of sea - all very favourable circumstances, so that the pictures taken (about 4,000) ought to be very effective when finished and projected upon the screen. The following day (the 7th inst.) the Worthing Swimming Club played some games of waterpolo, etc., in the big baths at West Worthing, while the mutograph was again actively looking on and taking it all in. [1]

Depending on who is right, the Scientific American, which says that the mutograph photographed at the rate of forty pictures a second, [2] or Ramsaye, who says that it photographed at the rate of thirty-six pictures a second, [3] these four thousand photographic impressions were made during a total shooting time of either one hundred and eleven or one hundred seconds; and because both the mutograph and biograph were motor driven, which made it possible to establish equal rates of projection and shooting, the four thousand pictures very likely occupied one of the above mentioned times when they reached the screen.

No matter who is right, this three-shot production represented a break from the episodic films of fity feet which took

---

1. "Notes," The Optical Magic Lantern Journal and Photographic Enlarger, ix (April, 1898). 54.

2. "The Art of Moving Photography," Scientific American, 76 (April 17, 1897). 248. Forty photographic impressions a second is described as the "ordinary speed." However, the camera could be speeded up to record at the rate of one hundred photographic impressions a second if necessary: e.g., flight of a projectile.

3. Ramsaye, p. 328.

a minute or much less to project. [1]

The three shots are not actually dependent upon one another for meaning. If necessary, any one of them could be exhibited independently in a mutoscope, and create interest among the patrons of such machines. But shown together as a biograph presentation the three shots assume additional meaning, for the expectancy of an answer to the question, will the man be saved?, creates a suspense which simply does not exist in any one of the shots alone.

"Views of the Pope" was another interesting Biograph production. This film showed views of Leo XIII in his carriage, in a sedan chair, in the act of walking, seated on his favorite bench in the Vatican gardens, and bestowing the papal blessing on an audience. They were merely a series of views, but they were given a kind of continuity by the regular appearance of Leo XIII in each view.

A presentation of this motion picture was given on Wednesday December 14, 1898, at Carnegie Music Hall in New York City. [2] It was probably quite an event, for Archbishop Corrigan attended the exhibition, and $1.50 was the top price charged for a reserved

---

1. Hugo Munsterberg, The Photoplay, p. 19.

2. "Biograph View of the Pope," The New York Times, December 15, 1898, p. 5 C.

seat.

In this section on longer motion picture productions
undertaken between 1895-1900 the efforts of Rich G. Hollaman
must be considered. Hollaman, manager of the Eden Musee in
New York City, is properly classified, insofar as his interests
centered on the motion picture, as an exhibitor; but by his
efforts in this field, and as a sometime backer of motion picture
productions, he managed to point the way to longer and more
imaginative motion pictures. Whereas most metropolitan showmen
seem to have exhibited motion pictures in a rather routine
fashion, Hollaman appears to have had an immediate comprehension
of the medium's possibilities.

Ramsaye says that the importance of the motion picture exhibitions at the Eden Musee cannot be too much emphasized:

> While elsewhere motion pictures were flitting from
> hall to hall in fitful lyceum appearances, and occupying
> the place of a turn in vaudeville programs, the Eden Musee,
> beginning in that first year of 1896, provided a permanent
> showing and exclusiveness of attention and policy accorded
> the film nowhere else in the world. [1]

When Hollaman first included films as one of the Musee
attractions, he scheduled an exhibition every half an hour.
But not very long thereafter he enlarged his program and presented

---

1. Ramsaye, p. 347.

thirty-five views every hour. [1] This was the beginning of an
interest in motion pictures at the Musee which persisted for
nineteen years. [2]

Hollaman apparently was prepared to present something beyond
the short films of fifty feet as early as the first two months
of 1897, for on January 10, 1897, the New York Times carried a
notice that,

> A new series of views will be shown by the cinemato-
> graphe at the Eden Musee this week. One will be the entrance
> of the Czar into Paris last fall, which occupies over three
> minutes and consists of 10,000 separate photographs. [3]

And on February 21, 1897, the New York Times advised its readers
that,

> The Eden Musee has a new cinematograph that is the
> invention of Joly of Paris. Where other instruments repro-
> duce short scenes, this one reproduces much longer ones....
> Many of the scenes last from three to five minutes, and
> each detail is exact. [4]

Unfortunately these two notes suggest rather than prove
Hollaman's interest in longer motion pictures. The exhibition
of a motion picture "which occupies over three minutes," six

---

1. "Notes of the Week," The New York Times, December 27, 1896, p. 11 A.

2. Ramsaye, p. 347.

3. "Notes of the Week," The New York Times, January 10, 1897, p. 11 B.

4. "Notes of the Week," The New York Times, February 21, 1897, p. 11 C.

weeks before the announcement of the acquisition of a machine which reproduces scenes lasting "from three to five minutes," needs clarification. And the "10,000 separate photographs" adds to the confusion. The cinematograph projecting at its normal rate of 16 pictures a second would have taken ten minutes and twenty-five seconds to project ten thousand pictures.

While manifesting an interest in longer productions Hollaman also sought more reliable projectors and a better selection of subjects.

The Joly machine, which replaced the Lumiere machine at the Musee, had, it is reported, the additional virtue of operating "without noise or the flickering of the light upon the screen." [1] But Hollaman was obviously not pleased with its performance, for on August 29, 1897, a little more than six months after the acquisition of the Joly projector, the Eden Musee manager announced that a new machine was being employed.

> The cinematograph is now a permanent feature at this amusement place. For months a skilled inventor has been working upon models, and a new cinematograph will be placed on exhibition today. It is a wonderful machine, and the vibration is reduced to a minimum. The light is stronger and the pictures are much clearer. Experts have pronounced it the best machine in the world. [2]

1. "Notes of the Week," The New York Times, February 21, 1897, p. 11 C.

2. "Notes of the Week," The New York Times, August 29, 1897, p. 8 B.

The "skilled inventor" is not identified, but Ramsaye reports that Hollaman, during his search for a better projector, hired Frank Cannock to work on the machine project. [1] Cannock, who had received his training as a mechanic in the Singer Sewing Machine plant in Scotland, was a very careful workman: "His notion of the requirements of machine fitting placed the thousandth part of an inch as the limit of latitude and on important parts a ten thousandth was his customary requirement." [2]

It also seems that Edwin S. Porter, of whom we shall hear more later, was hired by Hollaman to work with Cannock. [3] But Porter's stay with the Eden Musee was clearly very brief, for, according to Jacobs, he joined the Edison Company in 1896. [4] Inasmuch as motion pictures were first exhibited at the Musee during the summer of 1896, this would, it seems, hardly allow Porter time for more than a few months employment at the Musee at best.

While pursuing perfection in projection, Hollaman worked diligently on his program scheduling.

---

1. Ramsaye, pp. 347-348.

2. Ramsaye, p. 348.

3. Ramsaye, p. 348.

4. Jacobs, p. 35.

In addition to all the available American films the
Eden Musee purchased the output of Melies and Lumiere in
France, Robert W. Paul in London, and even the intermittent,
tentative products of Charles Pathe in Paris. [1]

The practice of securing the best of the American, as well as
the best of the European productions, was inspired by a desire
to keep the Musee programs up to the standard, and to allow frequent changes.

Hollaman's curiosity about the motion picture also seems to
have found expression in the presentation of unusual features.
An item in the May 2, 1897, issue of the New York Times reveals
that one of the views showing horses jumping hurdles, afterwards
"is reversed and the horses appear to jump over the hurdles
backwards." [2] Another item, appearing a week later, reveals
that "specimens of color photography" [3] were exhibited on the
Musee screen.

It may be argued that these examples simply indicate a
desire to present novelties. There may be some truth in this
assertion; but the examples also seem to reveal, on Hollaman's
part, a desire to keep abreast with the latest developments, and
a willingness to present unusual features.

---

1. Ramsaye, p. 348.

2. "Notes of the Week," The New York Times, May 2, 1897, p. 14 B.

3. "Notes of the Week," The New York Times, May 9, 1897, p. 4 A.

The quotations covering the Eden Musee manager's motion picture activities have been introduced into this paper in order partially to explain how it happened that Hollaman, towards the end of 1897, undertook what later turned out to be one of the most daring motion picture productions of the early period. These examples cited seem to reveal that he was prepared to take a chance with the motion picture.

The particular event leading up to this production occurred when W. B. Hurd, the Lumiere's representative in America, secured the right to make a motion picture of the folk presentation of the "Passion Play," which was given annually in the village of Horitz in Bohemia.

Hurd may have reasoned that if Rector could do as well as he had done with the long Corbett-Fitzsimmons motion picture there was no reason why he could not do just as well with a long motion picture of a subject as well-known as the "Passion Play." A prizefight motion picture was expected to appeal to men; [1] a religious subject like the "Passion Play" might very well appeal to the ladies and the children.

Hurd was willing to sell the rights to the Horitz "Passion

---

1. "Pictures of a Prize Fight", The Ithaca Daily Journal, October 5, 1897. p. 3 D. "The Veriscope reproduction of the Corbett-Fitzsimmons prize fight attracted a large audience to the Lyceum last night, composed almost solely of men, there being not more than ten or twelve members of the gentler sex present."

Play" for $10,000; and it was estimated that it would cost an additional $10,000 to send a crew to Europe to photograph the play. [1] In his search for a backer, Hurd turned to Hollaman, who readily agreed to buy the rights and finance the expedition. But before a contract could be signed Hurd turned about and sold the rights to Marc Klaw and Abraham Erlanger, who immediately sent a party to Europe to make the pictures. Hollaman was dissatisfied, but there was no course open to him except to wait.

When the finished motion picture was returned to this country it was shown in Philadelphia prior to its New York showing.

Hollaman, who was a member of the audience which saw the Philadelphia exhibition, "observed without overwhelming disappointment that the Horitz expedition had not been entirely successful in making a convincing picture." [2] Now the Eden Musee manager was ready with a plan.

He decided to stage his own version of the "Passion Play" explicitly for motion picture production.

In collaboration with Albert G. Eaves, who had in his possession the costumes and script of the Salmi Morse "Passion Play," Hollaman started work. L. J. Vincent of Niblo's Garden was appointed director, Frank Russell was given the role of the Christus, and the Grand Central Palace roof was selected as the

---

1. Ramsaye, p. 367.
2. Ramsaye, p. 368.

location for making the motion picture. Work on the production, which was done as secretly as possible, because Hollaman planned to release the film as an authentic European stage production, was completed during the early part of January, 1898.

Arrangements were made for an immediate release at the Eden Musee, and on January 31, 1898, [1] it was put on exhibition.

Nobody denies that it was a long motion picture, compared to the standard productions of the day, but as for its exact length there is some disagreement. Ramsaye says twenty-one hundred feet; [2] Talbot, "three reels, or about 3,000 feet, and some 48,000 separate pictures; [3] Munsterberg, "nearly fifty thousand pictures;" [4] and Rotha, "about three thousand feet long." [5] According to Talbot the "Passion Play" required "about 55 minutes to project." [6] and according to Munsterberg it "needed almost an hour for production." [7] The chief difference seems to exist between Ramsaye and the others.

----

1. Ramsaye, p. 371, dates the first exhibition, January 30, 1898. It was one day later, Monday January 31, 1898. See "Passion Play Represented," The New York Times, February 1, 1898, p. 7 E.

2. Ramsaye, p. 371.

3. Talbot, p. 106.

4. Munsterberg, p. 19.

5. Rotha, p. 23.

6. Talbot, p. 107.

7. Munsterberg, p. 19.

Apart from its length in feet the "Passion Play" seems to
have been presented in twenty-four scenes. [1]

And because continuity titles, [2] or titles of any kind, were
unknown at this time, the exhibition was accompanied by comments
from a lecturer. [3] And, as an additional "ornament," music was
provided by a choir of boys, [4] during "the two intermissions
between the three reels." [5] The choir probably sang songs like
"Ave Maria," "O, Holy Night," and "The Palms," numbers which
were sung by a young tenor during Henry H. Hadley's presentation
of the "Passion Play" at a later date. [6]

The "Passion Play", which ran for two hundred exhibitions, [7]
elicited newspaper comments favorable enough to be included in
a two column, four column-inch advertisement in the New York Times
of February 6, 1898:

---

1. Advertisement, The New York Times, February 6, 1898, p. 9 F
   and G.

2. Spottiswoode, p. 48. "Continuity Titles," Wording interposed
   in the film to record speech or to explain action.

3. Ramsaye, p. 372.

4. "Notes of the Week," The New York Times, March 27, 1898, p. 9 B.

5. Ramsaye, pp. 375-376.

6. Ramsaye, pp. 375-376.

7. "Notes of the Week," The New York Times, May 1, 1898, p. 9 C.

Follows quite faithfully the dramatic representation at
Oberammergau. - New York Herald.
The exhibition made a decidedly favorable impression and
will doubtless attract many visitors to this popular place
of amusement. - World.
Wherever it was done it was well done, and the pictures are
both artistic and interesting. - Evening Journal.
The pictures are life size, and all the action is brought
out in detail. - Daily News
One would prophesy that those who 'came to scoff' will
'remain to pray.' - Brooklyn Citizen. [1]

The Evening Journal comment, in the above advertisement,
discloses that information about the motion picture being produced on the roof of the Grand Central Palace had begun to leak
out; and also perhaps, that Hollaman, feeling sure that he had
a success on his hands, no longer considered it necessary to
give the impression that his production was a motion picture
of an authentic European staged version of the play.

The Klaw and Erlanger "Passion Play" went on exhibition at
Daly's Theatre on March 14, 1898. [2] It ran until Saturday,
March 26, 1898, [3] and does not seem to have affected the popularity of the Eden Musee production. On the day that the Klaw
and Erlanger production closed an Eden Musee newspaper advertisement announced: "Saturday next, 100th performance of "Passion Play." [4]

---

1. Advertisement, The New York Times, February 6, 1898, p. 9 F and G.

2. "Passion Play in Pictures," The New York Times, March 15,
   1898, p. 7 B.

3. Advertisement, The New York Times, March 26, 1898, p. 12 F.

4. Advertisement, The New York Times, March 26, 1898, p. 12 G.

Paul Rotha says that the Hollaman-Eaves "Passion Play"
has "a vague claim to be the first attempt to photograph a
story in pictures, but actually it was a mere photographic
record, with no attempt at narration." [1] Maybe Rotha is right;
but there is a suggestion that the production may have come a
little closer to being a respresentation of a connected succession of pictures than he thinks. It is true that it was
Vincent's practice, when a striking tableau had been achieved, to
rush out and cry, "Hold it," [2] but this situation was deplored
by Russell and the cameraman, who assembled the cast for additional
shooting after Vincent had departed for the day. [3] Though it
is unknown, at present, what was accomplished during these clan-
destine meetings, Russell and his colleagues may have had in
mind a production which would tell a story in terms of movement.
Obviously this is mere conjecture; but it does appear that they
made some effort to reject tableaux vivants.

On the other hand, if the "Passion Play" was merely a photographic record, and did depend on the narrator, the choir, and
the audience's knowledge of a well-known story to hold the twenty-
four scenes together, the production may have had the happy effect

---

1. Rotha, p. 23.

2. Ramsaye, p. 371.

3. Ramsaye, p. 371.

of making certain individuals, and perhaps Edwin S. Porter in particular, question the correctness of a technique which made the motion picture subordinate to the lecture. Such a technique was, of course, characteristic of the correctly managed lantern lecture, as G. R. Bryce indicates when he says: "Instead of having to explain the slides, the lecturer should have the slides explaining him." [1]

But apart from these speculative contributions, the "Passion Play" did exert a number of rather positive influences on the development of the motion picture. In the first place, on the basis of length alone it did suggest, like the Corbett-Fitzsimmons motion picture, something beyond the standard film of fifty feet. And in the second place it demonstrated very conclusively the feasibility of staged motion picture productions. And finally it bestowed a respectability upon the motion picture which it needed to neutralize the unsavory influence of the prizefight films.

In line with this last point it should be mentioned that Hollaman's endorsement of motion pictures apparently made it possible for many people to become acquainted with the new medium, who otherwise, because they avoided the vaudeville and variety houses, might have been oblivious of them. The New York Times comments on this situation in the edition of October 17, 1897:

---

1. G. R. Bryce, "Lantern Lecture," The Optical Magic Lantern Journal and Photographic Enlarger, viii (January, 1897). 29-30.

"Thousands of women and children who would not enter a variety theatre have seen the motion pictures at the Musee." [1]

According to Ramsaye the success of the "Passion Play" resulted in many similar attempts. [2] But none of them seem to have been of sufficient merit to receive the recognition given the Hollaman production. Sigmund Lubin of Philadelphia, according Hollaman the same recognition he had given Rector, produced another version of the "Passion Play." It seems to have been a very "rough and ready" production which apparently contained much in the finished film not existing in the script.

> Back of the stage was a dwelling. As the painted backgrounds flapped in the wind this house was occasionally revealed. Frank Tichenor, who in after years came to figure in the motion picture business, was startled to see on the screen the Philadelphia girl to whom he was paying attentions, revealed leaning out the window to watch the actors, in the midst of one of the "Passion Play's" most impressive scenes. [3]

Hollaman's search for longer productions also prompted him to arrange short subject into episodes or sets. This was, of course, a common practice among many exhibitors, but Hollaman's greater resources seem to have enabled him to do a more satisfactory job than most of the showmen. During the summer of 1898

---

1. "Notes of the Week," The New York Times, October 17, 1897, p. 21 B.

2. Ramsaye, p. 376.

3. Ramsaye, p. 377.

he assembled Spanish-American war films which he exhibited in
sets of twelve, [1] and during the fall of the same year he selected
representative productions from among the hundred odd he had
collected, and assembled them into "a panorama of the whole war
beginning with the arrival of the soldiers at Tampa and including
the various important movements that followed up to the surrender
of Tampe." [2]

Inspired by their success with the "Passion Play," Hollaman
and Eaves made other productions including a two-reel film with
the title, "The Opera Martha," which was accompanied by "allegedly"
synchronized phonograph records. [3]

This ambitious start in motion picture production by the
museum manager, and the costumer promised great things; but their
active interest in this field was suddenly cancelled by an event,
discussed in another section, which inhibited their efforts and
the efforts of other American producers right up to the end of
the first World War.

In Europe, Melies, in addition to making trick films, was
producing other motion pictures which, like Hollaman's, were not
too far removed from lantern slides. Though these productions

1. "Notes of the Week," The New York Times, July 24, 1898, p. 6 B.
2. "Notes of the Week," The New York Times, November 20, 1898,
   p. 17 D.
3. Ramsaye, p. 374.

may have been mere photographic records they did have the virtue
of length.

One of these productions made late in 1898,

> was a series of films in which he constructed (in little
> incidents barely sixty feet long) the principal events of
> the Dreyfus case. Among them were 'Dreyfus' Court-Martial --
> Arrest of Dreyfus,' 'Devil's Island -- Within the Palisade,'
> 'Suicide of Colonel Henry,' 'Dreyfus Meets His Wife at
> Rennes' and 'The Degradation of Dreyfus.' [1]

The Corbett-Fitzsimmons motion picture, "The Passion Play,"
and other "long" films produced during the first five years are
often passed off as curiosities, or as rather unimportant incidents.

Rotha, as has been noted, dismisses "The Passion Play" as
"a mere photographic record with no attempt at narration"; and
even Hampton has no more to say for the Hollaman production and
the fight motion pictures than "they were almost the only attempts
to produce movies of a thousand feet or more prior to 1903-4." [2]

But, if there were no other reasons for mentioning these
films, other than for their length, they would seem to have an
importance which deserves more attention.

The majority of producers were turning out films approximately

-----

1. Maurice Bardeche and Robert Brasillach, p. 15.

2. Hampton, p. 38.

fifty feet in length. These episodic films seem to have been very deliverately designed for both the peep show and the projector. On the other hand, the fight motion picture and "The Passion Play," because they were made up of a number of scenes, were evidently designed for the projector alone.

The long films, while they did not immediately revolutionize the business of motion picture production, did provide powerful precedents for the producers when they finally broke the peep show shackles, and began considering the production of longer motion pictures. In later discussions which were concerned with the money-making possibilities of long films, somebody undoubtedly said: "Back in '98, 'The Passion Play' ran two hundred performances. People must'a liked it. And the Corbett-Fitzsimmons movie ran a month at the Academy. And then they took it on the road."

Providing the producers with a reason for spending money on longer and better motion pictures was good, and probably is justification enough for labeling "The Passion Play" and the fight motion picture as very important films in the development of the motion picture.

But in connection with the achievement of length, we must

not forget that as long as the producers limited themselves to motion pictures fifty feet long, they were not going to produce story motion pictures. After all, story motion pictures require a "proper magnitude."

Twenty-three centuries ago, Aristotle said something which relates very directly to the episodic films, and their limitations:

> Hence an extremely minute creature cannot be beautiful to us; for we see the whole in an almost infinitesimal moment of time, and lose the pleasure that comes from a distinct perception of order in the parts. [1]

---

1. Aristotle, The Art of Poetry, Quoted by Lane Cooper, Aristotle on the Art of Poetry, p. 29.

CHAPTER VII

EARLY PRODUCTIONS BY THE SCIENTISTS, BUSINESS FIRMS, AND AMATEURS

Motion picture productions during the first years were not limited solely to entertainment films, nor to films like the "Passion Play" and "The Opera Martha" which were designed primarily for release in the commercial theatre.

Production was also accomplished by the scientists, business firms, and amateurs. While the scientists and amateurs did not generally seem to be interested in making motion pictures for profit, the business firms obviously aimed at stimulating trade with their films.

Almost as soon as cameras and projectors were made available to the public the scientists began using the motion picture with considerable purposefulness. This trend was forecast by the New York Times in its issue of May 26, 1897. In its editorial, "The Veriscope," which made observations on the Corbett-Fitzsimmons production, and on the motion picture's greater possibilities, the Times remarked:

> With the improvement in its mechanism it will no doubt be applied to more valuable purposes than those to which it has thus far been confined; and we may foresee that it will serve for the solution of many scientific problems for which the unaided human eye is too slow to furnish the necessary data. [1]

1. "The Veriscope," The New York Times, May 26, 1897, p. 6.

A month earlier the Scientific American after reporting
that the mutograph camera ordinarily recorded forty images per
second, but was capable of taking equally good pictures at the
rate of one hundred per second, observed that "the higher speed
would be used in photographing the flight of a projectile, or
any object that was in extremely rapid motion." [1] This article,
or one similar to it, may, as well as the veriscope pictures
of the fight, have inspired the editorial. At least, articles
such as the one appearing in the Scientific American, provided
a tip to the scientists that many events of scientific interest,
hitherto not susceptible of scientific description and explanation,
might now be susceptible of investigation with the motion picture
camera.

The New York Times' prophecy that the quick eye of the
camera would open up new worlds to the scientists was soon realized.
Dr. Robert L. Watkins, in the early summer of 1897, by combining
microscopy and motion pictures was able to photograph the motion
of bacteria under the microscope. According to the Scientific
American this achievement was important because:

> The fact is that on account of the motion of some
> bacteria, it has been well nigh impossible to photograph
> them. The books have had to depend upon the eye and hand
> of the draughtsman and vague description. This may not
> be of much importance either way, but as yet comparatively

1. "Art of Moving Photograph," Scientific American, lxxvi (April
17, 1897). 248-250.

little is known about bacteria. It is not yet known
whether they are the cause of disease or its result, or
neither. Photography, under the proper circumstances,
is most needed for the investigator, and it can be only
moving photographs.[1]

And as soon as efficient lighting facilities were developed,

it was promised that Dr. Watkins' micromotoscope would be able

to make motion picture records of the blood in actual circu-

lation in the thin tissue of the ear or the web of the fingers.[2]

In 1898, motion pictures were made of the French surgeon,

Dr. Doyen, performing an operation.[3] Doyen had these films

made so that he and his students could make a close study of

their operative techniques. Evidently the motion pictures were

very useful for the Bulletin Phonographique et Cinematographique

made the following report:

> Dr. Doyen states that many technical details, which
> appeared to him satisfactory, have had to receive further
> consideration since he studied the cinematograph records
> of his own operation. The cinematograph supplies him with
> a true picture of what he has done, and he can thus recon-
> sider the most minute details of the operation, with a
> view to their improvement in future cases.[4]

Among some layment the surgical films seem to have created

---

1. D. F. St. Clair, "The Micromotoscope," Scientific American,
   lxxvii (July 31, 1897). 75.

2. St. Clair.

3. Oscar W. Richards, "Photographic History," The Journal of the
   Biological Photographic Association, ii (January, 1933). 48.

4. "The Cinematograph and Surgery," British Journal of Photography,
   xlvii (January 26, 1900). 53.

a great scandal and much opposition because some critics thought
that the doctor was aiming to humiliate his patients. Doyen
stilled the opposition by declaring that "the films were solely
for his own education and that of his students."[1] Later, it
seems, he also had to meet the charge that the photographing of
an operation interfered with the welfare of the patient, for
during an address to his colleagues at the International Congress
of Medicine in Madrid in 1908 he remarked:

> As far as the patient is concerned, there is no dim-
> inution in safety, for, when about to operate under the
> eye of the cinematograph, your preparation will be made
> with exceptional care.[2]

But, on the whole, this method of studying surgery seems
to have received considerable encouragement, for motion picture
demonstrations were given in Monaco under the patronage of Prince
Albert I, and again in the same year at the University of Kiel
under the patronage of Emperor William II.[3] It is likely that
the patronage of Albert and William did much to allay the sus-
picions that first surrounded Doyen and his work.

In Germany, during the first year Doyen began his work,
1898, Oskar Messter duplicated the Frenchman's efforts by making
motion pictures of operations performed at the Surgical Clinic of

---

1. Oscar Richards.

2. Leonard Donaldson, The Cinematograph and Natural Science, p. 20.

3. Donaldson, p. 20.

the University of Berlin. [1] Perhaps the success of Messter's surgical films may have had something to do with William II's patronage of Doyen's exhibition at the University of Kiel.

The problems facing a cameraman photographing an operation cannot be passed over lightly, especially in 1898. First, he had to acquaint himself with the routine of the operating room so that he would not interfere with the activity of the surgeon and his assistants; next, he had to be enough of a scientist to follow intelligently, with his camera, the progress of the operation; and finally, he had to provide himself with adequate illumination so that he could photograph the subject. It would be interesting to know how the light problem was solved, for Ramsaye states that prior to the Jeffries-Sharkey fight film, photographed on the night of November 3, 1899, by the American Biograph Company, "all previous efforts at making motion pictures under light had failed." [2] However, Doyen and Messter seem to have succeeded where the commercial producers failed.

A year before both of these men began working on surgical films, Stenger reports that "x-ray motion pictures were first made with complete success by the Frenchmen, Roux and Balthazard." [3]

---

1. Stenger, p. 135.

2. Ramsaye, p. 408.

3. Stenger, p. 136.

Astronomers employed the motion picture camera too. In 1898, M. Flammarion took a globe on which he very carefully designed the seas and countries of the world. Then he constructed a mechanism which would completely revolve the globe within two minutes, thus obtaining "in this short space of time an exact representation of what regularly occurs (to the earth) every twenty-four hours." [1] After providing the globe with a star-studded background, and illuminating it with a concentrated light which represented the sun, M. Flammarion photographed the scene. The resultant motion picture, which was exhibited before the French Astronomical Society, created for the audience the effect of seeing a complete twenty-four-hour revolution of the earth from the moon in two minutes.

The production seems to have been successful enough to suggest other educational films; and the Optical Magic Lantern Journal and Photographic Enlarger felt compelled to speculate:

> Seeing the great and rapid strides which are being made with cinematograph projection, it might be safe to predict that it will, ere many years have passed, be in common use in certain colleges as a method of imparting instruction. [2]

Realization of this prediction has been a long time coming,

---

1. "Astronomical Illusion," Photographic News, 42 (1898). 115.

2. "Scientific Use of the Cinematograph," Optical Magic Lantern Journal and Photographic Enlarger, ix (March, 1898). 38-39.

but The Optical Magic Lantern Journal and Photographic Enlarger
during these early years was not alone in its speculations about
the possibilities of the motion picture.as a teaching device.
Wilhelm Leifeld believed that motion pictures would be invaluable
aid in the teaching of languages since it would enable the instruc-
tor to associate the act or object with the foreign word. Lei-
field contended:

> It is not possible for the teacher to actually show
> his class all the things that he must familiarise them
> with, but the lantern enables him to present them almost as
> vividly as the realities would appear, and so to fix
> quickly and permanently the foreign equivalent of them in
> their minds. [1]

In Germany, as early as 1897, the energetic Messter produced what Stenger describes as an "educational film." He photographed with his motion picture camera blossoming flowers over
a period of twenty-four hours, and then "compressed" the whole
film into a projected motion picture of one minute. [2] If
Messter's one-minute film was projected at the rate of sixteen
pictures a second he necessarily exposed one frame of the film
every one minute and a half while making the motion picture.

Messter was discovering like other producers that the motion

1. Wilhelm Leifeld, "The Lantern and Kinetograph as Aids to the
Teaching of Languages," Optical Magic Lantern Journal and
Photographic Enlarger, xi (February, 1900). 25-26.

2. Stenger, p. 134.

picture could be used for something more than a recording instrument. In this particular case he was employing "fast motion" [1] to make clear an event which would have been exceedingly difficult to study without the aid of the motion picture.

About 1900, Professor G. S. Moler of Cornell University, wishing perhaps to demonstrate to his classes the motion picture's capabilities, produced a film of a skeleton dancing. He employed frame by frame photography to make the picture. After adjusting the skeleton he photographed the figure exposing one frame, then after a slight change in position he exposed another frame, and so on. In the finished picture the skeleton appeared to be dancing under its own power. [2] Like Messter's blossoming flower film, Moler's skeleton dancing was an example of fast motion photography.

Similar "educational" motion pictures were very likely produced by physicists in other universities. Science demanded that they produce motion pictures in order to establish verification of persistence of vision, fast motion photography, etc. Furthermore, such work was not only instructive, but diverting as well.

By means of a mechanical device which exposed one frame of

1. Spottiswoode, p. 44. "Fast Motion. The film is passed through the camera more slowly than through the projector. Thus an object moves faster when projected than when filmed."

2. Walter H. Stainton, "A Program of Ithaca and Cornell Motion Pictures," Cornell University Theatre Program, May 9, 1942.

the film in the camera every half hour over a period of weeks
while the Star Theatre in New York was being demolished, the
American Mutoscope and Biograph Company produced a "step by step
stop motion picture" of the demolition. The resultant motion
picture projected at standard speed made it appear that the
building was wrecked in a matter of moments. This example of
fast motion photography is described by Ramsaye as a "notable"
motion picture. [1] Certainly if this film, the work of a commercial motion picture producing company can be described as
"notable," no less praise can be bestowed on Messter's and
Moler's productions.

"Slow motion" [2] photography was also employed in the interests of science, as early as 1899. Hopwood says that motion
pictures of girders subjected to the breaking strain, when photographed at high rates of speed and then projected at slower rates
of speed, were useful for "purposes of inspection." On the
basis of successful work in this kind of research Hopwood declared
that "The chief scientific use of the cinematograph will probably
be found in its applicability to the study of stresses and strains." [3]

---

1. Ramsaye, p. 329.

2. Spottiswoode, p. 44. "Slow Motion. The film is passed through
   the camera more quickly than through the projector. Thus an
   object moves slower when projected than when filmed."

3. Hopwood, p. 232.

Here again there is evidence that the American Mutoscope
and Biograph Company, as an expression of their "greater scope
of interest and abilities," [1] experimented with slow motion
photography. Photographs appearing in the April 17, 1897, issue
of the Scientific American show "mutograph" pictures of clay
pigeon shooting and of the firing of a ten-inch disappearing
gun at Sandy Hook. [2] In both cases the action was so fast
that the camera was probably operated at a high rate of speed
to catch the movement.

Since the American Biograph is praised for its bolder production methods, it would seem that the scientists were deserving
of considerable praise for their efforts during the period,
1895-1900.

Large commercial organizations quickly appreciated the
advertising potentialities of the motion picture, and by 1897
Kuhn and Webster of the International Film Company were making
advertising films for an agent who had accounts with Haig and
Haig Highland whiskey, Pabst's beer, and Maillard's chocolate.
These advertising films were projected on a screen billboard

---

1. Ramsaye, p. 328.

2. "The Art of Moving Photography," Scientific American, lxxvi
   (April 17, 1897). 248-250.

facing Broadway at Thirty-fourth Street. [1] The advertisers
were unquestionably delighted with the results for "the pictures
stopped the Broadway crowds. Throngs formed at vantage points
up and down the street. The car tracks were blocked and the
sidewalks filled to impassability." [2] But this was too much
for the police. They stopped the exhibition.

Apparently by March, 1898, the use of motion pictures as
an advertising medium had become fairly widespread, for the
Optical Magic Lantern Journal and Photographic Enlarger reported
that travelling showmen, who previously found it fairly simple
to secure an engagement at a very liberal remuneration, now found
their incomes threatened, not only by the opening of "shop"
theatres which charged one penny for a few minutes of films,
but also by the extensive use of advertising films which were
exhibited throughout the provinces "by several powerful soap and
other firms." [3]

It seems that the general public found the soap firm's motion
pictures "which represent the work carried on in certain depart-
ments of their place of business" as entertaining as the films

---

1. Ramsaye, p. 345.

2. Ramsaye, p. 345.

3. "Cinematographic Exhibitions," Optical Magic Lantern Journal
   and Photographic Enlarger, ix (March, 1898). 37-38.

turned out by Paul, Edison, Williamson, and the Lumieres. It must be said, however, that the soap companies generally admitted the public to their exhibitions on presentation of a coupon which could be secured by purchasing a package containing their wares; and furthermore the success of their programs seemed to depend as much on the variety troupe artists as it did on the motion pictures.

Also, less pretentious programs organized by the various companies probably included entertainment films ordinarily presented in the vaudeville houses, as well as advertising films. In 1902 it seems to have been the practice to sandwich advertising films in between the topical, scenic, and comedy films. [1] And in 1897 when the Kuhn and Webster advertising motion pictures were exhibited on Broadway, "The advertising was interlarded with short bits of current subjects and brief topical snatches of the day." [2]

The nature of the soap company advertising films, and of the Kuhn and Webster motion pictures advertising whiskey, beer, and chocolate is not revealed, but some idea of how the producers handled the problem can be gained by reading a description of a

---

1. "The Cinematographic Advertiser," British Journal of Photography, xlix (June 27, 1902). 506.

2. Ramsaye, p. 345.

motion picture prepared for the manufacturers of carpet-
sweepers in 1902:

> The virtues of a certain carpet-sweeper are extolled
> by means of a little drama in two acts. In the first one
> we see a servant raising dust in a sitting-room by means
> of an ordinary broom, much to the discomfort of an old
> gentleman taking his ease therein. In the second act,
> a room occupied by a young couple at dinner is swept with
> the patent appliance without raising a particle of dust. [1]

Shortly after the soap companies started their program,
the Mellin's Food Company began giving a series of advertisement entertainments with motion pictures. [2] Their programs
were probably very popular because they distributed samples of
their wares at the exhibition.

In reporting the Mellin's Food motion picture enterprise
the Lantern Journal noted that "this form of advertising is fast
becoming popular " [3]

There seems to be no denying this observation, for one
month earlier the Journal reported that Mr. J. S. Freer of Manitoba used the motion picture in most of the towns of England
in which he gave talks on the wonders of Canada in the interest
of the Canadian Pacific Railway Company. Mr. Freer spoke of the

---

1. "The Cinematographic Advertiser."

2. "Mellin's Food Cinematograph," Optical Magic Lantern Journal
   and Photographic Enlarger, ix (May, 1898). 70.

3. "Mellin's Food Cinematograph."

richness of the Canadian soil, and of the large free grants of
land which were given immigrants by the Canadian government; [1]
and he supported his remarks by exhibiting a series of films
showing harvesting in Manitoba. [2]

Following the Canadian Pacific Railway Company's lead, the
Northwest Transportation Company, beginning in 1899, used motion
pictures made by the Edison Company to publicize Alaska. Like
the Canadian Pacific, Northwest Transportation, which served
Alaska on a boat run from Puget Sound, depended for the success
of their enterprise on the opening up of new country. Their
films besides being shown in the United States were most especially
designed to be shown at the Paris Exposition in 1900. It was
felt that the films, which showed pictures of the country in
Alaska, would be most useful in persuading foreigners that the
United States Territory was the land of opportunity. [3]

But the motion picture did more than help open up new
countries. It also helped to publicize the growing industries
of the new world. Almost at the very time the wonders of Alaska
were being broadcast by means of motion pictures, a Toronto
manufacturer of agricultural appliances, in anticipation of

---

1. "Lecture on Canada," Optical Magic Lantern Journal and Photographic Enlarger, ix (April, 1898). 54.

2. Hopwood, p. 232.

3. Ramsaye, p. 401.

securing large orders, made plans to send to England sets of films which demonstrated the quality and efficiency of his horse rakes, self-binders, and other agricultural implements. [1]

The use of the motion picture as an advertising medium became so widespread that experiments evolved methods of exhibition which would lend themselves to the special demands of the advertising films. Hepworth, for example, devised a machine which, like the peep-show kinetoscope, projected an endless film, and did not require the constant attention of an operator. [2] Such a projector would, of course, be useful in a location where people were passing to and fro, and could find a moment to stop and look at the pictures.

Another method for exhibiting advertising films was advanced by Chadwick's Patent Advertising Company, Limited, of Manchester. They suggested projecting films on a screen erected at the rear of a van, from a projector placed at the front of the vehicle. The pictures were to be shown as the van was driven about the streets. [3] The practicability of the method was questionable should "the roads be at all uneven." But the suggestion of such a scheme demonstrated that the advertisers and agents were impressed

1. "The Cinematograph for Commercial Travellers," Optical Magic Lantern Journal and Photographic Enlarger, x (February, 1899). 18.

2. Hopwood, p. 222.

3. "New Style of Advertising," Optical Magic Lantern Journal and Photographic Enlarger, xi (August, 1900). 84.

with the motion picture's capacities as a publicizing medium.

In general, however, ordinary methods of exhibition seem to have been followed. The Hepworth machine, and the Chadwick plan were simply meant to accommodate the special wants of certain advertisers.

Business enterprises were not alone in appreciating the motion picture's persuasive powers. Even the War Office of the English Government, and the Salvation Army considered it worth while to adopt the medium.

The War Office, in order to encourage recruiting, prepared a series of films "illustrative of the life of a soldier from the raw recruit to the perfect soldier living a life of ease," [1] which were to be shown permanently in a London hall, and which were to be distributed throughout the country. In all cases recruiting sergeants would be on hand to take care of those who wanted to join the ranks.

There is evidence that the War Minister, on one occasion, at least, failed to exhibit suitable films to the prospective candidates, for Hopwood remarks: "It may be doubted whether an accurate reproduction of the horrors of a battlefield would to

-----

1. "Recruiting by Means of the Lantern," Optical Magic Lantern Journal and Photographic Enlarger, xi (October, 1900). 117.

any great extent facilitate recruiting; discretion is required in Cinematography as well as in every other path of life." [1]

The Salvation Army in West Australia, with General William Booth's daughter conducting the lectures, presented motion pictures of "their processions, rescue work, etc." [2] The exhibitions, which were augmented by the phonograph, which was used "to reproduce music from their bands, conversations in slumdom, etc.," [3] were so successful that the Salvation Army decided to create a special department to handle such programs. The new branch was called the "triple alliance" because it employed the cinematograph, the phonograph, and the magic lantern. Further plans purposed fitting out each Colony in West Australia with a lantern, a projector, and a phonograph. [4]

The relatively high cost of equipment, and the lack of a well-defined purpose inhibited the immediate use of the motion picture among the amateurs. But by 1900, things had taken such a turn that Hector Maclean wrote:

---

1. Hopwood, p. 232.

2. P. Newland, "A Few Lantern Notes from West Australia," Optical Magic Lantern Journal and Photographic Enlarger, x (February, 1897). 27-28.

3. P. Newland.

4. P. Newland.

Recent experiences,..., indicate that, so far from cinematography being outside the sphere of the amateur, it is steadily gaining ground in his favour; indeed, there is reason to think that, as the apparatus and materials become improved, not only will many amateurs take up the practice of Animated Photography, but they will on account of their number, and of their enthusiasm, at times obtain results which the comparatively few professional operators do not enjoy the opportunities of achieving. [1]

Early evidence of this turn can be found in the interest taken by motion picture equipment manufacturers in the amateur trade during the years 1898 and 1899.

The September, 1898, issue of the Optical Magic Lantern Journal and Photographic Enlarger announced that Messrs. Joseph Leir and Company of 97 Hatton Gardens, E.C., were preparing to retail a projector, named the "Cynnagraph," for "5 1. 5 s." [2] It was to be a very compact machine which could be packed up in a box 5½ by 5½ by 8 inches. Apparently this was one of the first machines designed for the amateurs.

The "Cynnagraph" may have been the "hit" it was promised to be, but it seems fairly certain that the "Biokam," another compact machine measuring 9½ by 5½ by 3¼ inches which was introduced to the public a few months later, soon replaced the earlier machine in popularity. The flexible biokam, which was manufactured

---

1. Hector Maclean, "Preface to Second Edition," Cecil M. Hepworth's Animated Photography.

2. "New Apparatus," Optical Magic Lantern Journal and Photographic Enlarger, ix (September, 1898). 138.

and sold by Messrs. John Wrench and Son, and the Warwick Trading
Company for "6 1. 6 g.", was a combined motion picture camera,
snapshot camera, printer, projector, reverser, and enlarger
"intended to meet the wants of the amateur." [1] It was such a
bargai, costing "rather less than the average price of an
ordinary hand camera" [2] that Hector Maclean remarked, "it is the
source of much wonderment how it can possibly be put on the
market at such a low figure." [3]

Quantity production probably explains in part the low cost,
for the manufacturers had about 2,000 biokams ready for distribution when sales began on April 15, 1899; and they had the
organization to produce about 100 additional machines for the
market each week thereafter. [4]

If the manufacturers of the biokam half realized the sales
they anticipated, their expectations certainly indicate considerable interest in the motion picture among the amateurs. And, of
course, their machine was only one of a number expressly constructed for the amateur.

---

1. "A Cinematographic Camera, Printer, Projector, and Snapshot
Camera in One," Optical Magic Lantern Journal and Photographic
Enlarger, x (April, 1899). 46-48.

2. Hector Maclean, "Notes on Cinematography in 1900," Cecil M.
Hepworth's Animated Photography, p. 124.

3. Hector Maclean.

4. "A Cinematographic Camera, Printer, Projector, and Snapshot
Camera in one," Optical Magic Lantern Journal and Photographic
Enlarger, x (April, 1899). 46-48.

W. C. Hughes, an optical specialist, designed a combination
motion picture camera, printer, and projector called "La Petite",
which retailed at "5 l. 10 s.", and was "suited to the amateur
or student." [1] While L.Kamm, an electrical engineer, designed
still another combination projector and camera which was "intended
for home use by the amateur photographer." [2] These were just
a few of the smaller English machines being made available to
the trade.

At the same time, on the European continent, Oskar Messter
designed a projector which was "intended for home use;" [3]
and in France, Faller designed still another "cinematographe des
familles" which was "une sort de jouet, mais que donne cependant
de petites images suffisantes." [4]

The following notes from the Optical Magic Lantern Journal
and Photographic Enlarger reveal how inexpensive the amateur
machines were compared to the professional machines:

Cinematographs at Moderate Price. - Those who have hitherto
purchased instruments of the Cinematograph class for exhibiting so-called living photographs, have been called on
to pay something like one hundred pounds for the outfit.

1. Maclean, p. 125.

2. "The Kammatograph," The British Journal of Photography,
xlvii (March 9, 1900).

3. Hopwood, p. 156.

4. Eug. Trutat, La Photographie Animee, p. 102.

Prices of this kind have received their death blow, for
Messrs. Wrench & Son are now supplying the trade with an
outfit to sell at "36 1." It can be used in conjunction
with any modern make of lantern; [1]

and,

The Lumiere Cinematograph Camera. - Messrs Fuerst Brothers
have made a reduction in the price of the Lumiere Cinematograph camera (which is capable of photographing, copying,
projecting, and reversing animated pictures) to "40 1."
The apparatus is an excellent one. [2]

Apart from the initial expenditure for a machine, a com-

parison of the costs between the sensitive film strips used in

the large commercial machines, and the sensitive film strips

used in the smaller amateur machines, seems to reveal that the

latter cost about a third as much as the large 35mm. strips.

In 1897, 35mm. negative film strips, 80 feet in length,

cost "1 1." apiece, [3] and in 1899, the smaller biokam negative

film strips, 25 feet in length, cost "3 s. 6 d." apiece. [4]

The 35mm. strips allowed for 16 photographic impressions a foot,

or 1280 in 80 feet.

----

1. "Notes," Optical Magic Lantern Journal and Photographic Enlarger,
   vii (September, 1896). 138.

2. "Notes," Optical Magic Lantern Journal and Photographic Enlarger,
   ix (January, 1898). 18.

3. Hepworth, pp. 7-8.

4. Hopwood, p. xiii.

The smaller strips allowed for 28.8 photographic impressions a foot, [1] or 720 in 25 feet. Thus the amateur wishing to make 1440 motion record pictures had to pay only "7 s." for 50 feet of film, while the professional had to pay "1 l." for 80 feet of film which enabled him to make 1280 motion record pictures. Positive film strips seem to have cost the same as negative strips: "1 l." for 80 feet of 35mm. positive film, and "3 s. 6 d." for 25 feet of the smaller biokam positive film. [2]

Film strips for the biokam seem to have been prepared in lengths of 25 feet so that the amateur could make film subjects with the "Same duration of exhibit as Films used for Public Cinematograph Entertainments." [3] The smaller strips were the equivalent of 48 feet of the large commercial films.

Hepworth does not explain why the 35mm. strips were sold in lengths of 80 feet. Some early English films seem to have been 40 feet long, [4] rather than the standard 50 feet, so it is conceivable that two films were made from the long strips. Then too, it is possible that the extra footage can be partially

---

1. "A Cinematographic Camera, Printer, Projector, and Snapshot Camera in One," Optical Magic Lantern Journal and Photographic Enlarger, x (April, 1899). 46-48. This article reports that Biokam pictures measured 7/12 by 5/12 of an inch.

2. Hepworth, pp. 7-8, and Hopwood, p. xiii.

3. Hopwood, p. xiii.

4. Talbot, p. 104.

explained by waste, [1] by the need for blank film at the beginning
of the film for threading purposes, and by the need of blank
film at the end of the motion picture to avoid a sudden flash
of clear light immediately after the last picture had been projected.

In addition to selling sensitive film for smaller machines,
the Warwick Trading Company also distributed biokam film subject,
25 feet long, for "10 s." each. [2] The small biokam film pictures which measured .583 by .416 inches were larger than the
16mm. pictures of today which measure .410 by .249 inches.

It is difficult to say how enterprising or how creative
the amateurs were in their use of the motion picture. Putting
aside men like Moler, who strictly speaking was an amateur, the
productions turned out by the amateur motion picture addicts of
1900 probably were of little consequence. But it seems that
they occasionally produced films which compared favorably with
the work done by the professionals. Maclean writes:

> Amongst some of the most popular of the films received
> from the front at South Africa were those taken by an ama-
> teur. Another, who has obtained interesting subjects when
> the professional has not had a look in, is Mrs. Main, whose
> animated pictures of snow sports in Alpine regions are
> examples in good point. [3]

---

1. Hepworth, p. 8.

2. Hopwood, p. xiii.

3. Maclean, p. 118.

The war films "taken by an amateur" may have included a
motion picture made in the Soudan by a war correspondent. The
cameraman's letter to Mr. Philippe Wolff, who "published" the
film, described the scene he had photographed:

> The cinematographic film which you have was taken by
> me on the battlefield of Omdurman the day before the battle.
> It is the only genuine Soudan film as nobody else had a
> cinematograph with them. There was a rumour that the
> dervishes were advancing to attack us, and all the men
> were told to lie down and be in readiness to fall in for
> anything. I therefore fixed my camera on the Grenadier
> Guards (Queen's Company) and when the brigade trumpeter,
> whom you see in the photograph, sounded the call, I took
> the men standing up, fixing bayonets, and marching off.... [1]

---

1. "A New Military Cinematographic Picture," Optical Magic Lantern
   Journal and Photographic Enlarger, ix (December, 1898). 174.

CHAPTER VIII

THE LAWSUITS

As we have seen, considerable progress in the development
of the motion picture was achieved during the years 1896 to
1897. The motion picture was finding an outlet to the public
in the vaudeville houses, and in the road shows. Problems of
exhibition were being solved. Longer films were being undertaken. Production and projection techniques were being evolved.
And even the creative possibilities of the camera were being
explored.

But, during the early winter of 1897-1898, this period of
experimentation and progress was suddenly retarded by the action
of Thomas A. Edison. Surveying the motion picture field through
the eyes of his general manager, W. E. Gilmore, Edison suddenly
saw that the motion picture had greater possibilities than he
had guessed. Now, encouraged by Gilmore, he was prepared to
fight to regain the business he had lost.

On December 7, 1897, Edison began a series of actions for
patent infringements against Rich G. Hollaman of the Eden Musee,
who had produced the "Passion Play;" Albert E. Smith and J.
Stuart Blackton of Vitagraph, who had converted one of his
projectors into a camera, and were producing motion pictures;

Maguire and Baucus, who had been his kinetoscope representatives
in London, and who were now importing and distributing foreign
motion pictures in the United States; Sigmund Lubin, Philadelphia motion picture producer; The American Mutoscope and
Biograph Company, which had his former employee, W. K. L. Dickson,
as a director; and sundry other organizations and individuals
who had entered the motion picture business.

Because Edison had failed to apply for European patents
on the kinetoscope, the field over which he hoped to exert control necessarily had to be limited to the United States. Thus
Paul, the Lumieres, and other Europeans interested in the motion
picture could proceed with their business unmolested as long
as they remained abroad.

Edison, who was willing enough to sell projectors and films,
had never sold a camera. Nor had he the intention of ever
selling one. Now by enforcing his control of the camera patents
he hoped to regain "his original possession of the motion picture
which he had brought into being." [1]

Edison's lawyers insisted that all inventors and manufacturers of motion picture equipment, and all producers of motion
pictures in the United States were operating in violation of the

---

1. Ramsaye, p. 465.

patents which he had secured on his peep-show machine.

The lineage of each machine, they alleged, could be traced back to Edison's kinetoscope; and no matter how many devices might have been added, his machine was father, or the grandfather, of the entire family. [1]

As an early consequence of the lawsuits, Edison forced Blackton and Smith, and Lubin to withdraw temporarily from the business. Lubin retired to Europe until the most serious part of the storm blew over, while Blackton and Smith eventually reached an agreement with Edison whereby the latter sold Vitagraph Company prints on a royalty basis.

The lawsuits also had the unhappy result of terminating Hollaman's activities as a motion picture producer. The Eden Musee manager, rather than battle with Edison, turned his negative of "The Passion Play" over to the inventor and gave up the idea of other productions. Hollaman's departure from the production field was unfortunate. He had an intense interest in the medium. He had taste. He had had a wide experience in the theatre. And, unlike the inventors and machinists who dominated the business, he had demonstrated with "The Passion Play," and with "Martha" a readiness to take a chance with longer and more ambitious productions.

Edison's attacks were sustained, and for the next ten years,

---

1. Hampton, p. 22.

right up until the end of 1908, there was no real peace for anybody in the motion picture industry in the United States. His agents instigated suits against every American, and against every European in this country, who could be accused of using illegal equipment.

But the whole business was futile because the promise of profit was too great. The men who had entered the field in 1896 and 1897 had already participated in the motion picture's first boom and as a result the majority of them were unwilling to quit without a struggle. As Hampton puts it:

> The Edison lawyers might just as well have attempted to enjoin a swarm of seven year locusts against entering a grain field. The irresponsible little offenders skipped around like fleas, selling their machines and devices and films to buyers who would take a chance of making profits before the law could reach them. [1]

During the period, 1898 to 1908, the men whom Edison attacked can be divided into two classes: those who owned permanent establishments like the Vitagraph Company, and the American Mutoscope and Biograph Company; and those whose sole asset was really nothing more than a camera. This latter group, because of their very scarcity of assets and consequent mobility, were difficult to bring to bay. And furthermore, once one of them

---

1. Hampton, pp. 64-65.

was eliminated there was always another fellow ready to jump
in and risk the attack in order to produce the short subjects
of fifty feet which seemed to have a never-failing market.

The former group, those who owned permanent establishments
and therefore were unable to scatter with the wind, had no
alternative but to stand and fight. But, because they had entered
the field early, and because they had introduced improvements
in motion picture equipment, they, when Edison went to court,
were able to enter counter-claims. Thus, when he challenged
Biograph, Selig, and Essanay, the American companies, and
Lumiere, and Pathe, the French companies, which were attempting
to conduct business in the United States, Edison discovered that
he was fighting well-established concerns, each of which claimed
that its patents gave it rights which enabled it to continue in
business without Edison's consent. These claims were frequently
valid enough so that until the Supreme Court could pass on them,
as well as Edison's claims, the position of none of the litigants
could be definitely established. [1]

When he challenged the American Mutoscope and Biograph
Company, probably the most enterprising American producer of
motion pictures during the period, 1896 to 1912, Edison found

1. Hampton, p. 65.

that he had engaged a Tartar. Unlike other film companies,
the American Mutoscope through connections with the Empire
Trust Company of New York City had connections with Wall Street.
As a consequence, it was

> better fortified both in the technology of the motion
> picture and in the craft of big-business-at-law than any
> other motion picture enterprise in the world against
> which Edison could press his claims. This defendant
> was an entrenched corporation. [1]

In the meantime, while the courts were considering the
claims of the litigants, "violations of Edison's patent rights,
and allegations of violations, increased in proportion to the
general prosperity of the industry in America." [2] Thus the
coming of the story motion picture in 1903, and the consequent
rise of the nickelodeon theatres in 1905 made the prospect of
profit so alluring "that law and patents and the ethical customs
of business were as futile as Prohibition." [3]

In this chaotic atmosphere, occasioned by the wild rush
for money, the few companies, in addition to Edison, which owned
legitimate patents, eventually found themselves in the curious
position of fighting off Edison's attacks with one hand, and
attacking the newcomers in the field with the other. The newcomers, who were identified as "crooks," stole cameras and

---

1. Ramsaye, p. 383.

2. Hampton, p. 64.

3. Ramsaye, p. 465.

other equipment, impartially, from both Edison, and the original
pioneer bandits.

As an inevitable result, the industry became a battleground;
and by 1907 every studio was a guarded stronghold. [1] The
extreme measure of fortifying the studios had to be adopted so
that the different producers, or litigants as they might more
properly be called, could conceal their production methods for
fear of having their own legitimate inventions stolen, and for
fear of being caught in a patent infringement.

In this warlike atmosphere, which prevailed from 1897 to
1908, the situation became so bad that people involved in the
film business were devoting more time to lawsuits than they were
to the production of motion pictures. Hampton goes so far as
to say that:

> a fourth of a producer's time and thought went to the
> making of pictures, and three-fourths were absorbed by
> legal battles with big and little competitors who sought
> to imitate his inventions or averred that he was stealing
> theirs. [2]

Hampton's estimate of the intensity of the struggle is
verified by a reference to the history of motion picture litigation in the United States cited by Ramsaye.

---

1. Ramsaye, p. 465.

2. Hampton, p. 65.

Motion picture patent litigation in the United States includes no less than 202 major actions, with a list of approximately three hundred replevins and the like. England had a dozen or more considerable litigations and France a handful. [1]

The quotation also indicates the comparative calm of which the European producer was possessed. This factor may have had some bearing on the emergence of Georges Melies as the first important film director in the development of the motion picture. In his Paris studio, the Frenchman was beyond the reach of the Edison agents, and the American courts. He could work in peace.

The situation began to resolve itself during the latter part of 1907, when the courts, after much deliberation, rendered an important decision favoring the Edison claims. On October 24, 1907, Judge Christian Kohlsaat, in the United States Court in Chicago, handed down a decision which held that the cameras used by William N. Selig infringed on the Edison patents. This was a blow that shook the industry.

Vitagraph, Lubin, Selig, Essanay, Pathe, Lumiere, Kalem, and George Kleine, chief targets of Edison's attacks, held council. Knowing full well that the Selig decision spelled the end for all of them, they authorized Kleine to approach Edison and ask for terms. Discussions among Kleine, the inventor, and

---

1. Ramsaye, p. 387.

Gilmore resulted in the establishment of the Edison Licensees
group.

The American Mutoscope and Biograph Company, however,
refused to go along. Insisting that it held patents as important as Edison's, Biograph demanded equal recognition. And
having acquired control of the Latham and Armat patents, which
greatly strengthened its position, Biograph succeeded in having
its demands recognized.

Finally agreeing upon a compromise, Edison and Biograph,
and the Edison Licensees announced the formulation of the Motion
Picture Patents Company on December 18, 1908. The Company,
composed of the most important producing units in the motion
picture business, had as its objective an iron-handed control
of distribution and exhibition. But the "trust," as it was
called by those producers who had been left out of the picture,
was destined to run into the same trouble, and worse, than Edison
had encountered when he began his lawsuits in 1897.

Though the litigation about the patents did not produce
an ideal atmosphere in which the motion picture might develop,
it must be said in fairness to the men who were trying to secure
a monopolistic control of the medium, that they were simply following a practice which had apparently become standard in other

businesses.

Edison, Biograph, and the other units in the newly organized Patents Company had in front of them as models: the Standard Oil Company, the American Sugar Refining Company, and certainly not least of all, the Theatrical Syndicate, which aimed to control "the legitimate theatre of the entire country through the control of its bookings." [1] All of these organizations had as their objective: exclusive control of the supply of the commodity or service in the market in which they were engaged. With such an objective set up almost as a business axiom, men in business expected no quarter and gave no quarter.

Certainly, Kalem and Selig and Essanay all complained bitterly when Edison began his lawsuits in 1897, but when peace was finally declared, and the Motion Pictures Patent Company was organized in 1908, the very men who had been most bitter in their denunciation of Edison and his methods joined hands with him and behaved just as arbitrarily (if his conduct can be described as such) as Edison had behaved in 1897: they tried to eliminate all competition in the production field; they tried to tell the exhibitors what they could show; and they resorted to physical

---

1. Alfred Harding, "The Theatre's First Three Thousand Years," in Our Theatre Today, Ed. Herschel L. Bricker, p. 114.

violence when the law failed to eliminate competition speedily
enough. That they, perhaps, did not have the moral right to
behave as they did, very likely never even occurred to them.
This was business, and business was a battle.

Gilbert Seldes says that the litigation about the patents
is important because it indicated "the growing popularity of
the movie from the moment it found its new material, the
story." [1] What he says is perfectly true, but the struggle
seems to have had other manifestations.

For one thing, the patent litigations seem to have indicated very clearly that the development of the motion picture
was in the hands of business men. "These men knew the commercial value of mechanical processes, and they could appreciate
the particular market value of this novelty," [2] therefore they
were ready to fight desperately for control, or partial control,
of the processes.

Furthermore, the litigations, which commenced in 1897, revealed the tremendous hold the motion picture exerted on the
public's fancy. Apparently its intrinsic quality of movement
was almost enought to command attention. Otherwise, considering

---

1. Gilbert Seldes, An Hour With the Movies and the Talkies, p. 22.

2. Alexander Bakshy, "The New Art of the Moving Picture,"
   Theatre Arts Monthly, xi (April, 1927). 277-282.

the amount of attention which the producers gave to the lawsuits, and the comparatively little attention which they gave to production, it almost seems that the motion picture would have disappeared in a paroxysm of self-destruction. But in spite of the chaos, and in spite of the shabby treatment it was frequently given during this period of adjustment, the new motion pictures continued to prosper.

CHAPTER IX

THE TRANSITION FROM EPISODIC MOTION
PICTURES TO STORY MOTION PICTURES. (1900-1903)

Gilbert Seldes is not an untypical observer when he asserts that "nothing whatever of interest" was accomplished by the motion picture producers prior to 1903. [1] And evidence is not wanting that portions of the public who attended the first programs felt pretty much about the motion pictures as Seldes indicates they might.

While many people had viewed the showings in 1896 and 1897 with enthusiasm, it does seem that a good number of them lost interest in the medium shortly thereafter. This about face is illustrated by the reception accorded the films at Keith's Union Square Theatre in New York. When motion pictures were first shown in this theatre in 1896 they increased the weekly gross receipts from $3500 to $7000. [2] Their success, however, was only temporary, for in little more than a year they were relegated to the position of "chaser". In the latter state the appearance of the pictures on the screen signaled the audience

----

1. Gilbert Seldes, An Hour With the Movies and the Talkies, p. 20.
2. Grau, The Theatre of Science, p. 9.

that the show was over, and that it was time to clear the house
for the next performance.

This condition prevailed in all vaudeville houses which
exhibited motion pictures. [1] And in some houses the films were
used only "when the crowds awaiting an entrance were overwhelming." [2]

The falling off of the public's interest in motion pictures
was foretold by the Showman, as early as June, 1897, when he
declared that while no novelty connected with optical projection
had secured so much of the public's attention as the motion picture, signs were not wanting that "interest had already begun
to flag." [3] His prophesy unfortunately came true, and even
late in 1900 we still find the motion picture occupying the sorry
position of "chaser" in the English music hall. A note written
by Messrs. Walker and Company, Cinematographers, of 19 Bridge
Street, Aberdeen, which was published by the British Journal
of Photography in 1900, reveals that the situation then was not
much better than it had been in 1897 and 1898. The Walkers
declare:

---

1. Ramsaye, p. 264.

2. Grau, The Theatre of Science, p. 12.

3. The Showman, "Animated Photographs and Projecting Machines,"
   The Optical Magic Lantern Journal and Photographic Enlarger,
   vii (June, 1897). 103-105.

If everyone connected with this form of entertainment
would take a personal interest in the subject, it would at
once place it on a higher platform, instead of relegating
it to the last turn in the music-hall programme. [1]

According to Grau the unhappy period of the "chaser" lasted
from 1898 to 1900. [2] But he goes on to say that the motion
picture in 1900 took a turn and regained some of the popularity
it had lost. Ramsaye supports him in this latter statement by
saying that the theatrical world began to see "possibilities
in the screen at the turn of the century. [3]

Notwithstanding, Seldes insists that nothing whatever of
interest was accomplished until 1903, and Jacobs goes right along
with him when he says that the producers for the most part continued to use the same techniques that they had used between
1896 and 1900, and that as a result the films continued to be
employed as "chasers" even after 1900. [4]

The opinions of Seldes and Jacobs would indicate that the
years immediately after the beginning of the new century were
of no particular account, as far as the development of the motion
picture is concerned; and that the films failed to enjoy a public.

---

1. "Commercial Intelligence," The British Journal of Photography,
   xlvii (November 9, 1900). 716.

2. Grau, The Theatre of Science, pp. 11-12.

3. Ramsaye, p. 407.

4. Jacobs, p. 5.

On the other hand the remarks of Grau and Ramsaye suggest that
something of interest may have happened; and that the motion
picture did enjoy a public.

Evidence seems to favor the opinions of the latter two
writers.

The first bit of evidence which favors the notion that
films gained in popularity after 1900, and that the motion picture producers began introducing new and important methods of
production at the same time can be found in the reception
accorded the motion picture in the large vaudeville houses of
the country during the strike of the "White Rats," in 1901.

On February 21, 1901, [1] the vaudeville actors, suddenly,
and without warning, refused to perform. Faced with the possibility of having to close their houses, the vaudeville managers,
in desperation, resorted to motion pictures as their principal
attraction. To their astonishment, "people came - and came
again." [2]

That the motion picture did meet with a favorable reception
during the strike is verified by Grau, who says:

----

1. Jacobs (p. 5.) as well as Grau (The Theatre of Science, p. 25),
   says that the strike occurred in the late part of 1900. According to the New York Times ("The Strike of the Vaudeville
   Actors, February 23, 1901, p. 9 A), the strike began on February 21, 1901.

2. Jacobs, p. 5.

Some of the play houses closed temporarily, others
were enabled to open solely through the help of the camera
man. At last, the latter, had come into his own. The
day of the 'chaser' had passed for all time as far as he
was concerned. Showmen all over the country were brought
to realize that a new manner of presenting an entire 'show'
was now possible without any need for worry as to whether
the 'ghost would walk' on salary day. [1]

If reports concerning the motion picture's reception during
the two weeks the strike lasted [2] are accurate, it seems evident
that the motion picture had moved beyond the early episodic
films, and that they were not quite as much out of favor with
the vaudeville public during the years 1900 to 1901 as Seldes
and Jacobs say.

And if the assumptions mentioned above are not correct, it
is difficult to understand how the vaudeville managers could
have successfully employed the films to keep their houses open.

Though he allows that the motion pictures were well received
during the strike, Jacobs denies that they were able to maintain
their position in the vaudeville program.

As the initial fascination and wonder of the audiences
waned and the strike ended, managers of the better-class
vaudeville theatres either abandoned the novelty entirely
or presented it at the end of their programs, so that the
people who did not care to see it could leave. Movies
became disdained throughout the theatrical world as 'chasers.' [3]

1. Grau, The Theatre of Science, pp. 26-27.

2. "White Rats Strike Ended," The New York Times, March 7, 1901,
   p. 2 D.

3. Jacobs, p. 5.

But an article in the June 29, 1902 issue of the New York Times seems to reveal that the motion picture was held in higher regard by the public after 1901 than Jacobs allows.

> There have lately been important developments in the 'moving picture' business. Practically every theatre in the country where vaudeville is either incidental or a feature has its own machine, which at each performance projects on canvas a dozen or more active views, the exhibition being given equal prominence on the programme with the comedietta preceding or the 'musical act' following. The views are changed weekly, so that the American public may not be surfeited. [1]

Certainly if most motion pictures had failed by 1900 and 1902 to move beyond their "first attempts," it seems unlikely that practically every vaudeville house in the country would have employed motion pictures in their programs on an "equal prominence" with their other acts.

Hampton makes the interesting suggestion that the motion picture's reception in the large vaudeville houses, and more pretentious music halls, does not present a true gauge of its popularity. He says that after they lost their popularity in the large theatres they continued to hold an important position in arcades and dime museums, and that here they found a truly responsive audience.

---

1. "New Things in Moving Pictures," The New York Times, June 29, 1902. p. 25 C.

The audiences in the arcades, whom he identifies as the "real movie devotees," [1] could not see films often enough, and they wandered from place to place trying to see films they had not already seen.

Hampton also identifies the arcade patrons as a "new class of amusement buyers," and he says that they "sprang into existence as quickly and apparently as magically as screen pictures themselves had appeared." [2]

His suggestion that the arcade and dime museum patrons constituted a more important segment of the motion picture public than the vaudeville patrons is especially interesting because Ramsaye says that "the vaudeville screen continued to be the principal avenue to the public for almost a decade." [3] – that is, from 1896 to 1905. There was evidently a considerable audience in at least one of these places.

The arcade managers accomplished the development and education of the new audience of amusement buyers by projecting on a screen the films which they used in their peep show machines. By joining together films from the peep shows they made up a reel of a few hundred feet, providing a screen performance of perhaps

---

1. Hampton, p. 17.

2. Hampton, p. 17.

3. Ramsaye, p. 264.

five minutes. Later, more films were included, and the program was extended to a half an hour.

The acquisition of projectors by the arcade owners was slow because manufacturers during 1896 and 1897, and for several years thereafter, had difficulty supplying the market; [1] and because arcade owners lacking the financial backing of the vaudeville managers had difficulty securing the little motion picture equipment which was available.

But once equipment became available, and projected pictures were introduced as one of the arcade amusements, the films became so popular that arcade managers "exerted themselves to the utmost to rent or buy more projectors and films, and to obtain other and larger rooms to accommodate the picture-hungry masses." [2]

It is significant that an arcade owner was one of the first to lead the way in establishing "moving pictures as a distinct feature attraction." [3] Thomas L. Tally, in 1902, finding that projected pictures were by far the most profitable of his arcade amusements discarded his other attractions and devoted all of his attention to the exhibition of films.

Up to this point we have discovered two groups of amusement

---

1. Hampton, p. 19.

2. Hampton, p. 17.

3. Jacobs, p. 7.

seekers, who as early as 1900-1903, had established a taste
for motion pictures: the vaudeville patrons, and the arcade
patrons. But there was still another group, which, though it
may not have been as large as the first two groups, cannot be
ignored--lantern lecture devotees.

Many lanternists, as has been pointed out, accepted the
motion picture as early as 1896, and from that date on because
their audiences enjoyed motion pictures made it a practice to
include them regularly in their programs.

The popularity of the motion pictures with the patrons
of the lantern shows was such, that by 1900, this group had
transferred its allegiance from slides to motion pictures.
Evidence of the switch can be found in the British Journal of
Photography:

> The introduction of animated photographs and the
> biograph and various other graphs, made a great change in
> the better class of lantern entertainments, and superseded
> to a large extent dissolving-view entertainments. No
> doubt the public like realism, and entertainments illustrated
> by triple lanterns, properly manipulated, such as used to
> be done by Mr. B. J. Malden, never failed to draw big
> audiences, but once the taste for moving photographs
> has become established the dioramic scenes and effects
> were at a discount." [1]

and,

---

1. "Lantern Mems.," The British Journal of Photography, xlvii
   (February 2, 1900). 9.

There has been nothing very new in the lantern world
this season, and all inventions seems to be stopped, as
far as ordinary apparatus is concerned, the optical lantern
and dissolving-view apparatus being eclipsed by the cinematograph and apparatus for showing animated photography. It
is now to be wondered at, when one sees representations
of scenes from the war and popular events portrayed by the
biograph and other good apparatus, and the reception given
to them by the audience. At a recent visit to one of the
halls of variety at the West-end, the only word that could
express the applause that followed the exhibition of the
pictures was 'enthusiastic.' [1]

In the preceding pages an effort has been made to show that

the public found a new interest in motion pictures after 1900;

and that the public's interest, once it had been revived, was

sustained right up to 1903, the year that "The Great Train

Robbery" was produced.

Now the question is, what was the content of the motion

pictures shown to audiences from 1900 to 1903, and how did it

differ from the content of the films shown to them from 1898 to

1900, when the motion picture experienced a slump.

In previous chapters we have learned that the early films

were generally restricted to scenes of simple movements, like

pictures of an onrushing train, a shoeblack at work, a dancer

doing a turn, a passing parade. And in the beginning it seems

---

1. "Lanters Mems., " The British Journal of Photography, xlvii
   (February 2, 1900). 9.

to have been quite enough "to photograph anything with movement, and the wonder of the projected picture was sufficient
to hold the attention of the audience." [1]

Jacobs says that technical difficulties like unwieldy
cameras and slow film limited producers to the photographing
of simple movements. [2] But this limitation did not bother most
producers, because the public was well satisfied with the simple
reproduction "in animation of scenes and incidents associated
with every-day life." [3]

The producers of motion pictures were in their glory.
"Nothing was too trivial to photograph;" [4] and most of them
failed to exert themselves beyond setting up a camera and
shooting whatever came in sight. As a consequence the motion
picture fell into disrepute beginning in 1898. To be sure,
there were a number of enterprising individuals, and firms were
experimenting with longer films, storyettes, and magical films,
but the results of their work was not enough to stem the tide.

In time, however, the effects of the depression began to
be felt, and the producers became alarmed. And like their

------

1. Hulfish, Vo. II, p. 75.

2. Jacobs, p. 11.

3. Talbot, p. 107.

4. Jacobs, p. 11.

Hollywood brothers of the twenties who introduced the novelty
of talking pictures only when business became so bad that no
other course was open to them, the early producers decided that
they must offer the public something different, if the motion
picture was to survive. Investigation of public taste was in
order, and as a result films of a "wider range" [1] and of "a
greater length" [2] began to appear on the market by 1900.

The first of the longer films, which simply supplemented
the regular fare of shorter motion pictures, were produced between 1900 and 1902; and were anywhere from two hundred and fifty
feet to four hundred feet in length. [3] Hampton says that some
embodied very slight themes; and he classifies them as "storyettes." [4]

Many storyettes appear to have been no more pretentious than
the little prearranged scenes photographed by the American Mutoscope and Biograph Company in 1897. Hampton's examples of a
storyette certainly make us believe that this was possibly the
case:

_____

1. Grau, The Theatre of Science, p. 28.

2. Hampton, p. 29.

3. Hampton, p. 36.

4. Hampton, p. 36.

> Employer flirting with stenographer - kisses her -
> wife enters office and creates disturbance.... Dignified
> man strolling in garden with young lady, budding romance
> destroyed as man steps on hose which turns upward and
> splashes water in his face; [1]

and production methods in 1900, described in "a little book

treating of the making of animated photographs," issued by Messrs.

Hepworth and Company, certainly do not persuade us that radical

new methods were employed. The little book says that studio

operators

> are continually preparing and executing miniature dramas
> for the amusement and entertainment of their patrons. Upon
> a well-furnished stage in the open air these dramas are
> enacted, after careful and elaborate rehearsal, amid all
> the requisite surroundings of scenery and accessories which
> the subject demands. In fact, quite an important branch
> of the business is continually occupied in the painting
> of scenery, the construction of 'properties,' and the
> manufacture of dresses and costumes for these short come-
> dies. The camera forgets nothing and notices everything,
> and the scenery and all accessories must be just as care-
> fully prepared for a play which has a run of one performance
> only, and that lasts but a single minute, as if a three
> hours' entertainment were contemplated in the hope of a
> run as long as that of Charley's Aunt. There is a little
> staff of actors within easy call, who rehearse again and
> again until they are proficient in their respective parts
> for each of their playlets. [2]

But the point seems to be, that by 1900, because the public

demanded it, producers turned more and more to the photographing

of films with prearranged scenes. Such films had been produced

in 1897, and even earlier; now they were simply produced in quantity;

---

1. Hampton, p. 29.

2. Hepworth Book (no title) quoted in "The Making of an Animated
   Photograph," Monthly Supplement of the British Journal of
   Photography, xlvii (July 6, 1900). 51.

and a bit more elaborately.

The years 1900 to 1902 saw the development of the "chase,"
which Hampton in 1931 says, "has persisted for more than three
decades as one of the surest methods of arousing spectators to
a high pitch of excitement." [1] Needless to say, "chases"
remain in 1949, even as in 1931, and in 1900, one of the motion
picture's most valuable assets.

According to David S. Hulfish:

> Chases are a division of the comedy class, in which
> the story involves the pursuit of some of the actors by
> others. A long series of ludicrous incidents may be strung
> together in a film, depicting the efforts of the pursued
> to evade his pursuers and the tribulations of the pur-
> suers, ending the film either with or without a capture. [2]

At first, motion picture audiences were satisfied with mere
pursuit, but rather soon they demanded that the pursuit become
a part of a fragmentary story. And gradually elements like suspense, conflict, and character delineation began to find their
way into these productions. These elements were employed only
in a sketchy manner, but they did add complications to the story
which did extend the length of motion pictures.

In addition to the chases, comedies and magical films also
became a regular part of the motion picture's bill of fare between

---

1. Hampton, p. 36.

2. Hulfish, Vol. II, p. 72.

1900 and 1902.

Comedies consisted of incidents which had been included in the clown's repertory of tricks for hundreds of years:

> a man hits another with a barrel-stave; well-dressed man kicks hat under which a brick is concealed; dignified (preferably snobbish) man passes under ladder and bucket of paint falls on him; dude sits down in a custard pie. [1]

And when these incidents were transferred to the screen, they were no less successful than they had been on the stage of a theatre, or on the actor's temporary platform erected in a public square.

The magical films employed fast motion, slow motion, reverse shooting, stop motion, and other camera tricks as a means of mystifying and startling audiences. Examples of such films are numerous; horses jumping over hurdles backwards, men disappearing in a puff of smoke, chairs unaccountably performing weird tricks, and vehicles moving along at remarkably high speeds.

Comedies and magical films had been produced during the years, 1896-1900, but apparently it was not until, 1900-1902, that they were produced in any quantity. The June 29, 1902 edition of the New York Times suggests that this was the case.

> Where a year or so ago those 'in front' were treated to realistic scenes of Niagara Falls, a trip across Brooklyn Bridge, or a view taken from the locomotive of an

---

1. Hampton, p. 36.

English railway train, they will now be shown with humorous exaggeration how Mrs. O'Grady deals with her husband when he comes unsteadily home on Saturday night minus his wages, or they will be permitted to gaze upon the remarkable spectacle of a clown ambling about the canvas, detaching his head or limbs at will. [1]

When Hampton says that the magical films achieved only "a moderate degree of popularity," [2] he indicates that they did not play an important part in reviving the public's interest in motion pictures.

However, Ramsaye does not hold a similar opinion. He says that the magical films, or "mysterious films" as they were called in 1902, actually "rescued" the motion picture following the slump of 1898-1900, and that they were "the sensation of the day." [3] And two articles appearing in 1902 editions of the New York Times appear at least partially to support his statement.

The first article appearing February 16, 1902, reveals that

A new series of mysterious moving pictures will be shown during the week at the Eden Musee . This addition makes over fifty mysterious pictures shown each day in addition to an equal number of comic and historical films. [4]

---

1. "New Things in Moving Pictures," The New York Times, June 29, 1902. p. 25 C.

2. Hampton, p. 38.

3. Ramsaye, p. 394.

4. "In Vaudeville Houses," The New York Times, February 16, 1902. p. 11 B.

And the second article, appearing June 29, 1902, reveals that

> of late nearly all the pictures produced have been either
> of a comic or mysterious nature, whereas a year or so
> a ago those 'in front' were treated to realistic scenes of
> Niagara Falls, a trip across Brooklyn Bridge, or a view
> taken from the locomotive of an English railway train. [1]

Before continuing with the development of the motion
picture during the period, 1900-1903, it would be well to stop
at this point and discuss briefly the work of the Frenchman,
Georges Melies, chief exponent of the magical or mysterious
films, and probably the foremost director of motion pictures
prior to 1903.

Georges Melies, a professional magician who was manager and
owner of the Theatre Robert-Houdin in Paris, had been invited to
the first private exhibition of the Lumiere's cinematograph in
1895. The first film show seemed to him "a sort of miracle";
and wishing to exploit the instrument in his theatre, he rushed
up to Auguste Lumiere before the private showing was over and
offered to buy it from him at once. Melies relates:

> 'I offered ten thousand, twenty thousand, fifty thou-
> sand francs. I would gladly have given him my fortune, my
> house, my family in exchange for it. Lumiere would not
> listen to me. "Young man," said he, "you should be grate-
> ful, since although my invention is not for sale, it would

---

1. "New Things in Moving Pictures."

undoubtedly ruin you. It can be exploited for a certain
time as a scientific curiosity but, apart from that, it
has no commercial future whatsoever." : 1

Undaunted, Melies secured a camera from Robert W. Paul in
London, and by April, 1896, he had produced and exhibited his
first motion picture.

Melies was peculiarly suited to his new occupation, having
been a newspaper caricaturist, a cabinetmaker, a painter, a
draughtsman, a mechanic, and a manufacturer before he had settled
on his managerial job at the Theatre Robert-Houdin.

At first he photographed moving objects at random: soldiers
marching, trains arriving at the station, people walking. Like
his contemporaries of 1896, he was pleased as long as the objects
he photographed displayed movement. Then chance revealed a new
aspect of the medium to him. One day while he was photographing
the traffic in Paris his camera jammed; the film had been caught
inside the aperture gate. Readjusting it, he continued shooting.
Later, when the film was developed and projected, Melies was
surprised to see on the screen, a bus turn into a hearse. He
had accidentally happened on stop-motion photography. This event
prompted him to explore the camera's capabilities for distorting
and concealing reality on the screen.

His accidental discovery made him realise that the director

_____

1. George Melies, quoted by Bardeche and Brasillach, p. 10.

can control everything in the motion picture. And, being a
magician, he immediately decided that it was the director's
job to deceive the public for entertainment purposes. From
mere reportage Melies turned to the creative realm of ingenious
trickery.

In his "One Man Band," Melies, employing multiple exposure,
appeared in several parts simultaneously. And, in other films,
deliberately using stop-motion photography, he made inanimate
objects appear to move. Stop-motion in "The Doctor's Secret"
also made it possible for a physician to reassemble a patient
who had been blown into six parts. The living man was sub-
stituted just as the doctor and his assistant screwed the dummy
head onto the straw body. [1]

Iris Barry credits Melies with having used a close-up as
early as 1896. [2] Though he never realised the possibilities
of the close-up, regarding it merely as a trick, he again demonstrated its feasibility in "A Trip to the Moon" by using a
tracking shot that led to a close-up of the moon. It is difficult to say whether he moved the camera towards the moon, or

---

1. In Rene Clair's "The Italian Straw Hat", furniture is made
   to scuttle from the house by means of stop-motion; and in
   the Russian film, "The New Gulliver," puppets are made to
   move by the same means.

2. Barry, Film Notes, Series I, Program 1.

the moon towards the camera, though the latter seems more likely.
In either case the effect is the same, and the possibility of
shooting a scene from more than a single position had been
demonstrated.

"Clearly Melies regarded the film literally as a series
of tableaux vivants, though he achieved continuity by over-
printing the end of each scene on the beginning of the next." [1]
He used these "rough dissolves" in all of his later films. As
with stop-motion, chance figured conspicuously in the development of the dissolve. "In the studio it had become customary
gradually to diminish the aperture of the lens while shooting
the last few feet of each scene, in order not to fog the film." [2]
Then, when the various shots were assembled in their chronological order, the portion that was underexposed was eliminated.
One day the cutter failed to eliminate the faded portion of the
film and it was projected onto the screen. Melies immediately
realised that if the aperture of the lens were slightly opened
at the beginning of the next shot, and then opened full as the
shot progressed, a smoother transition might be affected if the
under-exposed portion at the end of the first shot were super-
imposed onto the underexposed portion at the beginning of the

------

1. Barry.

2. Bardeche and Brasillach, p. 21.

second shot.

By developing the camera's capabilities, Melies, the
magician, was able to startle and mystify his film audiences.
In achieving these ends he mastered every trick of the camera:
fast motion, slow motion, dissolves, [1] stop-motion, fades,
animation, double exposure, and reverse shooting.

But he did not stop with camera technique. Having gained
a reputation with his early fantasies, which, like the majority
of motion pictures produced during the first five years, were
restricted to single scenes, Melies, in 1900, along with other
producers, turned to motion pictures which involved several
scenes.

"Cinderella," "Red Riding Hood," and "Bluebeard" were
among his first efforts in the field of the longer film; and
because they were popular with the public, they were probably
instrumental in not only encouraging the production of more
magical films, but also in extending the length of motion pictures.

Besides providing a more fertile field in which to work his
imagination, the longer subjects also demanded a more careful
preliminary preparation. Sets had to be constructed, properties
assembled, costumes designed. And being a man of the theatre,
he resorted to theatrical techniques in order to expedite the

----

1. Dissolves and fades are now chemically produced.

production of these motion pictures. Furthermore, he drew actors
from the music and variety halls to play the various roles in
his films. And probably influenced by his theatrical training
he rehearsed scenes before shooting them.

Melies did not recreate "Cinderalla" (1900), his first great
success after calling upon literature and the theatre's resources,
he illustrated it. The scenario follows:

1. Cinderella in the Kitchen
2. The Fairy
3. The Transformation of the Rat
4. The Pumpkin Changes to a Carriage
5. The Ball at the King's Palace
6. The Hour of Midnight
7. The Bedroom of Cinderella
8. The Dance of the Clocks
9. The Prince and the Slipper
10. The Godmother of Cinderella
11. The Prince and Cinderella
12. Arrival at the Church
13. The Wedding
14. Cinderella's Sisters
15. The King
16. The Nuptial Cortage
17. The Bride's Ballet
18. The Celestial Spheres
19. The Transformation
20. The Triumph of Cinderella [1]

Primitive though it was the order of scenes did form a coherent,
logical and progressive continuity. A new way of making moving
pictures had been invented. [2] Scenes could now be staged and
selected specially for the camera, and the movie maker could
control both the material and its arrangement. Movie making,

_____

1. Melies' "Star" Catalogue, 1900-1901, cited by Jacobs, p. 25.

2. "The Passion Play" (1898) also presented a coherent, logical
   and progressive continuity.

heretofore an unselective process, became with 'arti-
ficially arranged scenes' a creative enterprise, involving
planning, selection, direction, and control of material
and instruments, and fusing of all to produce a single
effect. [1]

Up to 1904 Melies was dominant in the field of the motion
picture. His prearranged scenes exerted a tremendous influence
on his contemporaries who had made it a point to publicize the
impromptu nature of their films. His work with the camera had
concentrated attention on its creative potentialities. And
larger scale productions gave the motion picture the magnitude
it needed before it could tell a story.

Melies, the first to grasp the theatrical potentiality of
the new medium, looked upon the motion pictures as an extension of stage art; and though "his style is monotonous and
his screen cramped, his films themselves are instinctive with
two vital elements - movement and imagination." [2]

After 1905, Melies failing to keep pace with the times,
both in technique and business methods, began to lose popularity.
By 1914 he was bankrupt.

Melies contemporaries also used stop-motion, dissolves,
fast motion and slow motion, and it is questionable whether he

---

1. Jacobs, pp. 25-26.

2. "Georges Melies, Magician and Film Pioneer: 1861-1938,"
   Film Notes.

was the first to employ these devices, but, what is more important, he was probably the first producer to use them extensively and intelligently.

Mysterious films from Paris were not simply advertised as mysterious films. They were given the tag, "from Paris." [1] Like Parisian styles, the Melies films seem to have been regarded as special.

While the chases, comedies, and magical films were finding a regular place in the motion picture programs, current events or news reel films, and travel films continued in popularity. These films had been as well received, it seems, all during the period, 1896-1900, as they are today; and they continued to occupy a conspicuous position in theatre programs after 1900.

The New York Times' observation in 1897 that the motion picture conveys the "fruits of travel" to those who stay at home more successfully than "all other inventions," [2] was substantiated by the reception accorded news reel and travel films in the theatres during the succeeding years. A sampling of notes from the New York Times during 1900, 1901, and 1902 seems to

1. "Notes of the Week," The New York Times, February 18, 1900, p. 16 G.
2. "The Veriscope," The New York Times, May 26, 1897, p. 6 D.

reveal that these films were shown regularly; and, because
theatre managers bothered to feature them in their advertising,
that they found public favor.

> Eden Musee. - A new series of moving pictures from South
> Africa has just been received. They include pictures of
> the massing of Boer troops and their movements toward the
> front. Among the pictures are also views of the English
> troops at drill and on their way to Ladysmith; [1]
> (January 28, 1900)
>
> Keith's Union Square Theatre. - ....In the biograph sketches
> views will be given of the British naval guns in action
> in the battle of Colenso; [2] (March 4, 1900)
>
> Keith's - Biograph: Ammunition Ox Train in Luzon; [3]
> June 3, 1900)
>
> Among the new moving pictures that will be shown at the
> Eden Musee during the present week are a number of foreign
> scenes of unusual interest. One is a scene upon the Ganges
> River, in India; another is a section of the Great Wall
> in China. Other pictures show historical places throughout
> China, India, Germany, and Russia; [4] (May 5, 1901)
>
> Cinematograph reproductions of the coronation of King
> Edward will be displayed at the Eden Musee beginning on
> Monday. The different tableaus will show the Archbishop
> administering the oath, the anointing, the obligation of
> the sword, the orb and sceptre, the crowning of Edward VII,
> and the king and queen in their chairs of state; [5] (August
> 17, 1902) and,

---

1. "Notes of the Week," The New York Times, January 28, 1900. p. 16 F.

2. "Notes of the Week," The New York Times, March 4, 1900. p. 16 G.

3. Advertisement, The New York Times, June 3, 1900. p. 8 G.

4. "The Week's Playbills," The New York Times, May 5, 1901. p. 20 C.

5. "Vaudeville and Concerts," The New York Times, August 17, 1902.
   p. 9 C.

The pictures of the Delhi Durbar were shown on the screen
of the cinematograph at the Eden Musee. [1] (February 15,
1903)

Some idea, as to the length of the various scenes shown
in the above mentioned programs, can be gained by reading a
note in the November 19, 1900, issue of the British Journal of
Photography:

Cinematograph Films of the C.I.V. Procession. - Messrs. W.
Butcher and Son, of Blackheath, inform us that the following
films were taken from the roof of Gloucester Gate Lodge,
Hyde Park; they show the procession coming from the Marble
Arch: No. 1, showing Mounted Police, Band of the Honorable
Artillery Company, Hussars, Colonel McKinnon, Major-General
Trotter, and other Officers and C.I.V.'s, 63 ft.; No. 2,
showing Battery of the C.I.V., Band of London Rifle Bri-
gade, C.I.V.'s, and Band of London Scottish Rifles, 71 ft.;
No. 3, C.I.V.'s, with flag captured from the Orange Free
State, 31 ft.; No. 4, Infantry Battalion of the C.I.V.
(remainder), Machine Gun Section of the C.I.V., Ambulance
Waggons with invalids and detachment of Guards, 68 ft. [2]

Because of the producers' preoccupation with chases, magical,
and comedy films, beginning in 1900, the travel and News reel
films apparently did not continue to receive the attention which
they had previously received. But they continued to be shown;
and it seems perfectly safe to say that as long as people enjoy
"Look," "Life," "The National Geographic," "The London Illustrated News," and the newspaper rotogravure section, they will
continue to enjoy news reel films.

---

1. "In Vaudeville," The New York Times, February 15, 1903, p. 25 C.

2. "Commercial Intelligence," The British Journal of Photography,
   xlvii (November 9, 1900). 716.

In their search for novelty during the years 1900-1903, producers apparently continued to make motion pictures which were simply designed to shock audiences. An example of such a film would be the motion pictures of the fountain in the Trocadero. "One view," according to the newspaper report, "is taken directly at the side of the fountain, and the vast sheet of water seems to be pouring directly upon the stage." [1] While the empathic response of the people seeing this film may not have been as pronounced in 1900, as it had been in 1897 when the audience "shuddered" at the sight of waves breaking upon the beach, [2] it can hardly be doubted that, at least, some souls in the twentieth century audience reacted as overtly, upon seeing the water appear to pour on the stage, as the earlier group had, when they felt that they were about to be inundated.

Another motion picture which very likely created a physical sensation in the audience was the "picture taken on the elevator of the Eiffel Tower" as it made its trip up and down. [3] The newspaper reporter covering the exhibition said that when the elevator started to rise "the vast crowd grew smaller until, when at the top of the tower they seem like small specks." [4]

1. "Notes of the Week," The New York Times, September 9, 1900. p. 18 D.
2. Edmund A. Robbins, "Animated Pictures," The Optical Magic Lantern Journal and Photographic Enlarger, viii (June, 1897). 99-101.
3. "Notes of the Week," The New York Times, September 16, 1900. p. 17 D.
4. "Notes of the Week," The New York Times, September 16, 1900. p. 17 D.

These films were simply later examples of the "punch" films of 1896 [1] which were calculated to raise the audience to a high pitch of excitement.

During 1902 and 1903, according to Hampton, motion pictures of three hundred to six hundred feet in length began to appear. [2] These films contained the framework of stores. [3]

Examples of the longer films are cited by Hampton:

'The Suburbanites,' 718 feet; a comic film in seven scenes, which depict the experiences of Mr. Cityman and his family in looking for rest and happiness in the suburbs.
'The Lost Child,' 538 feet; an exceedingly comical film, showing a series of laughable adventures which happened to a man suspected of stealing a baby.
'Impossible Voyage,' 1075 feet. This exceptional film shows the fanciful adventures of a body of scientists, who take a trip on an impossible train under the sea.
'From Christiana to the North Cape,' 426 feet; photographic reproduction of various places passed during a trip from Christiana to the North Cape. The film could be called 'In the Land of the Midnight Sun,' and shows some very artistic effects.
'The Adventures of Sandy McGregor,' 292 feet. A very humorous subject showing the adventures of Sandy who is caught by two young ladies on a lonely beach while preparing to take his bath.
'Locomotive Races; Electricity vs. Steam,' 266 feet; an unusual subject, showing the series of races between the powerful electric train which was tested by the New York Central Railway, and the regular Fast Mail Train. We consider this the most exciting as well as interesting railroad train scene that was ever made. [4]

---

1. Hampton, p. 14.
2. Hampton, p. 38.
3. Hampton, p. 38.
4. Hampton, pp. 38-39.

If "Impossible Voyage" was George Melies' production, as
it must be, since the description of the film fits the still
picture of Melies' "The Impossible Voyage" shown in Jacobs'
"The Rise of the American Film," there is a question about the
motion picture's production date. Hampton says 1902 or 1903; [1]
Jacobs says 1904. [2]

Ramsaye also cites examples of tiny, trivial efforts to
"use the screen to tell a story," [3] prior to 1903: Cecil Hepworth's "Rescued by Rover," and "The Burglar on the Roof."

However, here again there is a discrepancy. According to
Iris Barry, "Rescued by Rover" was produced in 1905. [4]

Though doubt may be thrown on the reliability of the other
examples cited by Hampton and Ramsaye, because of the date dis-
crepancies, examples of still other motion pictures are available
which substantiate Hampton's claim that films became longer, and
came a bit closer to telling a story during the period, 1902-1903.

The first of these films is Melies' "A Trip to the Moon"
made in 1902. [5] It was eight hundred and twenty-five feet long, [6]

---

1. Hampton, p. 38.
2. Jacobs, picture opposite p. 44.
3. Ramsaye, p. 414.
4. Barry, Film Notes, Series I, Program 1.
5. Barry, Film Notes, Series I, Program 1.
6. Jacobs, p. 27.

and consisted of thirty tableaus, [1] which told the story of an
expedition to the moon by a party of scientists.

With this film as a standard, Melies proceeded to turn out
other motion pictures of a similar magnitude; "Gulliver's
Travels," "Beelzebub's Daughters," "The Inn Where No Man Rests,"
and "Fairyland or the Kingdom of the Fairies."

In the United States, during the same period Melies produced
"A Trip to the Moon," Edwin S. Porter produced "The Life of an
American Fireman," which was about five hundred feet in length;
and shortly thereafter, Vitagraph produced "A Gentleman of France,"
apparently of about the same length.

Business expediency was probably the most important factor
behind the gradual lengthening of motion pictures.

In 1900, chances are, the number of exhibitors who projected
pictures on a screen were considerably fewer than the number of
exhibitors who used short film strips in peep show machines. If
this assumption is correct, it is understandable why, during
the first five years, the producers confined themselves to films
which averaged fifty feet in length.

But in 1900, as manufacturers of motion pictures began to
catch up with back orders, and as projectors became more

---

1. Barry, Film Notes, Series I, Program 1.

available, the men who operated peep show machines began dis-
carding them in favor of the machines which would throw pictures on a screen. Having acquired projectors they needed
films, so they took the short strips of film which they had
used in the peep shows, spliced them together, and projected
them on a screen.

Producers, while watching the new development with interest, continued to turn out short films; they wanted to see
how the public would react, before they decided to move into
the production of longer films. The peep show market and its
requirements were a known quantity, but the new business of
projected motion pictures, which very obviously opened up all
kinds of possibilities in regard to mass production of longer
films, was an unknown quantity, and had to establish itself
as a sound financial risk before the producers were willing
to change their production routine.

Melies being, perhaps, more interested in his job, and being,
perhaps, more of a gambler, produced his long film, "Cinderella,"
for the new market. It was a financial success, and he continued producing longer motion pictures. And other producers
having the same kind of confidence in the new market began
experimenting as well. Favorable results led to the gradual
lengthening of films, until by 1902, and 1903, films of from

three hundred to six hundred feet were appearing.

The first of the longer films turned out by the producers after 1900 probably consisted of no more than a collection of related shots, somewhat similar to Lyman Howe's "series of four shots , representing a fire alarm in New York City," [1] which had been exhibited in Ithaca, New York, in 1897. These shots, both those produced in 1897 and in 1900, could very likely have been shown as individual units in a peep show machine, as well as in series on a screen.

But probably as projected pictures began to supplant the peep show exhibitions in popularity, and as the producers saw less need for catering to the demands of the arcade customers, they decided to concentrate most of their time on films for screen presentation. This decision, as soon as the films achieved a magnitude which permitted the producers to photograph more than just fragmentary incidents, led to the inevitable result - story films.

Edwin S. Porter, an Edison cameraman, and James H. White, manager of Edison's Kinetograph Department, were the men who finally emerged with a motion picture which could be properly

---

1. "A Remarkable Exhibition," The Ithaca Daily Journal, May 10, 1897. p. 6 C.

identified as a story film.

In 1902, Edison and White finding that there were more exhibitors ready to buy long films, decided that it might be good business to turn out a long motion picture. Realizing that action and color are useful in making any story interesting, they selected the fire department as their subject. Then doing what any high school student would do, they collected their materials, in this case stock shots of fire department activities which were available in the Edison files. With this material in hand they decided that the story of a fire department rescuing a mother and child from a burning building might very well be a good unifying idea for their production. And because the files did not contain shots of all the scenes they wanted, so that they could tell the story as effectively as they had planned, Porter staged and shot the additional scenes they needed.

The resultant film, called "The Life of an American Fireman," consisted of ten shots. It involved exposition, action, suspense, crisis, and climax. It was probably different from other films of the day because it contained the additional shots which Porter bothered to photograph.

The scenario of "The Life of an American Fireman" follows:

THE LIFE OF AN AMERICAN FIREMAN

Scene 1: The Fireman's Vision of an Imperiled Woman and
          Child

    The fire chief is seated at his office desk. He
has just finished reading his evening paper and has
fallen asleep. The rays of an incandescent light
rest upon his features with a subdued light, yet
leaving his figure strongly silhouetted against the
walls of his office. The fire chief is dreaming,
and the vision of his dream appears in a circular
portrait on the wall. It is a mother putting her
baby to bed, and the impression is that he dreams
of hiw own wife and child. He suddenly awakens
and paces the floor in a nervous state of mind,
doubtless thinking of the various people who may
be in danger from fire at the moment.

Here we dissolve the picture to the second scene.

Scene 2: Close View of a New York Fire-Alarm Box

    Shows lettering and every detail in the door and
apparatus for turning in an alarm. A figure then
steps in front of the box, hastily opens the door
and pulls the hook, thus sending the electric current which alarms hundreds of firemen and brings
to the scene of the fire the wonderful apparatus
of a great city's Fire Department.

Again dissolving the picture, we show the third scene.

Scene 3:   Sleeping Quarters

A row of beds, each containing a fireman peacefully
sleeping, is shown. Instantly upon the ringing of the
alarm the firemen leap from their beds and, putting on
their clothes in the record time of five seconds, a grand
rush is made for a large circular opening in the floor
through the center of which runs a brass pole. The first
fireman to reach the pole seizes it and, like a flash,
disappears through the opening. He is instantly followed by the remainder of the force. This in itself
makes a most stirring scene.

We again dissolve the scene to the interior of the
apparatus house.

Scene 4:   Interior of Engine House

Shows horses dashing from their stalls and being hitched
to the apparatus. This is perhaps the most thrilling and
in all the most wonderful of the seven scenes of the
series, it being absolutely the first moving pictures ever
made of a genuine interior hitch. As the men come down
the pole and land upon the floor in lightning-like
rapidity, six doors in the rear of the engine house, each
heading a horse-stall, burst open simultaneously and a
huge fire horse, with head erect and eager for the dash
to the scene of the conflagration, rushes from each opening.
Going immediately to their respective harness, they are
hitched in the almost unbelievable time of five seconds
and are ready for their dash to the fire. The men hastily
scamper upon the trucks and hose carts and one by one the
fire machines leave the house, drawn by eager, prancing
horses.

Here we again dissolve to the fifth scene.

Scene 5:   Apparatus Leaving Engine House

We show a fine exterior view of the engine house, the great
door swinging open and the apparatus coming out. This is
the most imposing scene. The great horses leap to their
work, the men adjust their fire hats and coats, and smoke
begins pouring from the engines as they pass our camera.

Here we dissolve and show the sixth scene.

Scene 6: Off to the Fire

In this scene we present the best fire run ever shown.
Almost the entire fire department of the large city of
Newark, New Jersey, was placed at our disposal, and we
show countless pieces of apparatus, engines, hook-and-
ladders, hose towers, hose carriages, etc., rushing down
a broad street at top speed, the horses straining every
nerve and evidently eager to make a record run. Great
clouds of smoke pour from the stacks of the engines, thus
giving an impression of genuineness to the entire series.

Dissolving again we show the seventh scene

Scene 7: Arrival at the Fire

In this wonderful scene we show the entire fire department
as described above, arriving at the scene of action. An
actual burning building is in the center foreground. On
the right background the fire department is seen coming
at great speed. Upon the arrival of the different apparatus, the engines are ordered to their places, hose
is quickly run out from the carriages, ladders are adjusted to the windows, and streams of water are poured
into the burning structure. At this crucial moment comes
the great climax of the series. We dissolve to the interior of the building and show a bed chamber with a
woman and child enveloped in flame and suffocating smoke.
The woman rushes back and forth in the room endeavoring
to escape, and in her desperation throws open the window
and appeals to the crowd below. She is finally overcome
by the smoke and falls upon the bed. At this moment the
door is smashed in by an ax in the hands of a powerful
fire hero. Rushing into the room, he tears the burning
draperies from the window and smashes out the entire
window frame, ordering his comrades to run up a ladder.
Immediately the ladder appears, he seizes the prostrate
form of the woman and throws it over his shoulders as if
it were an infant and quickly descends to the ground. We
now dissolve to the exterior of the burning building.
The frantic mother having returned to consciousness, and
clad only in her night clothes, is kneeling on the ground
imploring the fireman to return for her child. Volunteers
are called for and the same fireman who rescued the mother
quickly steps out and offers to return for the babe. He

is given permission to once more enter the doomed building
and without hesitation rushes up the ladder, enters the
window and after a breathless wait, in which it appears
he must have been overcome with smoke, he appears with
the child in his arms and returns safely to the ground.
The child, being released and upon seeing its mother,
rushes to her and is clasped in her arms, thus making a
most realistic and touching ending of the series. [1]

The scenes had two functions; to communicate the
action and, more important, to relate it to the next action
so that a meaning was given to the whole. The scene thus
became a unit dependent upon all the other units; to be
fully understandable, it was inseparable from them. This
process of cutting film, is now known as editing, and is
what makes a film expressive. [2]

According to Jacobs, scene seven, "Arrival at the Fire," is

significant because it is broken up into three shots: the

arrival of the fire engines; the plight of the mother and the

child; and the descent down the ladder. "This is one of the

earliest signs of a realization that a scene need not be taken

in one shot but can be built by a number of shots." [3]

But actually, scene three, "Sleeping Quarters," scene four,

"Interior of Engine House," and scene five, "Apparatus Leaving

Engine House," even though the editor of the Edison bulletin

fails to bracket the three shots together as one scene, seems

to be as much of a sequence - "a succession of shots forming,

in the complete film, a subordinate unit of conception and pur-

pose" [4] - as scene seven. The three shots, or scenes, mentioned

above might be properly identified as a sequence, "Answering the

Alarm."

1. Edison Catalogue of 1903 cited by Jacobs, pp. 38-41.
2. Jacobs, p. 38.
3. Jacobs, p. 41.
4. Spottiswoode, p. 50.

Dissolves were used between every shot in the film, making it difficult to understand why the last three shots were identified by the bulletin editor as a scene. If cuts had been employed between the shots of scene seven, the segregation would be understandable; however, maybe fast dissolves were employed in scene seven, which might very well have given the shots a unity of conception which was not created among scenes three, four, and five because of slower dissolves.

Porter apparently employed dissolves in order to tie his shots together. Dissolves, while destroying cutting-tone, [1] did make abrupt transitions, due to the scarcity of supplementary shots, less jarring.

Close-ups (see scene 2) had been used for five or six years previous to the one in "The Life of an American Fireman," but they merely created a shock of surprise rather than act as an important element in the advancement of the story. The use of the close-up in scene two, as an integral part of the film, anticipated by six years Griffith's establishment of the defice as part of standard film technique.

"The Life of an American Fireman" created quite a stir among

---

1. Spottiswoode, p. 53. Cutting-tone - "The affective tone which,...., is produced solely by rate of cutting, through the agency of rhythmical montage."

the public when it was released, and Porter, feeling that he had
a good thing, determined to experiment further with his editing
method. [1] He reasoned that if he could make an interesting
film from stock shots he could certainly do better work yet
with shots of his own making. It was now his aim to adapt his
editing method to include direct story construction. Appreciating the public's interest in train robberies he decided to
produce for the screen a film about a train robbery.

This film which he called "The Great Train Robbery," being
longer by two hundred and fifty feet than "The Life of an
American Fireman," had more room for supplementary shots, consequently the scenes are more closely related one to the other,
making for a smoother continuity.

Despite its limitations, "the whole feeling of the film is
definitely cinematic." [2] Most of the scenes are played in pro-
file, but there is no evidence of this theatrical convention
in the chase scene, or the battle scene between the bandits and
the posse. The station and dance hall scenes are played before

---

1. Before Porter was allowed to proceed with his project Edison
   assigned him several other productions. One of these, "Uncle
   Tom's Cabin," is noteworthy because it was the most costly
   and elaborate film produced in the United States up to that
   time. Aside from its magnitude, which should not be overlooked, the film was a mere reproduction of the stage play,
   produced according to the Melies formula, scene by scene, in
   logical order, as in a play.

2. Barry, Film Notes, Series I, Program 1.

painted drops, but a real train pulls up outside the window in
the station scene. Tension and excitement, for the most part,
are created by the movement of the actors within the scene
rather than by the editing, but a certain amount of cutting-tone
is created by the parallel actions in the five scenes of the
chase (nine to thirteen). The camera is never moved from eye
level, but it does unbend momentarily to follow the action in
a pan shot in scene twelve. The foreground and middle-ground
are ignored in favor of the background, but a close-up - even
though it is not an integral part of the film-- is introduced,
demonstrating its feasibility. The movement of the actors in
almost every scene is directed horizontally in front of the
camera, but in some scenes it is directed forward and backward
as well.

The scenario for "The Great Train Robbery" follows:

THE GREAT TRAIN ROBBERY

Scene 1: Interior of Railroad Telegraph Office. Two
masked robbers enter and compel the operator to get
the "signal block" to stop the approaching train, and
make him write a fictitious order to the engineer to
take water at this station, instead of "Red Lodge",
the regular watering stop. The train comes to a
standstill (seen through window of office); the conductor comes to the window, and the frightened
operator delivers the order while the bandits crouch
out of sight, at the same time keeping him covered
with their revolvers. As soon as the conductor leaves,
they fall upon the operator, blind and gag him, and
hastily depart to catch the moving train.

Scene 2: Railroad Water Tower. The bandits are hiding behind the tank as the train, under the false order,
stops to take water. Just before she pulls out they
stealthily board the train between the express car
and the tender.

Scene 3: Interior of the Express Car. Messenger is busily
engaged. An unusual sound alarms him. He goes to the
door, peeps through the keyhole and discovers two men
tying to break in. He starts back bewildered, but,
quickly recovering, he hastily locks the strong box
containing the valuables and throws the key through
the open side door. Drawing his revolver, he crouches
behind a desk. In the meantime the two robbers have
succeeded in breaking in the door and enter cautiously.
The messenger opens fire, and a desperate pistol duel
takes place in which the messenger is killed. One of
the robbers stands watch while the other tries to
open the treasure box. Finding it locked, he vainly
searches the messenger for the key, and blows the
safe open with dynamite. Securing the valuables and
mail bags they leave the car.

Scene 4: This Thrilling Scene Shows the Tender and Interior
of the Locomotive Cab, While the Train is Running Forty
Miles an Hour. While two of the bandits have been
robbing the mail car, two others climb over the tender.
One of them holds up the engineer while the other covers
the fireman, who seizes a coal shovel and climbs up on
the tender, where a desperate fight takes place. They
struggle fiercely all over the tank and narrowly escape
being hurled over the side of the tender. Finally they
fall, with the robber on top. He seizes a lump of coal,
and strikes the fireman on the head until he becomes
senseless. He then hurls the body from the swiftly
moving train. The bandits then compel the engineer to
bring the train to a stop.

Scene 5: Shows the Train Coming to a Stop. The engineer
leaves the locomotive, uncouples it from the train, and
pulls ahead about 100 feet while the robbers hold their
revolvers to his face.

Scene 6: Exterior Scene Showing Train. The bandits compel the passengers to leave the coaches, "hands up," and line up along the tracks. One of the robbers covers them with a revolver in each hand, while the others relieve the passengers of their valuables. A passenger attempts to escape and is instantly shot down. Securing everything of value, the band terrorize the passengers by firing their revolvers in the air, while they make their escape to the locomotive.

Scene 7: The desperados board the locomotive with this booty, compel the engineer to start, and disappear in the distance.

Scene 8: The robbers bring the engine to a stop several miles from the scene of the "hold up," and take to the mountains.

Scene 9: A Beautiful Scene in a Valley. The bandits come down the side of a hill, across a narrow stream, mounting their horses, and make for the wilderness.

Scene 10: Interior of Telegraph Office. The operator lies bound and gagged on the floor. After struggling to his feet, he leans on the table, and telegraphs for assistance by manipulating the key with his chin, and then faints from exhaustion. His little daughter enters with his dinner pail. She cuts the rope, throws a glass of water in his face and restores him to consciousness, and, recalling his thrilling experience, he rushes out to give the alarm.

Scene 11: Interior of a Typical Western Dance Hall. Shows a number of men and women in a lively quadrille. A "tenderfoot" is quickly spotted and pushed to the center of the hall, and compelled to do a jig, while bystanders amuse themselves by shooting dangerously close to his feet. Suddenly the door opens and the half-dead telegraph operator staggers in. The dance breaks up in confusion. The men secure their rifles and hastily leave the room.

Scene 12: Shows the Mounted Robbers Dashing Down a Rugged Hill at a terrific pace, followed closely by a large posse, both parties firing as they ride. One of the desperados is shot and plunges headlong from his horse. Staggering to his feet, he fires at the nearest pursuer, only to be shot dead a moment later.

Scene 13: The three remaining bandits, thinking they have
eluded the pursuers, have dismounted from their horses,
and after carefully surveying their surroundings, they
start to examine the contents of the mail pouches.
They are so grossly engaged in their work that they do
not realize the approaching danger until too late. The
pursuers, having left their horses, steal noiselessly
down upon them until they are completely surrounded.
A desperate battle then takes place, and after a brave
stand all the robbers and some of the posse bite the
dust.

Scene 14: A Life-Size Picture of Barnes, leader of the
outlaw band, taking aim and firing point-blank at
the audience. The resulting excitement is great.
This scene can be used to begin or end the picture. [1]

During the next two years, Porter added two corollaries
to his editing technique: contrast construction and parallel
construction. In "The Ex-Convict" he employed contrast editing
to point up the environmental inequalities between the ex-convict
and the rich man who refused to give the social outcast work.

Scenes of the poverty-stricken home of the ex-convict
were opposed to scenes of luxury in the manufacturer's
household, and thus by implications and inference the sym-
pathy of the audience was directed. This new application
of editing, not straightforward or direct but comparative,
pointed to future subtelty in film expression. Not until
years later, however, was contrast editing to be properly
valued and developed. [2]

In "The Kleptomaniac," Porter employed parallel editing to
draw attention to causes of the acts, and the fates of two women

1. Edison Catalogue of 1904 cited by Jacobs, pp. 43-46.

2. Jacobs, p. 47.

shoplifters: one, rich; the other, poor. In the first sequence the rich woman is caught stealing; in the second the poor woman. In the third sequence they are arraigned before the judge, who released the rich woman into the custody of her husband, and sends the poor woman, who has stolen a loaf of bread to keep from starving, to jail.

"The Dream of a Rarebit Fiend" (1906) demonstrates the superiority of Porter's mthod over Melies'. In this film the American employed all the trick camera devices introduced by the Frenchman: stop-motion, dissolves, masking, double exposure; but Porter's editing principle gave his film, which was no doubt suggested by Melies' films of magic, "a fluency and rhythm lacking in the latter's work." [1]

Porter's contribution to the motion picture was intermittent composition.

Porter's "The Great Train Robbery" (1903) is frequently designated the first story film, [2] and as a consequence it has been given a conspicuous position in the history of the motion picture. Furthermore, because of its appearance in series I, program 1, of the Museum of Modern Art Film Library's series of

---

1. Jacobs, p. 49.

2. Rotha, The Film Till Now, p. 24, and Seldes, An Hour With The Movies and The Talkies, p. 21.

historical motion pictures, which has been rather widely distributed among individuals who have more than a normal interest in the motion picture, the film has continued to receive considerable attention.

But historically speaking, Porter's "The Life of an American Fireman" (1902) seems to be the really significant production in the development of the story film. This motion picture appears to contain all of the necessary elements required of a story. Also the various shots in the film seem to have a greater degree of dependence upon one another than can be exampled by earlier efforts. And the film seems to contain the first-known example of parallel action in a motion picture.

Unfortunately, no print of "The Life of an American Fireman" seems to be available, and judgment concerning the film's significance must depend on the scenario published in the Edison bulletin, the still pictures appearing in Jacob's "The Rise of the American Films," [1] and the statements of later writers.

Actually, the still pictures seem to indicate that the parallel action in "The Life of an American Fireman" was developed to a greater degree than the bulletin indicates. As has been noted, scene seven, according to the bulletin (and according to Jacobs, p. 41),

----

1. Opposite p. 45.

appears to be broken into three shots: arrival of the fire
engines, the plight of the mother and the child, and the descent
down the ladder. However, the still pictures show the arrival
of the fire engines (exterior), the rescue of the mother (interior), the fireman's descent down the ladder with the mother
(exterior), the rescue of the child (interior), and the fireman's
descent down the ladder with the child (exterior). So, scene
seven appears to have been broken into five shots rather than
three. If this really was the case, it is conceivable that the
cutting-tone produced by the assembling of the shots in "The Life
of an American Fireman" may have been more pronounced than that
produced by the assembling of the shots in "The Great Train
Robbery."

"The Great Train Robbery," because of its greater length,
and because of the practice Porter had had in producing "The Life
of an American Fireman," appears to be a more mature film production
than the earlier production. And "The Great Train Robbery" also
appears to have made more of an impression on the public than
"The Life of an American Fireman." But from a historical pointof-view,
at least, the earlier film seems to deserve more attention than it
has hitherto received.

The years 1900 to 1903 constitute an important transitional period in the development of the motion picture.

During these years the producers, in an effort to revive interest in the motion picture, moved away from short films, fifty feet in length, and began producing long films, three hundred to a thousand feet in length. And the eventual achievement of story films with their inevitable complications and greater detailization of images, helped to bring into use parallel action which introduced the methods of intermittent composition.

These years also saw the development of an audience, and the establishment of the first houses which employed motion pictures as a principal attraction.

In a sense, this was a period of experimentation in which the producers, with a sharp eye on the box-office, attempted to find out what would please an audience. The boom business of 1905 to 1908 established the correctness of their findings.

CHAPTER X

ORGANIZATION OF THE EXCHANGES

Between 1900 and 1902, the development of the story film, and the development of an audience, set the stage for the expansion of the motion picture industry into a big business.

But the problem of distribution was the inhibiting factor in any outline which attempted to forecast the medium's greater possibilities as a business enterprise.

Up until 1902 and 1903, all motion picture prints were still sold outright at ten or twelve cents a foot, [1] which meant that exhibitors paid anywhere from $100.00 to $120.00 for one thousand feet of film, or fifteen minutes of projected motion pictures. Of course, the method of selling prints outright imposed a very high percentage of the production costs on the individual who purchased motion pictures; so some exhibitors, making the best of the situation, took to the road where they could show the same films to a different audience each night, while others established themselves in a populous area where they could plan on an extended run at the same stand. In such a manner, showmen managed, during the years 1896 to 1902, to find an audience large enough to pay the expenses re-

---

1. Ramsaye, p. 427, and Bardeche and Brasillach, p. 7.

quired of an exhibitor.

Clearly, this method of distributing films was not con-
ducive to an extensive use of motion pictures. Showmen on the
road, depending on the number of times they were booked to
exhibit a program in one location during the course of a season,
could provide themselves with a proper number of films, which
most certainly was limited, and be prepared for the entire
year. While showmen in the cities, counting on the large number of people who lived there to see their motion pictures,
showed the same films for as long a period as they could make
money on one particular program, even though the income at
the door had shrunk considerably by the time they withdrew the
program.

Finding it advantageous, and at the same time expensive to
introduce new subjects into their programs, the exhibitors re-
lieved the situation somewhat by exchanging films among themselves; but even though a good number of them probably appreciated the need for establishing exchanges where films could be
rented rather than bought, nobody seems to have had the courage
or the cash to organize such a project.

But in 1902-03, conditions in the motion picture industry
were brighter. Longer films were being produced. Arcade managers were taking the business of exhibiting motion pictures more
seriously. Films were gaining in popularity among the amusement

seekers. And exhibitors were probably wishing that they might change their programs more frequently at less cost.

As this wish became more expressive, and began to sound more like a demand, Harry J. Miles, and his brother, Herbert, of San Francisco, decided that the time was ripe for the establishment of an exchange. They apparently reached their decision to act, around Christmas, 1902. [1]

The Miles Brothers had observed the routine followed by two of their friends who purchased motion pictures for exhibition in the San Francisco area. These men, David Grauman of San Francisco, and Anthony Lubelski of Oakland each payed $100.00 a reel for motion pictures; but neither one of them got his money's worth out of the reel because "the film exhausted its entertainment value in any community long before it was worn out. [2] So Harry and Herbert Miles decided to oblige their friends. They would purchase films from the producers, and then rent them in turn to Grauman and Lubelski for fifty dollars apiece. Thereafter, whatever the brothers could earn from other exhibitors in the San Francisco area, unquestionably a good area

---

1. Ramsaye says that Harry Miles instructed his brother Herbert, who was in New York at the time, to send him films in the summer of 1902 so that he could start operating the business (p. 472.). Jacobs says that the Miles Brothers' Exchange was established early in 1903 (p. 52.).

2. Ramsaye, p. 427.

for such business, would be so much profit.

This arrangement pleased the exhibitors, who, now, because they had to pay much less for films, could change their programs more frequently and even consider seriously the possibility of establishing exhibition halls in communities which could only support limited runs; it pleased the producers because the rental system, which reduced the cost of film, stimulated a greater use of their products by the exhibitors; and it most certainly pleased the exchange men who could continue to rent out films long after they had been paid for.

In time the Miles Brothers' Exchange, which began to make purchases at regular intervals from the producers, rented films at one-fourth the purchase price to the exhibitors. [1]

The exchange was a great success, and other men quickly adopted the Miles' plan.

Though the producers had sometimes been slow to appreciate the motion picture's possibilities as an entertainment medium, they soon enough saw the exchange's money-making possibilities, and in short order they were organizing their own exchanges in order to compete for the business. Thus, by 1907, "there were over a hundred film exchanges in the thirty-five key cities

---

1. Jacobs, pp. 52-53.

throughout the United States." [1]

Europe soon fell in line with the new method of distributing films. In 1904, three of Melies' assistants, Michaux,
Astaix, and Lallement opened a film-renting agency in France. [2]
"This enterprise, after initial difficulties, was so successful
that in 1907 Pathe decided to abandon the sale of films and
to organize instead a chain of renting offices all over France." [3]

Melies, for some unaccountable reason, continued to sell
his films outright. His defiance of the new commercial order
was one of the factors that speeded his deposition as a leader
in the motion picture world.

Though exchanges were first organized in 1902-1903, their
real rise "had to wait for the emergence of the screen theatre
1905-1908 , a permanently located exhibition, with a demand
for a change of program." [4] So even in 1904, we find Lubin
still selling prints of his productions at eleven cents a foot. [5]

Ramsaye, in connection with the founding of the Miles
Brothers' Exchange, says:

---

1. Jacobs, p. 53.

2. Bardeche and Brasillach, p. 23.

3. Bardeche and Brasillach, p. 23.

4. Ramsaye, p. 252.

5. Lubin's Films, The Great Train Robbery, August, 1904. An
   Advertising Bulletin.

It seemed an interesting but unimportant venture
then. But it was the most important development in the
motion picture since the invention of the projection
machine. [1]

1. Ramsaye, p. 427.

CHAPTER XI

THE SCREEN THEATRE

With films available on a rental basis, the establishment
of theatres devoted primarily to the showing of motion pictures
became economically feasible.

Of course, long before the Miles Brothers had established
their exchange several enterprising showmen had managed to
operate, rather successfully, a number of motion picture theatres,
but the relatively high cost of subjects had made it a precarious,
and, at best, a transient business.

William T. Rock's three month's stand in New Orleans, the
"shop" theatres in England, Bill Steiner's theatre in Chicago,
Alexander F. Victor's theatre in Newark, and Thomas L. Tally's
"Electric Theatre" in Los Angeles represent the best that could
be achieved by way of establishing permanent quarters for the
motion picture prior to 1903.

Even Tally's theatre, which was opened on April 16, 1902, [1]
and which seems to have been the first theatre devoted exclusively
to the showing of motion pictures, closed its doors eventually
because Tally felt that he could make more money touring the one

---

1. Jacobs, p. 7.

picture, "The Great Train Robbery".

But after 1903 attempts to establish permanent quarters for the motion picture were realized. Robert Grau declares that T. J. West carried on "extensive operations" in store theatres in England as early as 1904; [1] while Archie L. Shepard and William J. Gane, who were financed by Felix Isman, operated similar theatres in New York City, at the same time, or shortly thereafter. [2]

But, generally, Harry Davis and John P. Harris of Pittsburgh are credited with having instigated the screen theatre movement. Davis and Harris, who had a vacant storeroom on their hands, decided to make the best of their predicament by experimenting with motion pictures. So in November, 1905, they became exhibitors. Unlike the operators of earlier store theatres, they extended themselves to the point of refurbishing their establishment with discarded furnishings of the Grand Opera House. And probably best of all, they gave it the interesting name of "Nickelodeon".

Their enterprise was a tremendous success. And the fancy house furnishings contributed in no small part to the popularity

---

1. Grau, The Theatre of Science, p. 16.
2. Grau.

of their theatre.

The financial success of the Harris and Davis motion
picture theatre created a tremendous impression on showmen
throughout the country. Though the admission was only five
cents, and though the theatre only had two hundred seats, the
once vacant storeroom was yielding almost a thousand-dollars-
a-week profit, just two weeks after its conversion into a
motion picture theatre. [1]

It was now clearer than ever that anyone who could rent
a vacant storeroom, but a projector, and rent a few chairs,
was in a position to prosper. Showmen rushed to take advantage
of this great new opportunity to make money, and within a year
a thousand or more nickelodeons had been established throughout
the country. [2]

These thousand odd motion picture theatres were centered,
it seems, primarily in big industrial cities with large foreign
populations of poorly paid laborers. That such communities
would first foster the nickelodeons is reasonable enough. The
motion pictures were cheap, and they offered no language barrier
to the large polyglot populations beginning to crowd the industrial
cities of the United States at the turn of the century.

------

1. Ramsaye, p. 430.
2. Hampton, p. 46.

Pittsburg, which, because of its coal and steel industries, was attracting a high percentage of the emigrants, supported a hundred nickelodeons after the first year.

In his discussion of William F. Fox and his relationship to the phenomenal nickelodeon development, Upton Sinclair remarks:

> Not since the days of the forty-niners had there been such a way for the little fellow to get rich as in this new business. Everything depended upon a location where the crowds were passing. W. F. found that in order to get the right location, it would often pay him to lease the whole building - even though the fire laws required that the upstairs tenants be turned out before moving pictures were shown in the building.[1]

The small amount of capital needed to finance a nickelodeon is indicated by F. H. Richardson in his "Motion Picture Handbook" for managers and operators. Though the book was published in 1910, it does not seem unreasonable to assume that the financial responsibilities of an exhibitor varied little between 1905 and 1910.

> In figuring the matter of expense for a small town theatre the items may be estimated as follows: Operator, $15.00 per week; ticket seller and ticket taker, $5.00 to $6.00 each; piano-player - singer, $15.00; service, with express charges, $30.00 to $40.00; light, $6.00; rent, $10.00; or a total of about $100.00 per week.[2]

But this was for a "creditable" show. Richardson says that he knows that there are many small town theatres operating for

-----

1. Upton Sinclair, William Fox, p. 37.

2. F. H. Richardson, Motion Picture Handbook, p. 162.

much less. Some pay as little as $15.00 a week for film rentals.
But he declares that such theatres "don't and can't put on a
show worth seeing."

As a further spur to the nickelodeon movement the New York
Board of Aldermen passed a special ordinance categorizing the
exhibitions given in the five-cent theatres as "common shows."
Thus motion picture exhibitors were taxed only $25.00 for a
license contrasted to the five hundred dollars demanded of the
manager of a vaudeville or legitimate theatre. The determination
of a "common show" depended upon the seating capacity of the
theatre. If the total number of seats did not exceed 299 it was
designated a "common show"; if the number exceeded 299 it was
designated a "theatre". [1]

The establishment of a thousand nickelodeons in the larger
cities during the year following Davis and Harris' experiment
was indeed startling. But the expansion which took place during
1907 and 1908, when the motion picture moved out into the country,
was even more remarkable. By 1908 there were between eight and
ten thousand nickelodeons operating throughout the country. [2]

_____

1. Sinclair, p. 35.
2. Hampton, p. 46.

The expansion was so rapid that by 1910, Richardson was
compelled to tell prospective exhibitors that the saturation
point had just about been reached.

> The moving picture field has been so well covered
> that it is now well-nigh impossible to find a desirable
> location where there is no immediate competition. So
> true is this that the prospective owner may make up his
> mind at the outset that it is necessary to 'butt into'
> a field already more or less covered, unless he buys out
> some established house, and even there he cannot be assured
> of no competition, since another house may be put in at
> any time.[1]

The success of the nickelodeons was so great that the
vaudeville managers of the country felt compelled to enter the
field in order to forestall competition. [2] Of course vaudeville managers from the very beginning had found a place for
the motion picture in their programs, but this place had always
been a minor one, except during the initial period of excitement,
and during the strike of the White Rats. Now, however, it was
a different story, and they rushed to participate in the tremendous expansion of the motion picture.

Among the vaudeville managers who was first to appreciate
the nickelodeon's possibilities was J. Austin Fynes, who had introduced the Lumiere cinematograph to American audiences at Keith's

----

1. Richardson, p. 159.

2. Grau, The Theatre of Science, pp. 17-18.

Union Square Theatre in 1896. Fynes, seconded by B. F. Keith, was so impressed with the results that Davis and Harris had achieved with their nickelodeon that he personally visited Pittsburgh in order to see their theatre. And when he returned to New York he endorsed their idea by establishing in association with Charles S. Kline, nickelodeons in New York, New Haven, and Jersey City. [1]

F. F. Proctor, while continuing with B. F. Keith to conduct straight vaudeville theatres in the large cities, established combination vaudeville and motion picture theatres in the smaller cities with exceptionally good results. As an example of the success of the new policy, Grau cites Proctor's success with a combination vaudeville-motion picture theatre in Mount Vernon, New York, "a little town" where it had hitherto been impossible to maintain a theatre upon any basis whatsoever.

> It is no exaggeration to state that at least fifty per cent of the population of Mount Vernon enters this establishment at least once a week; an empty seat is unknown, while it is by no means uncommon, on ordinary days, to see a thousand persons, waiting in the lobbies and on the sidewalk for an opportunity to enter. [2]

But the energy of the vaudeville managers was as nothing

---

1. Grau, The Theatre of Science, p. 18.

2. Robert Grau, The Business Man in the Amusement World, p. 116.

compared to the energy of William Fox and Marcus Loew when they
decided to enter the motion picture business.

Fox is credited with having opened the first store theatre
in Brooklyn, July 12, 1906; and is "believed to have been the
first to combine moving pictures and vaudeville in the manner
that became the foundation for the prosperous chains of theatres
all over the country with a similar policy." [1]

His successful management of the Dewey Theatre in New York
City , where he presented motion pictures and vaudeville on the
same program, is illustrative, as Grau points out, of the up-
heaval caused by the new form of entertainment. Securing the
Dewey in July, 1908, Fox managed the theatre so expertly that
a daily attendance of seven or eight thousand was "so common as
to excite no comment." And on February 12, 1910, 16,080 persons
paid for admissions between the hours of 10 a.m. and 11 p.m. [2]

But Marcus Loew was the most conspicuously successful figure
that emerged during the rise of the screen theatre. In 1905-06
Loew operated penny arcades in New York City, one of which was
across the street from one of the newly established nickel theatres
owned by Fynes. The new nickelodeon played havoc with the arcade's
business. But to good purpose, for within a month after observing

---

1. Grau, The Theatre of Science, p. 20.

2. Grau, The Business Man in the Amusement World, pp. 131-132.

Fyne's success, Loew transformed all of his arcades into motion picture theatres. Having become acutely aware of the theatre's importance in the development of the motion picture, Loew proceeded to acquire during the next ten years, the control of "the largest number of theatres, most of which he owns outright, that were ever under one management." [1]

At first, it had satisfied Loew to manage nickelodeons, but with the organization of his "People's Amusement Company" he began acquiring and transforming legitimate theatres into "Pop" vaudeville and motion picture establishments. The capacity of these houses permitted him, without unduly raising his admission prices - in 1912 in a Loew Theatre the top admission price was twenty-five cents -, to more than absorb the increased overhead, and the increased cost of booking both better films and better vaudeville entertainers. This policy which had its beginning during the period, 1905 to 1908, eventually led to the undermining of the legitimate and straight vaudeville theatres, for in addition to carrying along with them the new audiences created by the motion picture, the managers of the combination film and vaudeville theatres, by presenting better programs at lower prices, actually weaned away from the legitimate theatre many patrons of the stage.

―――――――

1. Grau, The Theatre of Science, p. 19.

There was nothing extraordinary in this turn of events for
as Grau predicted in 1912,

> The head of a family will look into the matter of
> theatre-going with the same discernment that he practices
> in the purchase of other necessities, and he will discover
> that he can take a family of six to one of Mr. Loew's
> theatres and occupy the very best seats for a total outlay
> of $1.50. These theatres are quite as inviting as any
> in the city, and the audiences are gradually improving
> in quality, so that if Mr. Loew continues to improve the
> quality of his offerings on the stage, theatre-goers will
> refuse to pay nine dollars for six seats in the high-
> priced houses, when they can get quite as good entertain-
> ment for one-sixth of the outlay. [1]

The Loew and Fox policy of presenting motion pictures and
a number of vaudeville acts at low admission prices became so
popular that by 1910 the number of theatres in New York committed
to the same policy were in excess of those theatres committed
to straight vaudeville. [2]

But New York was no exception. In Philadelphia, at the same
time, there were twenty-five theatres with seating capacities
in excess of one thousand which were devoted to a combination
presentation. [3] And Grau adds what may be said of Philadelphia
may be said of every large city in the United States.

---

1. Grau, The Stage in the Twentieth Century, p. 47.

2. Grau, The Business Man in the Amusement World, p. 115.

3. Grau, The Business Man in the Amusement World, pp. 118-119.

Nickelodeon programs, according to Jacobs, lasted "from twenty minutes to a full hour, and often included a single reel melodrama, a comedy, and a novelty." [1] The accuracy of this statement is confirmed by Hampton's observation that one-reel story films became popular between 1906 and 1908, and that split-reels (300 to 600 feet) were common between 1903 and 1910. The comedy included in Jacob's typical nickelodeon program was probably a split-reel.

In the nickelodeons motion pictures were the feature attraction, but because the one-reel and split-reel subjects were apparently not strong enough to carry off the honors un-assisted, exhibitors seem to have depended on added attractions, or features, to help sustain the program.

Ballad singers, and song slides were regular features of the nickelodeon programs. The singer, accompanied by a pianist, and by illustrated, hand-colored slides projected on the screen, probably made a practice of singing through, alone, a verse and the chorus of a popular song, and then if current practices are indicative, he encouraged the audience to join him in repeating the song. This feature seems to have provoked enough interest among the patrons of the nickelodeons to encourage many of the

---

1. Jacobs, p. 56.

exhibitors to demand a daily change of song slides. [1]

As another "wrinkle" to bolster the program, C. Francis Jenkins and Oscar B. Depue suggested that exhibitors project on their screens announcements of war events, elections, et cetera. [2] And in order to produce the slides as rapidly as possible, they suggested that the announcements be typed on film, "and while the ink is still moist to dust it over with a tuft of cotton dipped in finely-divided lamp-black. The letters will appear in black against a white canvas." [3] The Trans-Lux theatres in New York with Associated Press wires installed in their lobbies, and their speedy news-reel coverage, are hardly more efficient.

Stereoscopic pictures were another novelty suggested by Jenkins and Depue.

> It is possible by means of a double lantern, a right and left stereoscopic picture superimposed on the same canvas, coloring them respectively, red and green with tinters. The resultant picture is a blurry smudge on the canvas but instantly springs into a monocrome (black and white) stereoscopic picture when viewed through red and green tinters held before the eyes. The tinters may be mounted in any suitable form, one of which is a paper fan. [4]

And strange as it may seem, Richardson recommended magic lantern lectures as a possible number for the nickelodeon program.

---

1. Richardson, p. 166.

2. C. Francis Jenkins, and Oscar B. Depue, Handbook for Motion Picture and Stereopticon Operators, p. 96.

3. Jenkins and Depue, p. 96.

4. Jenkins and Depue, p. 95.

But he cautioned that these must be properly managed.

> The lecturer <u>absolutely must speak slowly and dis-</u>
> <u>tinctly.</u> Reading the lecture impairs the effect very much.
> Naturally four-fifths of the effect as a whole depends
> on the lecturer himself, or herself. The sing-song
> talker, or the talker who speaks so fast or so slow that
> the words cannot be followed except by an effort, spoils
> it all. Properly done, the illustrated lecture is
> excellent. Wrongly done, it is worse than nothing at all. [1]

In the more prosperous nickelodeons vaudeville acts were introduced as a novelty. [2] But vaudeville never seems to have played more than a minor role in the nickelodeon program. Inferior stages, and the prohibitive cost of performers probably limited bookings to an occasional twenty-five dollar a week "single", or an even rarer fifty-dollar a week "double". Minimum requirements for the presentation of vaudeville in the nickelodeons included "a piano player who can read at sight, not only printed music but hand-written stuff as well," and a spotlight with color effects. [3]

It was not until the motion picture theatre moved from the nickelodeon stage to the combined motion picture-vaudeville stage that vaudeville became an important factor in the motion picture theatre.

"Amateur night" was another added attraction in the nickelodeon theatres. This feature, which was inexpensive, amusing,

---

1. Richardson, pp. 168-169.
2. Richardson, p. 168.
3. Richardson, p. 168.

and easy to stage, had been a regular and popular attraction in
the variety theatres, [1] so it was not particularly surprising
that the nickelodeon managers laid hold of this novelty to
strengthen their programs. [2]

And as a good will measure the exhibitors sometimes showed
a patriotic films, and a "strictly clean" comedy on Saturday
afternoon for the children. [3] In such cases the children were
admitted to the theatre for two or three cents; and the school
principal, if he were available, would be secured to deliver a
lecture supplementing the film subject. Richardson advises:
"The children will tell their parents all about it and the talk
will advertise your house, of course." [4]

Competition among the nickelodeon theatres, as has already
been pointed out, was intense, and the novelties and added attractions, besides strengthening frequently weak motion picture
programs, had the added virtue of making the patrons think they
were getting their money's worth.

During the nickelodeon days, as a part of the scheme to make

---

1. Grau, The Business Man in the Amusement World, pp. 242-243.

2. David S. Hulfish, Cyclopedia of Motion Picture Work, Vol. II, p. 201.

3. Richardson, p. 164.

4. Richardson, pp. 164-165.

"going to the movies" more attractive, there seems to have developed an awareness that the appearance and comfortableness of
a house had a bearing on a motion picture theatre's receipts.
And in the recommendations offered by Richardson to the exhibitors
in 1910 we can see the beginning of a sensitivity to surroundings
which, beginning about 1915, led to the construction of many
elaborate picture theatres.

Richardson, after advising exhibitors that the day of "the
flat floor" in a motion picture house is past, [1] and that it does
not pay to buy cheap fans because they are a source of noise,
continual trouble, and expense, goes on to suggest refinements
such as wire hat racks under each seat, and a ring or staple on
the back of each seat "through which the ladies may thrust a hat-
pin to hold their headgear instead of being obliged to hold them
in their laps." [2] These embellishments, he declared, would win
the audience's good will, and increase the number of dimes which
passed through the box-office window.

On other points of house management Richardson speaks with
heat. After declaring that the ticket taker should be neatly
dressed, in a uniform if possible, he remarks with contempt:

---

1. Richardson, p. 152.

2. Richardson, p. 151.

The writer has in hundreds of instances seen a ticket
taker in his shirt sleeves,unkempt, and even with a cigar
or cigarette in his mouth. Such a spectacle would convey
the impression to my mind that the show was likely to be
as slouchy as the man in the door. [1]

But contempt turns to anger when he comments on dusty seats
in a motion picture theatre.

There is nothing more annoying to a lady in a light-
colored dress than to find her costume soiled by a dusty
theatre seat. It amounts to an outrage. [2]

Unquestionably, clean, well-managed houses, in many instances,
served as well as the novelties and added attractions to draw many
customers into the nickelodeon theatre. After all, it was the
discarded grand-opera accessories, with which Harris and Davis
furnished the original Nickelodeon, "which distinguished it from
other store theatres and arcades and impressed the spectators." [3]

As an additional measure to set their five-cent theatres
apart from other nickelodeons, enterprising exhibitors did their
utmost to secure films at the earliest possible date following
release by the exchanges.

The speed with which an exhibitor received a print following
its release determined the rental price he paid for the film.

---

1. Richardson, pp. 163-164.

2. Richardson, p. 154.

3. Jacobs, p. 55.

Thus, a motion picture one day old cost more than one ten days old, and one ten days old cost more than one thirty days old.

Circumstances determined the kind of service exhibitors asked of the distributors. In the cities, for example, where the competition was apt to be intense, and the number of potential customers large, the exhibitor probably did his utmost to secure films no older than two or three days. And in the country where audiences were likely to be limited, and competition not quite so intense, the exhibitor probably contented himself with, say, one film no older than fifteen days, and a second film no older than sixty days. [1]

"Being first" was most always the guiding principle. And, furthermore, the sooner an exhibitor received a print from the exchange the better condition it was likely to be in. Prints, sixty days old, were sometimes badly scratched, and full of breaks.

It was common for the nickelodeons to change their programs every day; and it was not uncommon for them to change their programs twice in a day. [2] Jacobs explains:

> Profits from nickelodeons were quick and large but depended upon a constant turnover of customers. Since nickelodeons could only accommodate one to two hundred

---

1. Richardson, pp. 165-166

2. Jacobs, p. 57.

people at a time, programs had to be short and were run
continuously from morning to midnight. Changes of pictures
had to be made as often as possible so that people would
come again. [1]

That people would attend motion picture theatres with such

frequency, that an exhibitor could justify a change of program

once or twice a day, is really remarkable. But it seems to have

actually been the case, and it seems to demonstrate that the

American people - a considerable segment at any rate - had taken

the motion picture to its heart, even at this early date.

As further evidence that a large body of devotees was being

nurtured during the nickelodeon days, Richardson relates that in

one place on North Clark Street, in Chicago, where six motion

picture theatres are located within three blocks of one another,

"people often start in at one end and go to all of them." [2]

Towards the very end of the decade some of the exhibitors

began to question the advisability of booking a new program each

day. They apparently began to feel that "good" motion pictures

might profitably be held over for a second- or third-day's showing.

The views of these more "advanced" showmen were held in con-

tempt by the die-hard exhibitors, who, not sensitive to the

----

1. Jacobs, p. 57.

2. Richardson, p. 166.

improvements being made in motion picture production around 1908, hated to take a chance with a new idea. They declared that they had steady patrons who came to their theatres daily, and that they must have a new program for them every day or lose them. Richardson reasoned with the conservatives:

> But have you enough of them to make up for the added cost of such service? I very much doubt it. I am fairly convinced that the managers who give three changes a week will have more clear profit on the week's business than the ones who pay for daily changes. 1

And, probably drawing on personal experience, he continued his argument:

> As a rule,...., taking cost into consideration, I do not believe it pays, especially if film must be shipped a considerable distance. It is seldom that any considerable portion of the community will see the picture in one day. If it be a good picture and it is retained two or three days it will advertise itself and then bring added patronage. 2

Some managers, of course, continued to make daily changes.

The nickelodeon period was a period of apprenticeship for the motion picture exhibitors. During the years they operated these small theatres, they learned the showman's tricks, and prepared themselves for the day when they were to move into more pretentious quarters.

---

1. Richardson, p. 166.

2. Richardson, p. 166.

CHAPTER XII

THE PRODUCERS PREPARE FOR MASS PRODUCTION

"The Great Train Robbery" (1903), which was almost one-reel
long, was the first story film produced in America. But it was not
until about three years later, 1906, that the production of story
films of similar length became general.

The mass production of the one-reel films had to wait upon
the establishment of the nickelodeons, which would assure the
longer films of an outlet to the public; the development of the
exchanges, which would assure the films of an expeditious distribution; the adjustment of production methods which would permit an
economical and regular production of such films; and the development of the public's tastes, which would assure the film's favorable
reception.

During the years 1900 to 1903, when the transition from the
short subjects of fifty feet, to subjects of between three hundred
and six hundred feet was accomplished, many producers had the opportunity to experiment with simple stories, chases, and "mysterious"
films, all of which involved staging, acting, simple plot construction,
and a variety of other problems beyond those faced by the newsreel
cameraman; thus they were not totally unready to follow Porter's
lead when he finally produced "The Great Train Robbery" in 1903.

Appreciating Porter's success, producers adopted his film as their Bible, [1] and assiduously imitated his technique. And some, like Lubin, even went so far as to undertake exact copies of the first story motion picture. Lubin's "The Great Train Robbery", produced in 1904, except for one or two trifling changes, is exactly the same as Porter's film. The synopsis of scenes in the Lubin bulletin reveals the similarity:

Scene I. The Chief and His Band.

    The first scene shows the chief as he explains to his followers the plan of the Great Train Robbery.

Scene II. The Interior of a Railroad Telegraph Office.

    Two masked robbers enter and compel the operator to stop the approaching train. They make him write an order to the engineer to take water at this station instead at the regular watering stop.
    The train stops, the conductor comes to the office window, where the operator delivers the order while the bandits keep their revolvers trained on him. No sooner has the condutcor left, when they bind and gag the operator and hastily depart to catch the moving train.

Scene III. At the Watering Stop.

    This scene shows the train at the water tank. The bandits are hiding behind the tank and just before the train pulls out they quickly board the express car wherein the messenger is busily engaged with his duties.

---

1. Jacobs, pp. 41-43.

Scene IV. The Interior of the Express Car.

Alarmed by the unusual sound, the messenger locks the
door, peeps through the key-hole, discovers the bandits and
quickly looks the iron boxes which contain the valuables. He
then throws the key through the small window and pulls out
his revolver to defend the valuables entrusted to him. Two
robbers succeed in entering the car. The messenger bravely
attacks them and discharges his revolver, but he is quickly
laid low by a bullet. The bandits bind and gag him and
then try to open the treasure box. When they find it locked
they search the messenger for the key, and as they do not find
it, they blow up the strong box with dynamite. They take the
valuables and the mail bags and quickly leave the car. During
all this time, the train is seen flying past beautiful scenery.

Scene V. Fight on the Tender.

While two of the robbers blow up the strong box in the
express car, two other ones hold the engineer and the fireman
at pistols' point. The fireman takes a coal shovel and climbs
up on the tender to defend himself and his position, but he
soon finds himself overpowered and is thrown from the swiftly
moving train. The two bandits then compel the engineer to
stop the train.

Scene VI. The Engine Ahead.

Forced by the robbers, the engineer brings the train
to a stop, uncouples the engine and pulls ahead about two
hundred feet, always covered by the bandits' pistols.

Scene VII. Looting the Passengers.

In the meantime, two of the bandits compel the passengers
to leave the coaches with hands up. They line them up along
the tracks, go through their pockets and relieve them of all
their valuables. One passenger makes an attempt to escape,
but is instantly shot down by one of the bandits. As soon
as they have all the booty the bandits mount the engine and
make good their escape, while the passengers lend their helping
hand to their unfortunate friend who was badly wounded by
one of the bandits.

Scene VIII. The Flight on the Locomotive.

The bandits bring all their booty on the locomotive and command the engineer to pull the lever, and pretty soon we see them disappear in the distance.

Scene IX. The Escape.

Far out in the rough countries the bandits command the engineer to stop, descend from the engine and escape to the mountains with the stolen goods

Scene X. Crossing the River.

This scene shows the bandits coming down from the mountains into the valley, where they cross a stream to get to a place of safety. The scenery is truly beautiful. One of the robbers, in his hurry, slips and falls into the water, but he quickly arises and makes good his escape.

Scene XI. The Signal for Help.

This scene brings us back to the interior of the telegraph office, where the operator lies bound and gagged on the floor. After a desperate struggle he succeeds in reaching the table where his instruments stand. He telegraphs for help and manipulates the key with his mouth, and then falls to the floor, fainting from exhaustion.

Scene XII. The Operator's Daughter.

The operator's little daughter enters to bring him his daily dinner. She finds her father bound, kneels down, praying to the Lord to give her strength to help her poor father, throws quickly a glass of water in his face, restoring him to consciousness, takes a knife and cuts the ropes and removes the gag from his mouth.

Scene XIII. In a Western Dance Hall.

This typical Western dance hall shows some men in company with women. A tenderfoot appears upon the scene and is made to dance in the regular Western style. Suddenly the door opens, the operator's little daughter enters and relates what has happened. The men quickly stop their merriment, take their guns and leave in pursuit of the outlaws.

Scene XIV. After the Bandits.

The bandits are seen dashing through the woods on spirited horses, followed closely by the Sheriff and a large posse. There is much firing from both parties. One of the bandits is shot and falls from his horse, but he staggers to his feet again and kills one of the Deputy Sheriffs before he expires.

Scene XV. The Law is Avenged.

This scene shows the bandits in a fierce fight with the Sheriff's posse. The bandits dismount their horses, and, not thinking that the Sheriff and his Deputy were so near, are just beginning to look over their booty when suddenly the Sheriff and his Deputy appear on the scene. A desperate battle takes place, and after a brave stand the bandits and several of the pursuers breathe their last.

Scene XVI. The Bandits' Chief.

This scene shows a life-size picture of Daniels, the chief of the bandits, as he takes aim and fires into the audience. The picture is so realistic that women scream, and even though no sound is heard, they put their fingers in their ears to shut out the noise of the firing.

THE END [1]

"The Chief and His Band," Scene I in the Lubin film, does not

---

1. Lubin's films, THE GREAT TRAIN ROBBERY, August, 1904. An advertising bulletin. (A copy, in possession of Professor Walter H. Stainton, Cornell University, Ithaca, N.Y.)

appear in the Porter production. This seems to be Lubin's one touch of originality. Elsewhere he copies Porter's film so meticulously that in Scene X, "Crossing the River," he even goes so far as to have a robber slip and fall in the stream, the exact piece of business which probably occurred in Porter's film by accident. It almost seems that Lubin was making sure that his film would be mistaken for Porter's. Apparently he wished to capitalize to the fullest possible extent on the publicity received by the earlier film.

Porter followed his initial success with "The Great Bank Robbery". And as can be guessed from the title, it was very similar to his first film. Lubin, of course, produced the "Bold Bank Robbery".

Other companies followed the Porter and Edison lead by turning out story films. Selig in Chicago produced "Trapped by Blood -hounds; or, A lynching in Cripple Creek"; Biograph produced "Personal" and "The Moonshiners"; and Vitagraph, "Raffles the Amateur Cracksman." All of these motion pictures, produced during 1904 and 1905, were approximately a thousand feet long. They were not, however, typical films of the period. Shorter films continued to dominate the market.

Even though the story film idea had been born, the motion picture progressed "none too rapidly" during 1904 and 1905. [1]

---

1. Ramsaye, p. 423

Progress had to await the arrival of the nickelodeon. Then the sudden demand for story films, created by the rise of the motion picture theatre revolutionised the industry.

With the rise of the nickelodeon, the producer who could merely crank a camera and develop film was no longer adequate. The new motion picture audiences were no longer satisfied with episodic comedy and newsreel films alone; they also wanted long comedy and drama subjedts, [1] and in quanity. Now the medium had to reach out for actors, stories, directors.' And a creative technique had to be established.

The industry began to accommodate itself to mass production. And as a first step in this direction, the older and more prosperous companies, as a matter of necessity and convenience, expanded their studio facilities. Many of the new story films required interiors, and the staging and shooting of such productions could be accomplished more readily in a studio; and now that there was a steady demand for films, a production schedule could be maintained with more certainty under a roof out of the weather.

In the studios, with their glass roofs, the producers still largely depended on daylight, even though the mercure-vapor lamp, introduced in 1906, made the photographing of scenes under artificial light a possibility. [2] Apparently it took the engineers

---

1. Hulfish, Vol II, P. 75

2. Ramsaye, p. 532

several years to bring the lamp to a point of efficiency which
satisfied the motion picture producers.

Lesser companies, unable to afford artificial lighting
facilities, and the large upkeep of a studio, continued to shoot
all of their films on location: in the city streets and parks,
and on the countryside. 1

Previous to 1905 production had been pretty well centered
in New York, Chicago, and Philadelphia. And with the advent of
the nickelodeon, work in these centers was accelerated. But as
competition among the producers became more intense, and as the
public's desire for novelty began to express itself, some producers,
in an effort to excite new interest in their motion pictures,
chose interesting new locales outside the cities as backgrounds
for their films.

For example, Sidney Olcott, a director at Kalem, made the
first western pictures among "the picturesque badlands of the
Palisades of New Jersey." 2

But westerns with a Jersey background were abandoned when
G. M. ("Broncho Billy") Anderson discovered the real west. In
the spring of 1908, Anderson, who was an actor, author, and producer,
left Chicago for Golden, Colorado, where he produced the first of

----

1. Jacobs, p.58

2. Ramsaye, p. 460

the "Broncho Billy" western adventure films which were released
every single week thereafter for the next three hundred and
seventy-six weeks. [1] Subsequently, he and his company moved to
Niles, California; but his weekly release was not interrupted.

But the exodus from the cities had another motive beyond the
desire for new locales. Sunshine, which was frequently at a
premium in the eastern cities during the winter months, was
another factor which impelled the producers to explore Cuba,
Florida, and California, soon after the birth of the motion picture
theatre created a demand for motion pictures. And as early as
the latter part of 1907 a Selig unit moved to Los Angles to complete
the shooting of a one-reel film, "The Count of Monte Cristo." The
interiors for this film had been shot in Chicago, and now with an
entirely new cast the exteriors were shot in California. The Selig
expedition was among the first to visit the west coast. The mass
migration however was still a few years off.

While the innumerable problems related to production were
being worked out, the matter of story material for the films
began to press the producers. Though Melies had established the
precedent of going to literature for his film subjects, the majority
of producers ignored his practice. Having little knowledge of

----

1. Ramsaye, p. 444

literature, [1] they chose instead to concoct simple stories out of their own minds.

But as soon as the demand for story films increased, the producers changed their entire routine. They hired special writers to create original scripts, and adapt short stories for the screen.

H. N. Marvin of Biograph was one of the first producers to recognize that better films could be made, and more efficient methods introduced, if the method of extemporization were dropped. And he hired Stanner E. V. Taylor, a free lance newspaper man, to turn out motion picture ideas. Taylor, who was paid fifteen dollars for each "idea" was so impressed with the pay - he had been receiving about eight dollars a column as a newspaper man - that he decided right then and there to devote all of his time to the motion picture business. Other newspaper men who heard of his good fortune immediately accepted the tip and became scenario writers.

When the scenario writers first began adapting stories for the screen they did not bother to acquire the motion picture rights from the author or the publisher. Such a thing as motion picture rights were unknown. And, as Ramsaye remarks,

> It was not at all certain that there was any such thing. And in all instances of the kind the motion picture industry always

---

1. Homer Croy, How Motion Pictures are Made, p. 104

generously gave itself the benefit of the doubt. [1]

But the parties possessing the rights to the literary works "borrowed" by the motion picture could hardly be expected to continue viewing with equanimity the "pilfering" of their property, so in January, 1908, the inevitable happened, and Kalem which had just produced and released a one-reel film version of "Ben Hur" found itself hailed into court by Harper and Brothers, publishers of the novel, Klaw and Erlanger, producers of the drama version of the novel, and Henry Wallace, administrator of the estate of Susan E. Wallace, deceased, heir of Lew Wallace, author of the novel.

Kalem certainly could not have been too surprised by the action, for in 1896, Lew Wallace, author of the novel, Walter C. Clark, the owner of the dramatic rights, and Harper Brothers had sued Messrs Riley Brothers of New York,

> 'optical lantern and slide makers, from issuing or causing to be issued, their set of 72 lantern slides illustrating the story; and from issuing or causing to be issued any opitomised reading of the same. [2]

But, even so, Kalem was probably willing to risk a court action because the complainants had not been altogether successful in 1896. They had merely succeeded in restraining the Rileys from distributing the epitomised readings of "Ben Hur." Their

---

1. Ramsaye, p. 462

2. Citation from an unknown source, Quoted by The Optical Magic Lantern Journal and Photographic Enlarger, vii (October, 1896). 166-167.

effort to restrain the Rileys from publishing and selling the slides
had been denied. So Kalem probably considered that it had a fair
case.

In the 1896 case the judge in denying the complainants' con-
tention that the presentation of the seventy-two slides constituted
a "dramatic representation", remarked:

> 'in the first place he could not be sure the life models
> or drawings had been originally prepared specially for the purpose
> of illustrating "Ben Hur," but that even taking it for granted
> that they were so prepared, it would hardly be contended that no
> one, except with permission of complainants, might produce and sell
> copies of drawings, the motif of which was suggested in the book.' [1]

But in 1908 the judge rationalized differently, and Kalem
realizing this, settled the matter out of court for $25,000.

This was the first suit covering motion picture rights, and
as Ramsaye remarks: "It was the precedent making action that was
to establish the legal character of the motion picture as a medium
of dramatic and literary expression." [2]

As the story films became more complex, demands on the people
playing roles in the motion pictures became greater. A studio
mechanic, or a relative of the producer, no longer sufficed as an
actor. [3]

---

1. Citation from an unknown source, quoted by The Optical Magic
   Lantern Journal and Photographic Enlarger, vii (October, 1896) 166-167.

2. Ramsaye, P. 463.

3. Bardeche and Brasillach, pp. 13-14.

Professionals who could sustain a scene, and who were practiced in pantomime were in demand.

Because the motion picture had little to offer by way of salary and even less by way of prestige, securing professional actors to play roles in the films was frequently a problem. But the failure to secure a part in a play, and the enticement of five-dollars-a-day pay, did finally compel some of the "hungry" actors to hide their shame and work for the motion pictures. And when Vitagraph, in order to insure the dependability of their players, organized a stock company and promised actors steady work and a regular weekly salary of twenty to forty dollars, [1] more and more of the professionals flocked to the screen.

When they were not acting the professionals were given jobs as carpenters, seamstresses, and painters. Thus, Florence Turner, an actress at Vitagraph,

> drew eighteen dollars a week as the mistress of the wardrobe. That was a minimum guarantee, in effect. If she acted in pictures, then she received a total of five dollars a day, and might, when production conditions were especially fortunate, earn a total of thirty dollars a week. [2]

This practice became common among the other film companies, and the actors, if they wanted steady incomes, had to submit to the policy. But, eventually, the humiliated actors under the leadership

---

1. Jacobs. p. 41.

2. Ramsaye, pp. 442-443.

of Maurice Costello, who insisted," I am an actor and I will act, but I will not build sets and paint scenery, "forced the producers to abandon such methods, and recognize acting as a special skill. [1]

Credit titles apparently did not exist prior to 1908, and their absence did not bother either the producer or the actor. The producer, on the one hand, had no wish to build up the reputation of his actors for fear they would ask for more money, and the actors, on the other hand, had no wish to have their names associated with the motion picture, for fear that they would lose prestige in the legitimate theatre.

By 1910 and 1911, when the motion picture began to achieve a little repuation, the actors lost their enthusiasm for this arrangement, and they did their utmost to follow the lead of G. M. Anderson of Essanay, who had had his name flashing on the screen as leading man, producer, and author of the "Broncho Billy" western films since the spring of 1908.

Ultimately, the recognition of the players was to create a revolution within the motion picture industry. [2] But the full force of the star system was not to be felt until the years of World War I.

While the motion picture was developing a tremendous popularity in the United States, other countries throughout the world were not slow in bestowing their favor on the medium. In addition

---

1. Jacobs, p. 61.

2. Hampton, pp. 146-169.

to France and England, where motion pictures had been popular from
the very beginning, Germany, Austria, Denmark, Russia, Sweden,
Argentina, and Italy were among the other countries demonstrating
a very positive taste for films.

Though American companies penetrated the foreign market with
their productions - Biograph, for example, had offices in England
and Holland -, it seems that Pathe Freres, and other French producers, as well as the Great Northern Film Company, or Nordisk,
of Copenhagen, were the chief sources of supply for the
markets outside of the Untied States. As a result, the direction
taken by American films seems to have had a limited influence abroad.

Ramsaye in speaking of the world-wide reputation of Pathe
Freres says:

> Following on the producing precedents of Melies of Paris,
> the Pathes were rapidly rising to an important place in the
> world market for film. Because all the Latin peoples of the
> world came to Paris to shop Pathe films in even that remote
> day had well near covered the globe, figuring in every market
> except the United States. 1

And Grau, after establishing The Great Northern Film Company's
pre-eminent position as a supplier of film says:

> Other concerns have made efforts with more or less success,
> and at great expense, to create a similar impression on the
> public, but the Great Northern Film Company retains the lead by
> far. It has branch offices at St. Petersburg, Berlin, Vienna,
> London, Genoa, Christiania and Buenos Aires. 2

---

1. Ramsaye, p. 444.

2. Grau, The Business Man in The Amusement World, p. 126

European films were shown in the United States during these early years, but they were not altogether popular. Americans seem to have preferred comedies, westerns, and films which were filled with movement.

As might be expected, Melies occupied the foremost position in the French motion picture business during the years 1900 to 1905, and his contemporaries closely followed the producing precedents laid down by him. [1] Ferdinand Zecca, Emil Cohl, and Jean Durand, conspicuous French producers of the period 1905 to 1910, all employed stop motion, reverse motion, and all the various trick devices introduced by Melies.

Zecca, especially, showed a "particular facility" for trick films. [2] In "Whence Does He Come?," produced in 1906, he employed reverse motion in a simple but very amusing fashion, by photographing a man removing his clothes and diving into a stream, and then projecting the film in reverse. And in "Slippery Jim," produced the same year, Zecca, by employing stop motion, allowed Jim to "persistently defeat or pervert the laws of space, time, gravity and ordered reason. [3] To be sure these films are amusing, but they do not seem to represent any particular advance over Melies, nor, as a matter of fact, do they represent much of an improvement over

---

1. Ramsaye, p. 445.
2. Iris Barry, "Three French Film Pioneers," Film Notes.
3. Barry.

the American "mysterious" films produced in 1902.

Other trick films produced in the Melies tradition were Cohl's "The Pumkin Race," (1907), and Durand's "Onesine Harloger" (1908). But these producers did not always adhere to the Melies' ideal, which assumed that motion pictures were a series of gags and divert - ing trick effedts; and that the plot of the film was inconsequential. They, like the Americans, though not to the same degree, were interested in story films.

Zecca's "The Story of a Crime" (1901) seems to have been the production which revealed to the French the possibilities of the story film, [1] and it may be said that it provided the precedent for Pathe's "Quo Vadis" (1902), "Faust" (1905), and "Underworld in Paris" (1906), and the other story films which were produced in France prior to 1908.

But the similar lines of development being traced by the Amer- ican and French motion picture producers during the years immediately following the birth of the story film were not destined to run parallel, or nearly parallel, for very long. A wide divergence occurred in 1908. In this year, at their congress of film producers, which met on February 2, the French producers, in an effort to "raise the prestige of the cinema and erase the memory of its lowly past," decided to cast their lot with the theatre. They would

---

1. Bardeche and Brasillach, pp. 24-25.

photograph stage plays.

And because the new films would be so terribly elegant, they decided that they would "stop renting films to the little cafes that showed them without charge to their customers." [1] This action indicated rather clearly that the motion picture did not belong to the mass of people in France, as it belonged to the mass of people in the United States.

Although the older producing companies had sounded the call for "films of quite another kind", [2] it was a new firm, the Film d'Art, which heralded the new day with its first production, "Assass-ination of the Duc de Guise," which was exhibited publicly for the first time on November 17, 1908. The exhibition created a sensation.

Henri Lavedan wrote the scenario, actors from the Comedie Francaise played the various roles, and Charles Camille Saint-Saens composed the music.

It was the greatest array of big names that had ever participated in the making of a motion picture up to that time.

Saint-Saens' music, which was arranged for piano, two violins, viola, chello, bass violin, and harmonium, [3] almost without question

---

1. Bardeche and Brasillach, p. 39.

2. Bardeche and Brasillach, P. 39.

3. A copy of the score in possession of Mr. Arthur Kleiner, museum of modern art film library, New York City.

added tremendously to the effect created by the exhibition.

And apart from brief appearances by Jefferson, Bernhardt, Coquelin, and some few other celebrated actors, in some of the early episodic films of 1895-1900, this was the first time that actors as eminent as those of the Comedie Francaise willingly lent their names to the motion picture.

Though Lavedan, a member of the Academic Francais, was a "trivial writer," [1] he had a large popular following, and a reputation as an Academician; so even he played a large part in contributing to the sensation created by the film.

According to Bardeche and Brasillach, the motion picture in France was now prepared to bid farewell to tents, circuses, and little cafes in order to woo "a buskined Muse." [2] The new attitude was given hearty support by the public (not the masses, certainly), and by the Academie Francais. [3]

The latter's acknowledgement was especially gratifying to the film makers; for with the Academie's approval the motion picture had achieved the pinacle of respectability.

Now began the "years of horrors." [4] Producers throughout

---

1. George Freedley and John A. Reeves, A History of The Theatre, p. 355.

2. Bardeche and Brasillach, p. 43.

3. Bardeche and Brasillach, p. 43.

4. Bardeche and Brasillach, p. 46.

Europe became self-conscious and affected. A Societe Cinemato-
graphique des Auteurs et Gens de Lettres was founded. Pathe, in
collaboration with the Italian Film d'Art, introduced a Serie d'Art
Pathe. Gaumont, not to be outdone, introduced a Film Esthetique.
And Eclair organized the Association Cinematographique des Auteurs
Dramatiques. The new development moved along unabated, so that,

> By 1909, a sea of artistic pretentiousness threatened to
> swamp the films. Everything was pressed into service - prose
> and poetry, tragedies, novels, light comedies, history, Georges
> Ohmet and Brieux, Francois Coppee and Michelet and, of course,
> Lavedan and Sardou. The Film d'Art produced Theodora, For the
> Crown, Madame Sans-Fene, The Abbe Constantin, Louis XI, The
> Red Robe, The Iron-Master, Oliver Twist, La Tosca and even
> Werther with Andre Brule. France, Italy and Denmark all flung
> themselves into adaptations from the stage or from books. The
> art of the film suffers to this day from the results. 1

Following the first exhibition of the "Assassination of the Duc
de Guise," M. Charles Pathe turned to the Lafitte brothers, producers
of the film, and exclaimed: "Ah, gentlemen, you are our masters!" 2
But this condition did not continue for long. Pathe Freres, in
very short order, established themselves as the foremost producers
of art films.

Grau, between 1910 and 1914, was able to report that Pathe had
established factories 3 in Paris, Joinville-le-pont, Montreuil,
Sons Bois, and Vincennes; and that the firm employed the foremost

---

1. Bardeche and Brasillach, pp. 43-44.

2. Bardeche and Brasillach, p. 43.

3. Until around 1908 motion picture studios were called factories.

writers and actors of France in their productions. Among the writers
were: Henri Lavedan, Jules Le Maitre, and Jules Sandeau. And among
the actors and actresses were: A. Bargy, Albert Lambert, Henri Krauss,
Silvain, Severin, Max Dearly, Monet-Sull , Prince, Max Linder, Melles,
Tessandier, Barat, Robinne, Taillade, Cecil Sorel, Bartel, Megard,
Geniat, Mau, Catherine Fontenay, and Trouhanowa. [1]

However, other European producing firms were not far behind
Pathe in the employment of great names for their productions. Le
Film d'Art was fortunate in acquiring the services of Sarah Bern-
hardt, Lou Tellegen, and Rejane. [2] And the Italian firm of Ambrosio-
Caesar-Film featured Eleonora Duse. [3]

As these famous players and writers became a regular part of
the motion picture scene, the motion picture directors came to have
less and less to say about the methods of producing a film.
Probably overawed by the reputations of these stars, the producers
and directors sat back and let the actors take charge. M. Jourjon
of the Eclair Company, a French concern, which was one of the first
motion picture companies to engage stage stars, actually felt
compelled to explain the new arrangement by evolving a theory.

---

1. Grau The Theatre of Science. p. 196.
2. Iris Barry, "Great actresses of the past," Film Notes.
3. Iris Barry, "Great actresses of the past," Film Notes.

M. Jourjon believes in the theory of supplying the camera
to the directors of a group of famous players; passing upon
the merits of the finished film, and then arranging the
marketing on a royalty basis, not unlike the practice of
book publishing. [1]

M. Jourjon's motion picture directors were apparently not good

enough to manage these distinguished actors. He must allow the

players of that famous tradition-laden theatre, the Comedie Fran-

caise, who had probably never even been inside a motion picture

theatre, have control of the production. Under such conditions it

is little wonder that the art films never developed into anything

more than photographed plays. Such traditions and techniques as the

motion picture had developed, very laboriously, over a period of

fourteen or fifteen years, were completely ignored, and the camera

once more became simply a reproducing instrument.

Lou Tellegen in his memoirs reveals how the motion picture in

France retrogressed in the hands of the famous players. Speaking of

his experience in "Queen Elizabeth", which featured Sarah Bern-

hardt, he reveals:

> Suffice it to say that we hadn't the remotest idea of camera
> angles, make-up for the camera, or anything. The camera didn't
> even move, but photographed everything from the same position. [2]

And "Queen Elizabeth" was produced in 1912, the year that marks

"the beginning of Griffith's deeper feeling about the movie," and the

first appearance of Mack Sennett's "Keystone Comedies." While the

Americans were developing the creative aspects of the motion picture,

---

1. Grau, The Theatre of Science, P. 181.

2. Lou Tellegen, Women Have Been Kind, p. 283.

the French were using it as a recording instrument.

Adolph Zukor introduced European art films to the United States in 1912. And according to Grau they immediately gained "undisputed sway" in this country, [1] as well as abroad. Ramsaye, however, differs with Grau on this point. He declares that "Europe's efforts to make the screen the vehicle of the classics were largely wasted on the American market;" the Americans wanted Indians and action. [2]

But no matter how popular these films were, there is no denying the fact that they made an impression on American motion picture production. The length of the foreign films - some were from four to eight reels in length - was one of the factors which released the American films from the bondage of one-reel lengths, imposed by the Motion Pictures Patents Company. And the art films did attract the attention of American stage stars, some of whom, under the influence of Griffith, Sennett, and Ince, did manage to adjust themselves to the new requirements of the motion picture as set forth by the American directors.

Significantly, the European art film movement which began in 1908 with the "Assassination of the Duc de Guise," preceded by less than six months, the introduction of David Wark Griffith to the American motion pictures as a director. Griffith, unlike the European

---

1. Grau, The Theatre of Science, p. 196.
2. Ramsaye, p. 515.

~~American motion pictures as a director.~~ ~~Griffith, unlike the~~
~~European~~ directors, was the master of his productions. He was not
forced to accede to the wishes of star stage performers, and consequently his productions developed along lines totally unlike those
of the Europeans.

But in spite of Griffith's films, the westerns, the serials,
and slapstick, the European art films "gave the movie a direction
in which it proceeded for many years, almost to the point of destruction." [1] And the fact that the American motion picture was not
submerged in a sea of art films simply bespeaks the genius of men
like Griffith.

---

1. Gilbert seldes, An Hour With The Movies and The Talkies, p. 50.

CHAPTER XIII

DAVID WARK GRIFFITH

This study is limited to the development of the motion
picture through 1908, the year in which the schism between
American and European production methods took place. But in
order to reveal more clearly the line of development followed
by the American film, as compared to the line of development
followed by the Europeans, and by the French in particular, it
is necessary to cover very briefly the work accomplished by
David Wark Griffith during his first few years as a director
with the American Mutoscope and Biograph Company. Griffith
shortly after joing Biograph became the outstanding director of
motion pictures in this country, and a study of his early work
is quite enough to bring into focus the difference between the
American approach and the European approach to motion pictures
prior to World War I.

In the early months of 1908, Griffith joined the American
Mutoscope and Biograph Company as an actor. [1] The theatre, in

---

1. Iris Barry (Film Notes, Series V, Program 1) says that Griffith,
   "apparently," went to work for Biograph in January, 1908; while
   Lewis Jacobs (p. 98) fixes 1907 as the date. Mrs. D. W. Griffith (When the Movies Were Young, pp. 36-37) agrees with neither
   Barry nor Jacobs. She places the date as February, 1908, or
   a few weeks later.

which he had had considerable experience both in acting and writing, was his major interest; [1] but being out of work, and in an unsteady financial position, Griffith had turned to motion pictures as a temporary measure to tide him over a slack period.

Despite his initial distaste for the motion picture, he worked diligently at his job, soon becoming a director. At first he had hesitated to accept the new position fearing that if he failed he would lose his acting job as well. But when Henry N. Marvin, vice-president of Biograph, assured him that he might return to acting if he failed at his new post, Griffith quickly accepted the offer, for he felt that he could produce better motion pictures than those being turned out by other directors. [2]

Griffith's first films differed little from those produced by Edwin S. Porter. They did, however, show greater discrimination in direction and acting, [3] for he selected his casts with more care,

---

1. In addition to playing stock in Louisville and Chicago, Griffith had toured Iowa with Walker Whiteside, played a season with Nance O'Neil, and acted briefly with Helen Ware, Ada Gray, and J. E. Dodson. And Griffith's play, "A Fool and a Girl," one of twenty plays he had written, had been produced by James K. Hackett with Fanny Ward in the lead. (Henry Stephen Gordon, "David Wark Griffith I","Photoplay Magazine, x (June, 1916). 28-37.

2. In the spring of 1908 Griffith was offered a job in summer stock which he turned down. The consideration, "You don't know what's going to happen down at Biograph, you might get to direct someday," affected his decision (Mrs. D. W. Griffith, p. 43). Furthermore, the casualness of the Biograph Studio bespoke opportunity: "What would happen if some one really got on the job down there some day?" (Mrs. D. W. Griffith, p. 41).

3. His stage experience no doubt made him more aware of the deficiencies in acting and directing, both of which he declared "insufferably careless." (Mrs. D. W. Griffith, p. 45)

and, in order to achieve a more realistic impression, he rehearsed his scenes before they were shot.

In August, 1908, three months after assuming his directorial duties, Griffith's influence, "dependent on the instinct and acumen of technical discovery rather than on the stimulus of his thought," [1] began to exert itself. Working on a Jack London story, "Just Meat," renamed, "For Love of Gold," he was faced with the problem of making an audience aware of the distrust two thieves held for each other. Eschewing the double exposure "dream balloon," the conventional method of expressing the actor's thoughts, Griffith, in the midst of a scene in which their distrust begins to express itself, moved his camera in close for a large full-length view of the actors thus enabling them to project their feelings through facial expression alone.

The implications of the innovation were tremendous. Up to this time it had been conventional to shoot every scene as a long shot, and in its entirety as a single shot. Now Griffith had demonstrated the possibility of breaking up a scene into a number of shots, and of releasing the camera from a position corresponding to that of a spectator in the theatre.

Having discovered that the camera is not merely an inert medium, Griffith proceeded to give the instrument a still greater

---

1. C. A. Lejeune, _Cinema_, pp. 36.37.

flexibility in "After Many Years" (1908), a screen adaptation of Tennyson's "Enoch Arden." [1] In this film, since the story called for quiet suppressed emotion, he moved his camera in even closer to the actor than he had in "For Love of Gold," showing a large close-up of Annie Lee's face in order to catch the subtlest expression.

Up to this time, close-ups, for the most part, had simply been used as trick shots. But in "After Many Years" it became "the natural dramatic complement of the long and full shot." [2]

Griffith made still another innovation in this production. Following the scene showing Annie Lee waiting for her husband, he inserted a shot of Enoch cast away on a desert island. This was the first example of a flashback in the motion pictures. [3]

Officials of the Biograph Company were distressed. In "For

---

1. Iris Barry gives October, 1908, as the production date of "After Many Years" (D. W. Griffith, American Film Master, p. 38); while Lew Jacobs says that it was produced November, 1908 (p. 102).

2. Jacobs, p. 103.

3. "At first, when the plots were simple and the technique still elementary, a straightforward stringing together of a series of scenes was all that was considered necessary for unfolding the story. Later, the more complicated stories and the greater detalization of images helped to bring into use the flashback and the parallel action, the two devices of cutting which introduced the method of intermittent composition. In this way the content matter of images became for the first time a formal element of cinematic composition. This formal character of the treatment of images, be it noted, had nothing to do with their visual form; it was merely a means of organizing their content—a means which unquestionably has its origin in the peculiar mechanical structure of the motion picture, but which also has its analogues in other non-visual arts, as for example, in fiction and poetry." (Alexander Bakshy, "Dynamic Composition," Experimental Cinema, (February, 1930).

Love of Gold" Griffith had broken up a scene into a number of shots, but these shots, the long and close shots of the thieves sitting at the table, had been coherent in space and time. Now he had placed in juxtaposition shots which were disassociated in time and space. His employers asked, "How can you tell a story like that? The people won't know what it's about." [1] He justified his action on the grounds that Charles Dickens employed the same technique in fiction. Griffith's intuition was correct. The shots of Annie Lee and her husband, though unrelated temporally or spatially, "were unified in effect by theme." [2]

While he was developing the intermittent method of composition, Griffith sought still other means of enhancing the reputation of his productions. Lacking the restraint of his cameramen, Marvin and Bitzer, who were inhibited by a convention which decried shadows as amateurish, and by a timidness which overemphasized the inadequacies of the raw film, Griffith in "The Drunkard's Reformation" (March, 1909) forced them to photograph a scene in which the characters were to be illuminated by a fireside glow. Marvin and Bitzer insisted that they would not be able to record

1. Mrs. D. W. Griffith, p. 66.

2. Jacobs, p. 103.

an image in such poor light. He simply demanded that they try.
The results were gratifying; and from this point on lighting
was regarded as an important element in contributing to the dramatic and pictorial effectiveness of the motion picture.

The "fireside glow" in "The Drunkard's Reformation," as
well as the "sunlight effect" in "Pippa Passes," which he produced in September, 1909, and the "dim, religious light" in "Threads
of Destiny," which he produced during the winter of 1910, contributed to the correct atmospheric and dramatic quality of
these productions, and gave to the settings, because of the
directional nature of the light, which created shadows, a plastic
quality unknown in motion pictures, and unusual in the theatre
at the time. [1]

The lighting problem posed by "Pippa Passes" had been one
of the reasons Griffith had made a screen adaptation of the
Browning poem. But the unusual lighting effects to be achieved
in the films were, at this time, a minor consideration. He wanted
to produce a motion picture which would make the legitimate actors,
the critics, the writers, and a "better class" of public recognize
his work. And he calculated that "Pippa Passes" would provide

---

1. See stills opposite p. 118 in Mrs. D. W. Griffith's When the
Movies Were Young.

a subject so unlike the subjects of the ordinary run of motion pictures that it would make the discriminating part of the public notice his film; his judgment was correct. On October 10, 1909, six days after the film's release, the New York Times carried a review of the film, commenting that the production had been well received and that "there seems to be no reason why one may not expect to see soon the intellectual aristocracy of the nickelodeon demanding Kant's Prolegomena to Metaphysics with the 'Kritick of Pure Reason' for a curtain raiser." [1]

This was the first time that a conservative New York newspaper had taken the Biograph Company, and Griffith, "seriously." [2] And Mrs. Griffith remarks: "Suddenly everything was changed. Now we could begin to lift our heads, and perhaps invite our lit'ry friends to our movies." [3]

Even before he had produced "Pippa Passes," Griffith, seeking better stories for his films, had turned for material to Shakespeare, Poe, Scott, Tolstoy, O. Henry, Stevenson, Bret Hart, and Dickens, as well as to London and Tennyson. This tendency was influenced by his belief that it would take more than a chase

---

1. Cited by Mrs. D. W. Griffith, p. 130.

2. Mrs. D. W. Griffith, p. 130.

3. Mrs. D. W. Griffith, p. 130.

melodrama to attract a discriminating audience to the motion picture, and probably also by popular opinion which was beginning to express itself through the Board of Censors of the People's Institute.

The People's Institute wanted to do away with the "sensational blood-and-thunder variety" of films, and Griffith accommodated them by going to the classics; but he never for a moment, despite his envy of literary people, forgot the importance of movement and of the visual image. Otherwise, he might very well have fallen into the unfortunate ways of the French, who relied on literature and the theatre to such an extent that they worked themselves into a state of complete immobility.

In "The Adventures of Dolly," the first film he directed for Biograph, Griffith immediately demonstrated an interest in acting. Hearing that the company planned to assign him inferior actors, [1] Griffith anticipated his employers by choosing his own cast. His wife, Linda Arvidson, was given the part of Dolly's mother, not because she was Griffith's wife, but because she was " a good actress." [2] And Charles Inslee, "an excellent actor," [3] whom

---

1. Mrs. D. W. Griffith, p. 49.

2. Mrs. D. W. Griffith, p. 48.

3. Mrs. D. W. Griffith, p. 49.

Griffith had known in California, was given the part of the
gypsy. The part of Dolly's father presented the greatest
problem. Griffith wanted somebody who had the appearance of
a husband and father, and "who looked as though he owned more
than a cigarette."[1] Finding nobody in the studio who met
this qualification, Griffith picked up Arthur Johnson, a
Broadway actor, for the role. Though Johnson had never been in
the films before, he vindicated Griffith's judgment by later
developing into one of the screen's great favorites.

With the cast assembled Griffith proceeded with the production. Biograph was very satisfied with his results for
within a month of the film's release, the company had him sign
a contract for $45.00 a week and a royalty of one mill for every
foot of film sold. "Viewed in the perspective of time 'The Adventures of Dolly' would seem rude indeed, but it was a burst
of new genius in '08. It told a plausible story in a natural,
logical manner."[2]

In addition to the care given to the selection of casts,
Griffith carefully rehearsed each scene "until everyone was easy
in his role and the cameraman satisfied that all would go well,"[3]

1. Mrs. D. W. Griffith, p. 49.

2. Ramsaye, p. 458.

3. Barry, D. W. Griffith, American Film Master, p. 18.

This procedure was uncommon, and considered a waste of time by other producers. Later, however, other directors saw the wisdom of the practice, and took it up calling it "the 'once again' idea." 1

And in 1909, after he had established himself at the studio, Griffith, in "The Lonely Villa," insisted on retaking scenes which had turned out unsatisfactorily during actual shooting. This was regarded as extravagance of the first order.

As Griffith in "For Love of Gold" and "After Many Years" moved his camera in closer to the scene it became unnecessary for the actors to use the more emphatic gestures required by the long shot. That Griffith was aware of the effect of the close shot would have on acting is evidenced by a remark made to Henry Stephen Gordon by W. C. Cabanne, one of Griffith's assistants:

> 'When Mr. Griffith began to direct,' says Mr. Cabanne, 'we used to act as people do on the stage, preserving distances, and as the story seemed to demand, standing quite a distance from the camera.
> '"What's the good of this?" he said one day; "your legs and your feet do not act; it's your faces that tell the story."' 2

---

1. Jacobs, p. 101.

2. Henry Stephen Gordon, "The Story of David Wark Griffith III", Photoplay Magazine, x (August, 1916). 78-88.

Griffith did not reduce his films to a series of close-ups, nor did he renounce long shots, as Mr. Cabanne's remark might indicate. He was simply making it possible for his actors to give expression to the smaller gestures.

Having discovered that acting must be more natural and "less a matter of 'artistic attitudes,'" [1] Griffith went to the theatre for talent, seeking there actors who could adjust themselves to a realistic style. When he failed to entice the good legitimate actors with the ordinary $5.00 a day salary that it was customary to pay motion picture actors he went to $10.00 and to $20.00, managing as a consequence to attract Frank Powell, who had been with Ellen Terry, and James Kirkwood and Henry Walthall, who had been with Henry Miller. The triumverate of Powell, Kirkwood, and Walthall became under Griffith, "America's earliest anonymous screen idols." [2] They remained anonymous because Biograph, like the other producing companies, which deliberately avoided crediting either directors or actors wished to prevent any one person from building up a public following that would permit him like the stars in the legitimate theatres to demand higher salaries.

---

1. Jacobs, p. 105.
2. Jacobs, p. 105.

Griffith did not have as much luck persuading legitimate
actresses to join Biograph. According to Mrs. Griffith, they
failed to find in the dingy motion picture studio the glamour
they accustomed to find in the theatre. [1] Even so, Griffith
in 1916 told Henry Stephen Gordon that all the "picture
actresses of note" came from the stage in the early days. [2]
Mary Pickford and Dorothy Gish illustrate this last point.
Before she joined Biograph in 1909, at the age of sixteen, Mary
Pickford had played for Belasco in "The Warrens of Virginia,"
and had acted in stock in Toronto from the time she was four. [3]
And Dorothy Gish had had her first part on the stage when she
was seven.

Griffith's romanticism, [4] as well as the sharpness of the
Biograph camera which revealed every line in an actor's face, [5]
explain in part his inclination to cast very young girls for
leading roles in his motion pictures. However, the fact that he
was the "star" of his own productions, [6] must be reckoned as

---

1. Mrs. D. W. Griffith, p. 105.

2. Henry Stephen Gordon, "David Wark Griffith IV", Photoplay
   Magazine x (September, 1916). 79-86, 146, 148.

3. Mrs. D. W. Griffith, pp. 103-104.

4. Jacobs, p. 96.

5. Barry, D. W. Griffith, American Film Master, p. 18.

6. Mrs. D. W. Griffith, p. 221.

another important explanation for this tendency. Young people
were more flexible, and consequently easier to mold. Furthermore, because of their youth, and because in most cases they had
not achieved the prominence of stardom, they were not in a
position to make demands of him. [1]

Griffith was very exacting in his efforts to secure the
correct expression from his actors. Henry Stephen Gordon relates
that he saw Booth's leap in "The Birth of a Nation" rehearsed
twenty times with the camera before Griffith finally secured the
desired execution of the feat. [2] And, in one instance, when
Mae Marsh [3] was attempting with little success to make a sudden
transition from tranquility to terrible alarm, Griffith, while
keeping her within the range of the camera, affected the turn
for her by having one of the company fire off a double-barrelled
shotgun while she was going through her scene. Mrs. Griffith
remarks that the resultant exhibition of fear would have satis-
field the most exacting director. [4]

Having discovered in "After Many Years" that two shots unrelated in space and time could be juxtaposed and have meaning,

---

1. Mrs. D. W. Griffith, p. 228.

2. Gordon, "David Wark Griffith IV."

3. Mae Marsh was one of the few actresses in the Biograph Company
who had not had stage experience.

4. Mrs. D. W. Griffith, pp. 216-217.

Griffith in "The Lonely Villa" (1909) took advantage of an opportunity to experiment with a last-minute -rescue, a development of the chase. Referring to his past experiments, and to Porter's efforts in "Rescued from an Eagle's Nest," [1] in which the director depicted scenes occurring simultaneously, as well as in chronological order, Griffith cut back and forth between a mother and her children who were being harassed by burglars, and the father who was rushing to the rescue, creating suspense and tension in the audience by showing alternately the fears of the mother and the children, and the anxiety of the father. As the tension increased, the length of the shots was reduced. And as a consequence of the cutting, the relief at the rescue was intensified.

Finding the disjunctive method of narration effective, Griffith continued refining his technique, and within two years produced in "The Lonedale Operator" (1911), a last-minute-rescue which created a much greater degree of tension than had been effected in the earlier "The Lonesome Villa." Cutting with great conciseness, Griffith retained only that portion of the film which contributed to the urgency of the story. In "The Lonesome Villa" he had, like other directors, recorded in long shots the entrances

---

1. Griffith had worked as an actor in "Rescued From an Eagle's Nest." It was his first job in the films.

and exits of his actors even when these entrances and exits had
no special significance. This practice approximates the stage
where "the eye follows characters from point to point with perfect
smoothness; they never vanish, to reappear the next moment in a
different place." [1] In "The Lonely Villa," however, Griffith by
catching his characters more in mid-action than he had in the earlier
film suggested what he was to do later in "The Birth of a Nation,"
where with the greatest rapidity and precision he cut from one vital
point of interest to another. The movement of the actor in these
briefer shots was, of course, made more emphatic. But Griffith
gave even more momentum to "The Lonedale Operator by placing his
camera on board the train of the engineer-hero who was coming to
the rescue of his operator-sweetheart. [2]

1. Spottiswoode, p. 159.
2. By treating his audience to the illusion of a moving train at a
   standstill, while the stationary landscape appeared to be flying
   swiftly into the distance, Griffith made it possible, quite by
   chance, perhaps, for the audience to identify itself more closely
   with the feelings of the engineer-hero. For this effort he would
   have been applauded by the Russian stage director, Evereinov,
   who advocated the use of all available effects in the theatre to
   illustrate the changing moods and standpoints of the protagonist.
   In his "The Path of the Modern Russian Stage" (p. 80), Alexander
   Bakshy says that under these circumstances he has, as far as his
   own experiences go, never been under the impression that it was
   he who was seated in the speeding engine, and the hero of the
   occasion. He said this in 1919. At that time he had not had
   the opportunity to see the news-reel shots taken from a British
   warship in the Mediterranean which was a target of the Italian
   fleet. As the enemy shells hit the water all around the English
   ship it was not difficult to associate yourself with the feelings
   of the men aboard the ship. Another convincing monodramatic
   effect was created in "Tortilla Flat" (Victor Fleming, M-G-M,
   1942) when Fleming had an actor throw stones at the camera which
   was placed in a position corresponding to that of a group of
   men the solitary man was attacking. As the stones came hurtling
   through the air towards the camera creating an illusion of stones
   being thrown into the auditorium of the theatre, the audience
   protected itself with as much celerity as did the group of men
   being attacked.

While Griffith's ideas governing acting and staging were unusual for his day, it was in his free use of the camera, and in his editing that he stood apart from the Europeans.

The European producers of "art films" regarded the motion picture camera as a recording instrument; and when they produced motion pictures they did little more than set up the camera and shoot scene after scene in chronological order. "A straight-forward stringing together of a series of scenes was all that they considered necessary for unfolding the story. [1]

Griffith, on the other hand, saw the motion picture as a new medium of expression, and he employed the flashback, and parallel action, "the two devices of cutting which introduced the method of intermittent composition," [2] as new and effective methods of communicating ideas on the screen.

Though the "art films" managed to win considerable approval for more than a decade, Griffith's ideas about the arrangement of shots finally prevailed, and have become basic precepts in the production of motion pictures. And his influence, even today, is such that nobody can deny the correctness of Dorothy Gish's instructions to a man seeking Griffith: You can find him,

---

1. Bakshy, "Dynamic Composition."
2. Bakshy, "Dynamic Composition."

"on every movie screen in America." 1

While not wishing to detract one iota from the greatness of Griffith, it is necessary, once in a while, to protest a bit, when some of his admirers, in an unprofitable effort to secure his already impregnable position in the development of the motion picture, over indulge themselves in praising his accomplishments. These paeans, such as the one cited below, because they are generally incorrect, and need, as a consequence, to be corrected, simply draw attention away from Griffith's true merit.

> Here, to sum up, are the meaning and also the tragedy of Griffith: he was the greatest creative genius which the new art of the moving picture has thus far brought forth. By an odd stroke of history, he came at the beginning instead of later in the medium's development. Other media offer no parallel to this phenomenon. 2 In literature, for example, before Shakespeare, there was Cervantes; before Cervantes there were the Greek playwrights and poets. But what was there in the realm of the cinema, before Griffith? A few trick shots invented by the Frenchman, Melies? A few 500-foot trailers, directed by Porter, chiefly at the insistence of the Edison Company, and devoid of either cinematic technique or important content? Before Griffith there was nothing. Griffith was the real beginning of the motion picture, owing so little to the few men who preceded him that their very names have been all but forgotten. 3

---

1. Cited by Leonard Lyons, "Lyons Den," The Syracuse Post Standard, August 2, 1948. p. 16 D.

2. Did Shakespeare appear later in his medium's development? Did Haydn appear later? Did Giotto appear later? And how about Aeschylus?

3. Seymour Stern, "D. W. Griffith: An apreciation," The New York Times, August 1, 1948. Section 2, p. X 3 A.

"Before Shakespeare, there was Cervantes; before Cervantes
there were the Greek playwrights and poets." Without wishing to
seem presumptuous, we think it only fair to ask Stern what chronological position Griffith holds in the history of the arts. Before
the Greek Playwrights and poets, or after them?

Stern is positive that Cervantes influenced his contemporary,
Shakespeare, yet he denies that Griffith was influenced by Shakespeare. In effect, he says that the development of the motion
picture took place in a vacuum. But his assumption that the motion
picture had nothing to learn from the other arts is denied by
Griffith himself who explained his use of the flashback by saying
that Dickens employed the same device in literature.

Certainly it is unfair to Griffith to spead so slightingly
of his background, which was one of the very things which distinguished him from his early contemporaries in the motion picture
industry. They, being business men and mechanics, had had little
contact with the arts, and they constantly betrayed their inadequacies
because of this shortcoming. Griffith, on the other hand, because
of his contact with literature had a mind which "was stored with
plots, situations, and incidents." [1] And his experience in the
theatre had taught him the tricks and "business" of dramatic
expression, and had made him keenly aware of the fact that acting

---

1. Hampton, p. 50.

and directing in motion pictures was "insufferably careless." Actually, the experience of hundreds of artists was behind him.

"Before Griffith there was nothing." "A few trick shots...by ...Melies. A few 500-foot trailers...by Porter." Stern's "appreciation" of Griffith is fine and right, but his lack of appreciation for the work accomplished by the men who came before Griffith is unfortunate.

These men whose "very names have been all but forgotten" created for Griffith an audience, and ten thousand nickelodeon theatres in which his films could be exhibited. Furthermore, by the time Griffith had cast his lot with the motion picture, they had set up over a hundred exchanges in the key cities of the United States to facilitate an easy, economical, and rapid flow of films throughout the country. If Stern thinks that this was "nothing," he is not aware of the relationship between the art of the motion picture, and the business of the motion picture. The organizational set up created by the pioneers permitted Griffith to experiment with one new motion picture every week for hundreds of weeks so that when he finally decided to film "The Birth of a Nation" he approached the problem with skill and confidence.

These "forgotten" men also had made progress in the development of the motion picture's technical resources before Griffith appeared. Scenic craftsmen by 1908 had grown skilful and were ambitious to build substantial settings. [1] Electric lamps for lighting indoor sets had been devised. Motion picture equipment, though still not perfect, was constantly being improved. And the sensitivity of film which formerly could record only sharp blacks and whites had been developed to a point where it could respond to a "fireside glow."

These last remarks are not made in any attempt to belittle Griffith's accomplishments. They are simply aimed at correcting, as has been the whole study, a misapprehension about the importance of the work accomplished by the men who worked with the motion picture, prior to the time Griffith appeared and consolidated the tools, material, and personnel in the creation of better motion pictures.

Griffith was daring in the use of his knowledge, and he never hesitated to "try for the unattainable in story or dramatic effect," [2] but he had behind him, and supporting him at all times, the important accomplishments of the men who had worked in the motion picture, and in other fields of art.

---

1. Hampton, p. 50.

2. Hampton, p. 50.

BIBLIOGRAPHY

AGNEW, FRANCES. Motion Picture Acting. New York City, 1913.

ARNHEIM, RUDOLF. Film. Translated by L. M. Sieveking and Ian ·
F. D. Morrow, London, 1933.
> ("Parts II and III of "Film" contain an analysis of the
> relation between what is seen and what is shot, which
> is not likely to be soon surpassed." - Spottiswoode,
> A Grammar of the Film, p. 28.

BAKSHY, ALEXANDER. The Path of the Modern Russian Stage and other
Essays. London, 1916.

BALCON, MICHAEL, and LINDGREN, ERNEST, and HARDY, FORSYTH, and MAN-
VELL, ROGER. 20 Years of British Film, 1925-1945. Second
impression. London, 1948.

BARDECHE, MAURICE, and BRASILLACH, ROBERT. The History of Motion
Pictures. Translated and Edited by Iris Barry. New York, 1938.

BARRY, IRIS, and LEYDA, JAY. Film Notes, being the Program Notes
for the Film Library's Circulating Programs. New York, n.d.,
c.1938.

BARRY, IRIS. D. W. Griffith, American Film Master. Museum of
Modern Art Film Library Series No. 1. New York, 1940.

BEBENDSOHN, WALTER A. Selma Lagerlof, her Life and Work. Adapted
from the German by George F. Timpson. London, 1931.

BESSY, MAURICE, et LO DUCA. Georges Melies. Paris, 1945.

BRAZIER, MARION HOWARD. Stage and Screen. Boston, 1920.

BRUNEL, ADRIAN. Filmcraft. London, 1933.

BUCHANAN, ANDREW. The Art of Film Production. London, 1936.

------. Film Making, from Script to Screen. London, 1937.

CAMERON, JAMES R. Motion Pictures with Sound. Manhattan Beach,
N. Y. 1929.

CARTER, HUNTLEY. The New Theatre and Cinema of Soviet Russia.
London, 1924.

------. The New Spirit in the Russian Theatre, 1917-28. New York,
1929.

CROY, HOMER. How motion pictures are made. New York, 1918.

DONALDSON, LEONARD. The cinematograph..and Natural Science: the Achievements and Possibilities of Cineomatography as an Aid to Scientific Research. London, 1912.

DRESSLER, MARIE. My Own Story, as told by Marie Dressler to Mildred Harrington. Boston, 1934.

DRINKWATER, JOHN. The Gentle Art of Theatre Going. London, 1927.

------. The Life and Adventures of Carl Laemmle. New York, 1931.

EISENSTEIN, SERGEI. The Film Sense. Translated and edited by Jay Leyda. New York, 1942.

ERNST, MORRIS L., and LORENTZ, PARE. Censored: the Private Life of the Movie. New York, 1930.

FAURE, ELIE. The Art of Cineplastics. Translated from the French by Walter Pach. Boston, 1923.

FERGUSON, FRANK S. English Melodrama in the Early Nineteenth Century. A Master's Thesis, Cornell University. Ithaca, N. Y., 1932.

FITZGERALD, PERCY. The World behind the Scenes. London, 1881.

GRAU, ROBERT. The Business Man in the Amusement World. New York, 1910.

------. The Stage in the Twentieth Century. New York, 1912.

------. The Theatre of Science. New York, 1914.
          (Grau knew many of the pioneers, and in all three of his
          books he has many interesting things to say about the
          invention of the motion picture, the nickelodeons,
          combination motion picture-vaudeville shows, etc.)

GREEN, PAUL. The HawthorneTree: Some Papers and Letters on Life and the Theatre. Chapel Hill, N. C., 1943.
          (On pages 38 through 40 Green relates briefly the
          important part played by music in the exhibition of
          Griffith's "The Birth of a Nation.")

------. "The Theatre and the Screen," reprinted from the New York Times in Modern Plays and Playwrights by Caro Mae Green Russell. University of North Carolina Library, Extension Publication, July, 1930. Vol. II, no. 6.

GRIFFITH, Mrs. D.W. When the Movies Were Young. New York, 1925.

HAMPTON, Benjamin B. A History of the Movies. New York, 1931.
(Business and art in the motion picture appear to be inseparable. Any consideration of one seems to demand a consideration of the other. Hampton probably knows the business of the motion picture better than any other man who has written on the subject.)

HARDING, ALFRED. "The Theatre's First Three Thousand Years," in Our Theatre Today, edited by Herschel L. Bricker. New York, 1936.

HARDY, FORSYTH. See BALCON, MICHAEL.

HARRINGTON, MILDRED. See DRESSLER, MARIE.

HEPWORTH, CECIL M. Animated Photography, the A B C of the Cinematograph. Second edition, revised and brought up to date by Hector Maclean. London, 1900.

HOPWOOD, HENRY V. Living Pictures. London, 1899.

HULFISH, DAVID S. Cyclopedia of Motion-Picture Work: a general reference work on the optical lantern, motion head, specific projecting machines, talking pictures, color motography, fixed camera photography, motography, photo-plays, motion-picture theatre, management and operation, audience, program, etc. Chicago, 1911. 2 vols.

HUNTER, WILLIAM. Scrutiny of Cinema. London, 1932.

JACOBS, LEWIS. The rise of the American Film. New York, 1939.

JEANNE, RENE. "L'Evolution Artistique Du Cinematographe," in Le Cinema. Paris, n.d. c. 1932.

JENKINS, C. FRANCIS, and DEPUE, OSCAR B. Handbook for Motion Picture and Stereopticon Operators. Washington, D. C., 1908.

JENKINS, ------. Picture Ribbons. Washington, D. C., 1897.

JOHNSTON, ALVA. The Great Goldwyn. New York, 1937.

KOMISARJEVSKY, THEODORE. Myself and the Theatre. London, 1929.

KROWS, ARTHUR EDWIN. Play Production in America. New York, 1916.

LAWSON, JOHN HOWARD. Theory and Technique of Playwriting and Screenwriting. New edition. New York, 1949.

LEJEU E, C. A. Cinema: A Review of Thirty Years Achievement. London, 1931.

LINDGREN, ERNEST. The Art of the Film. New York, 1948.

-----. See Balcon, Michael.

LINDSAY, VACHEL. The Art of the Moving Picture. New York, 1916.

LONDON, KURT. Film Music. Translated by Eric S. Bensinger. London, 1936.

LONG, ROBERT EDGAR. David Wark Griffith. New York, 1920

LOPEZ, MANUEL VILLEGAS. Cine del Medio Siglo. Buenos Aires, 1946.

LOW, RACHAEL and MANVELL, ROGER. The History of the British Film, 1896-1906. London, 1948.

MACLEAN, HECTOR. See HEPWORTH, CECIL M.

MANVELL, ROGER. See LOW, RACHAEL, and BALCON, MICHAEL.

-----. Film. Revised and enlarged edition. London, 1946.

MUNSTERBERG, HUGO. The Photoplay. A Psychological Study. New D York, 1916.

NICOLL, ALLARDYCE. Film and Theatre. New York, 1936.

NILSEN, VLADIMIR. The Cinema as a Graphic Art. London, n. d., c. 1936.

PAINE, ALFRED BIGELOW. Life and Lillian Gish. New York, 1932.

POWELL, MICHAEL. 200,000 Feet on Foula. London, 1938.

PUDOVKIN, V. I. Film Acting. Translated by Ivor Montagu. London., 1937.

PUDOVKIN, V. I. Film Technic. Translated and annotated by Ivor Montagu. London, 1935.

QUIGLEY, MARTIN Jr. Magic Shadows. Washington, D. C., 1948.

RAMSAYE, TERRY. A Million and One Nights: a history of the motion picture. New York, 1926. 2 vols.

RICHARDSON, F. H. Motion Picture Handbook: a guide for managers and operators of motion picture theatres. New York, n. d., c. 1911.

ROBSON, E. W., and ROBSON, M. M. The Film Answers Back. London, 1939.

ROTHA, PAUL. Celluloid: the film to-day. London, 1933.

-----. Documentary Film. London, 1936.

-----. The Film Till Now: a survey of the cinema. New York, 1930.

-----. Movie Parade. London, 1936.

SARGENT, EPES WINTHROP. Technique of the Photo Play. Second edition. New York, 1913.

SEABURY, WILLIAM MARSTON. Motion Picture Problems. New York, 1929.

SELDES, GILBERT. An Hour with the Movies and the Talkies. Philadelphia, 1929.

-----. The Movies Come from America. New York, 1937.

-----. The Seven Lively Arts. New York, 1924.

SINCLAIR, UPTON. William Fox. Los Angeles, 1933.

STAUFFACHER, FRANK. Art in Cinema. San Francisco, 1947.

STENGER, ERICH. The History of Photography. Translation and footnotes by Edward Epstean. Easton, Pa., 1939.

SPOTTISWOODE, RAYMOND. A Grammar of the Film. London, 1935.

TALBOT, FREDERICK A. Moving Pictures: how they are made and worked. Philadelphia, 1912.

TELLEGEN, LOU. Women Have Been Kind. The Memoirs of Lou Tellegen. New York, 1931.

THORP, MARGARET FARRAND. America at the Movies. New Haven, Conn., 1939.

TRUTAT, EUG. La Photographie Animee, avec une preface de J. Marey. Paris, 1899.

WRIGHT, BASIL. The Use of the Film. London, 1948.

The Film Index, a Bibliography. Vol. 1, the Film as Art.
Compiled by Workers of the Writers Program of the
Work Projects Administration in the City of New York.
New York, 1941.

The Theatre and Motion Pictures. A selection of articles
from the New 14th edition of the Encyclopaedia Britannica. Britannica Booklet No. 7. New York, 1933.

Le Cinema: Des origines a nos jours. Preface par Henri
Fescourt. Paris, n.d., c. 1932.

The following special sources have been consulted:

Saint-Saen's score for Film d'Art's "Assassination of the Duc de
Guise." (A copy in possession of Mr. Arthur Kleiner, Museum of
Modern Art Film Library, New York City.)

An advertising bulletin: Lubin's Films, "The Great Train Robbery,"
August, 1904. (A copy in possession of Walter H. Stainton, Cornell
University, Ithaca, New York.)

Cornell University Theatre Program, May 9, 1942. Note by Walter
H. Stainton: "A Program of Ithaca and Cornell Motion Pictures."

Issues of the following newspapers and periodicals have been
consulted:

The British Journal of Photography,
Close-Up,
The Electrical World,
Experimental Cinema,
Harper's Weekly,
Hollywood Quarterly,
The Ithaca Daily Journal,
The Journal of the Biological Photographic Association,
The London Times,
McClure's,
The New York Daily Tribune
The New York Times,
The Optical Magic Lantern Journal and Photographic Enlarger,
The Photographic News,
Photoplay Magazine,
The Scientific American,

The Syracuse Post Standard, and
Theatre Arts Monthly.

No record of a large number of notes and articles which have
been used in the preparation of the thesis appears in either the
bibliography or in the foot-notes. (other than a listing of the
magazines and newspapers from which they have been secured.)

The decision to leave out these notes, which would require
ten or twelve pages of listings, has been considered not unwise,
because their inclusion does not seem necessary to the purpose
of the thesis, and because, in most cases, the notes which have
not been recognized, particularly advertisements of motion picture
exhibitions, simply repeat other notes which are fully credited
in either the bibliography or in a foot-note.

The articles listed below will be of special interest to
students studying the early history of the motion picture. They
represent, of course, only a smattering of the many notes and
articles on the early history which can be found in several of
the publications noted above.

"The Kineto-Phonograph," The Electrical World, xxiii (June 16,
1894). 799-801.
           (Edison predicts that eventually sound motion pictures
           will be made of the operas performed at the Metro-
           politan Opera House in New York.)

"The Art of Moving Photography," The Scientific American, lxxvi
(April 17, 1897). 248-250.
           (A well-illustrated, and detailed re ort on the activi-

ties of the American Mutoscope and Biograph Company in 1897.)

"The Tragedy of the Charity Bazar Fire," The Scientific American, lxxvi (May 15, 1897). 307.
        (An account of the disastrous Charity Bazar Fire in Paris.)

St. Clair, D. F. "The Micromotoscope," The Scientific American, lxxvii (July 31, 1897). 75.
        (Microscopy and motion pictures combined.)

"Astronomical Illusion," The Photographic News, xlii (, 1898). 115.
        (M. Flammarion with a short motion picture lasting two minutes creates for the audience the effect of seeing a complete twenty-four hour revolution of the earth.)

"The Cinematograph and Surgery," The British Journal of Photography, xlvii (January 26, 1900). 53.
        (Dr. Doyen finds the motion picture useful in the study of operative techniques.)

" A Cinematographic Feat," The British Journal of Photography, xlvii (April 13, 1900.) 230.
        (Fifty feet seems to be the average length of a motion picture in 1900.)

"The Cinematographic Advertiser," The British Journal of Photography, xlix (June 27, 1902). 506.
        (Description of an advertising motion picture made in 1902.)

"New Things in Moving Pictures," The New York Times, June 29, 1902. p. 25, c, d, e.
        (State of the motion picture "business" in 1902.)

Bakshy, Alexander. "The New Art of the Moving Picture," Theatre Arts Monthly, xi (April, 1927.) 277-282.
        (How it happened that "men of artistic culture" were slow in grasping the motion picture's possibilities as an art medium.)

Richards, Oscar W. "Photographic History," The Journal of the Biological Photographic Association, ii (January, 1933). 48.
        (Motion pictures of a surgical operation made in 1898.)

THE OPTICAL MAGIC LANTERN JOURNAL AND PHOTOGRAPHIC ENLARGER.

    The Optical Magic Lantern Journal and Photographic Enlarger, a British Journal published between 1889 and 1902, appears to be one of the richest sources of information on the early history of the motion picture. For this reason, and because the publication

is not available in most libraries, very brief summaries of certain
articles and notes which have been useful in the preparation of this
thesis have been included in the bibliography so that the reader may
better understand the value of this particular source.

Rachael Low and Roger Manvell, who identify the journal as
the motion picture's first trade paper, say:

> The Optical Magic Lantern Journal and Photographic Enlarger
> was founded in 1889, and edited for thirteen years by John Hay Taylor.
> Animated photography became its especial concern from the article on W.
> Friese-Greene's experiments, in the June 21st issue of 1889, onwards. In
> March 1902, John Hay Taylor retired, and was succeeded as editor by
> Alfred H. Saunders. In November of the same year the name was altered
> slightly to The Optical Lantern Journal and Photographic Journal. [1]

1895

"The Kenetoscope, and Photoramic Effects," vi (January, 1895) 3.
>   (Exhibition of Edison's kinetoscope in London; and a reference to
>   an article published in the Optical Magic Lantern Journal and
>   Photographic Enlarger of November 15, 1889, concerning the early
>   efforts of Mr. Friese Green in the motion picture field.)

"General Wants, & c.," vi (February, 1895).
>   "Sets of slides for sale: e.g., "SLIDES, set 25, Temperance,
>   'Which side wins'.")

"Dr. Henry Morton of the Franklin Institute of Pennsylvania," vi
(December, 1895). 202.
>   (Dr. Morton presents a lantern show in which he employs dis-
>   solves, and creates the effect of a tracking shot. [1])

1896

Dreamer, The. "Topical Notes," vii (April, 1896). 71.
>   (Lumieres are credited with having given the first public
>   exhibition of motion pictures in London.)

"Theatrograph." vii (April, 1896). 71-72.
>   (Robert Paul's theatrograph "is now being exhibited at Olympia,
>   and is creating a great sensation.")

Lomax A. "Kinetoscope and Lantern," vii (August, 1896). 132-134.
>   (There are only a few reliable motion picture machines on the
>   market.)

"Films," vii (October, 1896). 162.
>   (Messrs. Watson & Son establish a projection room where their
>   customers can see motion pictures before purchasing them.)

"Wallace and others v. Riley Brothers, New York," vii (October, 1896).
166-167.
>   (The Riley Brothers are restrained from distributing the epito-
>   mised readings of "Ben Hur," but they are permitted to sell sets
>   of seventy-two lantern slides illustrating the story.)

---

1. Low and Manvell, pp. 120-121.

"Wrench's Cinematograph," vii (October, 1896). 168-169.
(Mr. Wrench is working on a cinematograph which will
sell for 36 1. rather than for the "usual" price of
100 1. or more.)

"Animated Photographs at Brechin," vii (November, 1896). 173-174.
(Mr. C. W. Locke, showman, manipulates the cinematoscope in the cities of Scotland.)

1897

"Cinematographic Films," viii (January, 1897). 2.
(Mr. Philipp Wolff's films are "about 75 feet long,
and very clear.")

Bryce, G. R. "Lantern Lectures," viii (January, 1897). 29-30.
("Instead of having to explain the slides, the lecturer
should have the slides explaining him.")

"Sausages from Dogs and Cats," viii (May, 1897). 78.
(A comedy film showing cats and dogs being thrown into
a hopper and ground into sausages.)

Robins, Edmund A. "Animated Pictures," viii (June, 1897). 99-101.
(Motion pictures are very popular with the public, and
now that competition has been set up better results
are expected. Audiences "shudder" as they view motion
pictures of waves breaking through the mouth of a cave.
The Lumiere and Paul machines suffer from flicker,
and from a slight jumping of the picture.)

Notes," viii (June, 1897). 101-102.
(L. Gaumont of Paris is selling a fan-like device,
pierced with holes, which he says will eliminate flicker
in the motion picture if it is held between the eyes and
the projected pictures with a slight "to and fro" motion.
The fan is called "La Grille.")

Showman, the. "Animated Photographs and Projecting Machines,"
viii (June, 1897). 103-105.
(There are signs that interest in the motion picture
is beginning "to flag." Many exhibitors have failed
because they "were quite unable to tell a good machine
from a bad one." Good motion picture machines are "few
and far between.")

"Fuerst's New Cinematographic Slides." viii (August, 1897). 126.
(Motion pictures advertised as "cinematographic slides.")

"Life of a Cinematograph Film." viii (November, 1897). 177.
(With ordinary care a film can be exhibited three hundred
times.)

"Death of Nelson," viii (November, 1897). 177.
(A special film commemorating the anniversary of Trafalgar.)

1898

"A Hanging Cinematographed," ix (January, 1898). 3.
("The set of slides illustrating the gruesome spectacle
have been pronounced 'good,' and these are to be duplicated and public exhibitions given in various towns.")

"Cinematograph Fire," ix (February, 1898). 18.
(No serious damage; the operator, however, was burned
about the hands.)

"Cinematographic Exhibitions," ix (March, 1898). 37-38.
(Motion picture exhibitions sponsored by "several powerful soap and other firms" threaten incomes of motion
picture showmen.)

"Sceintific Use of the Cinematograph." ix (March, 1898). 38-39.
(A prediction that motion pictures before long will
be "in common use in certain colleges as a method of
imparting instruction.")

"Lecture on Canada," ix (April, 1898). 54.
(Motion pictures used by the Canadian Pacific Railway Company to promote emigration to Canada.)

"Notes," ix (April, 1898). 54.
(Mr. Wm. K. Laurie Dickson photographs the Worthing
(England) life-saving crew in action. Detailed account.)

"Mellin's Food Cinematograph," ix (May, 1898). 70.
(Mellin's Food Company decides to use motion pictures
for advertising purposes.)

"Cinematographic Pictures at Westminster," ix (July, 1898). 102.
(A motion picture of the "funeral procession of the
late Mr. Gladstone.)

"Fire at a Cinematographic Entertainment," ix (August, 1898). 114-115.
    (None of the spectators were hurt, but the canvas roof
    of the tent took fire, and the fire brigade had to be
    called out.)

"1899 Cynnagraph," ix (September, 1898). 138.
    (The new projector is small and costs only 5 1. 5 s.)

"A New Military Cinematographic Picture," ix (December, 1898). 174.
    (A motion picture taken on the battlefield at Andurman.)

"New Cinematographic Regulations," ix (December 1898). 175.
    (The London County Council regulates motion picture
    exhibitions.)

1899

"Half a Mile of 'Bull Fight' Film," x (January, 1899). 2.
    (The writer is amused that an exhibitor would dare adver-
    tise a film half a mile in length: "It might be interest-
    ing to determine how long this would take to pass the
    condenser, what size of room such a film would carpet,
    etc.")

"Cinematograph Fire," x (February, 1899). 18.
    (The loss of a thousand dollars worth of property at
    a motion picture fire seems to have prompted an exhibitor
    to shoot himself.)

"A Novelty in Films," x (February, 1899). 18.
    (Each of the three verses of the well-known humorous
    song, "Simon the Cellarer," is illustrated by a separate
    film of about fifty feet in length.)

"The Cinematograph for Commercial Travellers," x (February, 1899).
18.
    (A Toronto firm uses motion pictures to advertise
    its agricultural appliances in England.)

Newland, P. "A Few Lantern Notes from West Australia," x
(February, 1899). 27-28.
    (The Salvation Army has created a new department.
    "They call it the triple alliance, i.e., lantern (three-
    decker), cinematograph, and phonograph.)

"The Cinematograph and Birmingham Town Hall," x (March, 1899). 34.
(Insurance rates make it impossible to show motion pictures
in Birmingham Town Hall.)

"Cinematograph Fire." x (April, 1899). 45.
(Motion picture fire at the Hammersmith Theatre undetected
by the audience because of the fireproof room designed
by the London County Council.)

"A Cinematographic Camera, Printer, Projector, and Snapshot Camera
in one," x (April, 1899). 46-48.
(The Biokam. This camera is intended to meet the wants
of the amateurs.)

"What the Cinematograph has done for Constantinople," x (July, 1899).
82.
(The Sultan, wishing to see a motion picture show, permits
the exhibitor to install the first electrical lighting
plant in Constantinople.)

"A Lantern Entertainment well worth a Visit," x (November, 1899).
143.
(An account of the sound effects employed in one of
the early motion picture exhibitions.)

"The Correct Presentation of Dioramic Effects," x (November, 1899).
153.
("The best days" of the motion picture are over.)

1900

"Cinematograph Fire," xi (January, 1900). 1.
(Film tightly wound is difficult to ignite.)

Leifeld, Wielhelm. "The Lantern and Kinetograph as aids to the
Teaching of Languages," xi (February, 1900). 30.
(By using motion pictures it is "possible for the teacher
to actually show his class all the things that he must
familiarise them with.")

"Sham War Cinematograph Films," xi (March, 1900). 30.
(The editors attempt to tell a perplexed correspondent
how to distinguish real from sham war films.)

"Trick Film Tableau," xi (June, 1900). 70.
(A detailed description of a trick motion picture produced by R. N. Paul.)

"New Style of Advertising," xi (August, 1900). 94.
      ("At the tail end of a large van a screen is erected,
when by means of a cinematographic lantern placed in
front, animated advertisement films are projected on
the screen, meantime the van is hauled about the streets.")

"Recruiting by Means of the Lantern," xi (October, 1900). 117.
      (The War Office has prepared a series of motion pic-
tures illustrating "the life of a soldier from the raw
recruit to the perfect soldier living a life of ease.")

"The Cinematograph at Newcastle-on-Tyne," xi (November, 1900)
137.

      (A sub-committee of the Newcastle Town Improvement
Committee are drawing up regulations for the control of
the motion picture.)

The Arno Press Cinema Program

THE LITERATURE OF CINEMA

Series I & II

Agate, James. **Around Cinemas.** 1946.

Agate, James. **Around Cinemas.** (Second Series). 1948.

American Academy of Political and Social Science. **The Motion Picture in Its Economic and Social Aspects,** edited by Clyde L. King. **The Motion Picture Industry,** edited by Gordon S. Watkins. *The Annals,* November, 1926/1927.

L'Art Cinematographique, Nos. 1-8. 1926-1931.

Balcon, Michael, Ernest Lindgren, Forsyth Hardy and Roger Manvell. **Twenty Years of British Film, 1925-1945.** 1947.

Bardèche, Maurice and Robert Brasillach. **The History of Motion Pictures,** edited by Iris Barry. 1938.

Benoit-Levy, Jean. **The Art of the Motion Picture.** 1946.

Blumer, Herbert. **Movies and Conduct.** 1933.

Blumer, Herbert and Philip M. Hauser. **Movies, Delinquency, and Crime.** 1933.

Buckle, Gerard Fort. **The Mind and the Film.** 1926.

Carter, Huntly. **The New Spirit in the Cinema.** 1930.

Carter, Huntly. **The New Spirit in the Russian Theatre, 1917-1928.** 1929.

Carter, Huntly. **The New Theatre and Cinema of Soviet Russia.** 1924.

Charters, W. W. **Motion Pictures and Youth.** 1933.

Cinema Commission of Inquiry. **The Cinema: Its Present Position and Future Possibilities.** 1917.

Dale, Edgar. **Children's Attendance at Motion Pictures.** Dysinger, Wendell S. and Christian A. Ruckmick. **The Emotional Responses of Children to the Motion Picture Situation.** 1935.

Dale, Edgar. **The Content of Motion Pictures.** 1935.

Dale, Edgar. **How to Appreciate Motion Pictures.** 1937.

Dale, Edgar, Fannie W. Dunn, Charles F. Hoban, Jr., and Etta Schneider. **Motion Pictures in Education: A Summary of the Literature.** 1938.

Davy, Charles. **Footnotes to the Film.** 1938.

Dickinson, Thorold and Catherine De la Roche. **Soviet Cinema.** 1948.

Dickson, W. K. L., and Antonia Dickson. **History of the Kinetograph, Kinetoscope and Kinetophonograph.** 1895.

Forman, Henry James. **Our Movie Made Children**. 1935.

Freeburg, Victor Oscar. **The Art of Photoplay Making**. 1918.

Freeburg, Victor Oscar. **Pictorial Beauty on the Screen**. 1923.

Hall, Hal, editor. **Cinematographic Annual, 2 vols**. 1930/1931.

Hampton, Benjamin B. **A History of the Movies**. 1931.

Hardy, Forsyth. **Scandinavian Film**. 1952.

Hepworth, Cecil M. **Animated Photography: The A B C of the Cinematograph**. 1900.

Hoban, Charles F., Jr., and Edward B. Van Ormer. **Instructional Film Research 1918-1950**. 1950.

Holaday, Perry W. and George D. Stoddard. **Getting Ideas from the Movies**. 1933.

Hopwood, Henry V. **Living Pictures**. 1899.

Hulfish, David S. **Motion-Picture Work**. 1915.

Hunter, William. **Scrutiny of Cinema**. 1932.

Huntley, John. **British Film Music**. 1948.

Irwin, Will. **The House That Shadows Built**. 1928.

Jarratt, Vernon. **The Italian Cinema**. 1951.

Jenkins, C. Francis. **Animated Pictures**. 1898.

Lang, Edith and George West. **Musical Accompaniment of Moving Pictures**. 1920.

London, Kurt. **Film Music**. 1936.

Lutz, E ⌈dwin⌉ G ⌈eorge⌉. **The Motion-Picture Cameraman**. 1927.

Manvell, Roger. **Experiment in the Film**. 1949.

Marey, Etienne Jules. **Movement**. 1895.

Martin, Olga J. **Hollywood's Movie Commandments**. 1937.

Mayer, J. P. **Sociology of Film: Studies and Documents**. 1946. New Introduction by J. P. Mayer.

Münsterberg, Hugo. **The Photoplay: A Psychological Study**. 1916.

Nicoll, Allardyce. **Film and Theatre**. 1936.

Noble, Peter. **The Negro in Films**. 1949.

Peters, Charles C. **Motion Pictures and Standards of Morality**. 1933.

Peterson, Ruth C. and L. L. Thurstone. **Motion Pictures and the Social Attitudes of Children**. Shuttleworth, Frank K. and Mark A. May. **The Social Conduct and Attitudes of Movie Fans**. 1933.

Phillips, Henry Albert. **The Photodrama**. 1914.

Photoplay Research Society. **Opportunities in the Motion Picture Industry**. 1922.

Rapée, Erno. **Encyclopaedia of Music for Pictures**. 1925.

Rapée, Erno. **Motion Picture Moods for Pianists and Organists**. 1924.

Renshaw, Samuel, Vernon L. Miller and Dorothy P. Marquis. **Children's Sleep**. 1933.

Rosten, Leo C. Hollywood: The Movie Colony, The Movie Makers.
1941.

Sadoul, Georges. French Film. 1953.

Screen Monographs I, 1923-1937. 1970.

Screen Monographs II, 1915-1930. 1970.

Sinclair, Upton. Upton Sinclair Presents William Fox. 1933.

Talbot, Frederick A. Moving Pictures. 1912.

Thorp, Margaret Farrand. America at the Movies. 1939.

Wollenberg, H. H. Fifty Years of German Film. 1948.

RELATED BOOKS AND PERIODICALS

Allister, Ray. Friese-Greene: Close-Up of an Inventor. 1948.

Art in Cinema: A Symposium of the Avant-Garde Film, edited by
Frank Stauffacher. 1947.

The Art of Cinema: Selected Essays. New Foreword by
George Amberg. 1971.

Balázs, Béla. Theory of the Film. 1952.

Barry, Iris. Let's Go to the Movies. 1926.

de Beauvoir, Simone. Brigitte Bardot and the Lolita Syndrome. 1960.

Carrick, Edward. Art and Design in the British Film. 1948.

Close Up. Vols. 1-10, 1927-1933 (all published).

Cogley, John. Report on Blacklisting. Part I: The Movies. 1956.

Eisenstein, S. M. Que Viva Mexico! 1951.

Experimental Cinema. 1930-1934 (all published).

Feldman, Joseph and Harry. Dynamics of the Film. 1952.

Film Daily Yearbook of Motion Pictures. Microfilm, 18 reels,
35 mm. 1918-1969.

Film Daily Yearbook of Motion Pictures. 1970.

Film Daily Yearbook of Motion Pictures. (Wid's Year Book).
3 vols., 1918-1922.

The Film Index: A Bibliography. Vol. I: The Film as Art. 1941.

Film Society Programmes. 1925-1939 (all published).

Films: A Quarterly of Discussion and Analysis. Nos. 1-4, 1939-1940
(all published).

Flaherty, Frances Hubbard. The Odyssey of a Film-Maker:
Robert Flaherty's Story. 1960.

General Bibliography of Motion Pictures, edited by Carl Vincent,
Riccardo Redi, and Franco Venturini. 1953.

Hendricks, Gordon. Origins of the American Film. 1961-1966. New
Introduction by Gordon Hendricks.

Hound and Horn: Essays on Cinema, 1928-1934. 1971.

Huff, Theodore. **Charlie Chaplin.** 1951.

Kahn, Gordon. **Hollywood on Trial.** 1948.

New York Times Film Reviews, 1913-1968. 1970.

Noble, Peter. **Hollywood Scapegoat: The Biography of Erich von Stroheim.** 1950.

Robson, E. W. and M. M. **The Film Answers Back.** 1939.

Seldes, Gilbert. **An Hour with the Movies and the Talkies.** 1929.

Weinberg, Herman G., editor. **Greed.** 1971.

Wollenberg, H. H. **Anatomy of the Film.** 1947.

Wright, Basil. **The Use of the Film.** 1948.

DISSERTATIONS ON FILM

Karpf, Stephen L. **The Gangster Film: Emergence, Variation and Decay of a Genre, 1930-1940.** First publication, 1973.

Lounsbury, Myron O. **The Origins of American Film Criticism, 1909-1939.** First publication, 1973.

Sands, Pierre N. **A Historical Study of the Academy of the Motion Picture Arts and Sciences (1927-1947).** First publication, 1973.

North, Joseph H. **The Early Development of the Motion Picture, 1887-1909.** First publication, 1973.

Rimberg, John. **The Motion Picture in the Soviet Union, 1918-1952.** First publication, 1973.

Wolfe, Glenn J. **Vachel Lindsay: The Poet as Film Theorist.** First publication, 1973.